THE BLACK PRESS IN MISSISSIPPI
1865–1985

THE BLACK PRESS
IN MISSISSIPPI
1865–1985

Julius E. Thompson

University Press of Florida
Gainesville/Tallahassee/Tampa/Boca Raton
Pensacola/Orlando/Miami/Jacksonville

Library of Congress Cataloging-in-Publication Data

Thompson, Julius Eric.
    The Black press in Mississippi, 1865–1985 / Julius E. Thompson.
      p.   cm.
    Includes bibliographical references and index.
    ISBN 0–8130–1174–4
    1. Afro-American newspapers—Mississippi—Bibliography—Union
lists. 2. Afro-American periodicals—Mississippi—Bibliography—
Union lists. 3. Catalogs, Union—Mississippi. 4. Afro-American
newspapers—Mississippi—Directories. 5. Afro-American periodicals—
Mississippi—Directories. I. Title.
Z1361.N39T52   1993
[PN4882.5]
013′.03960730762—dc20   92–28135
                                                                    CIP

Parts of this study were originally published as chapter 6, "Mississippi," in *The Black Press in the South, 1865–1979*, ed. Henry Lewis Suggs (Westport, Conn.: Greenwood Press, Inc.). Copyright © 1983 by Henry Lewis Suggs. Reprinted by permission of the publisher.

The University Press of Florida is the scholarly publishing agency for the State University System of Florida, comprised of Florida A & M University, Florida Atlantic University, Florida International University, Florida State University, University of Central Florida, University of Florida, University of North Florida, University of South Florida, and University of West Florida.

University Press of Florida
15 Northwest 15th Street
Gainesville, FL 32611

To
W. E. B. Du Bois (1868–1963)
and
Ida B. Wells-Barnett (1862–1931)

CONTENTS

Illustrations and Maps

Illustrations

PREFACE

Since the period of American Reconstruction, Afro-Americans in Mississippi have produced several hundred newspapers, more than fifty magazines and journals, and hundreds of pamphlets, newsletters, and other related press materials. Given the historical conditions of poverty, illiteracy, and fear that prevailed in Mississippi from the era of slavery to the end of the twentieth century, two questions emerge: why were blacks in Mississippi able to create a viable black press institution in the state, and how did they accomplish it? In this study, I explore these phenomena and the relationship of the black press in Mississippi to the economic, political, and social conditions of the Afro-American people in the state from 1865 to 1985.

This work examines six major topics on the black press in Mississippi: development; content; advertising; economics of publishing; role in politics, economic affairs, and social conditions; and radio and television. I examine the needs of the Mississippi black community over time, at least as seen by the members of the black press (reporters, editors, announcers, and publishers) from the 1860s to the mid-1980s.

In chapter 1, I review the historical background of Mississippi's black press from 1865 to 1939. During these years, in spite of great hardships, the state produced the largest number of black papers in its history. Yet the period also witnessed a great decline in black press outlets. The reasons for this growth and subsequent decline are juxtaposed against the changing nature of the black economic, social, and political conditions in Mississippi. In chapter 2, I continue this analysis with an emphasis on the role and nature of the Mississippi black press during World War II and the cold war period that followed. In chapters 3 and 4, I define the relationship between the press and the major black civil rights movements of the 1950s and 1960s. In chapters 5 and 6, I explore the post-movement era, 1970–85, and examine the multifold efforts of Mississippi's blacks to renew the press's earlier strengths.

The literature on the black press in the United States is weak, especially in books. The only essay on Mississippi was written by me and appeared in Henry Lewis Suggs, ed., *The Black Press in the South* (1983). The best book-length studies on the history of the black press in the United States are I. Garland Penn's *The Afro-American Press and Its*

Editors (1891); Frederick Detweiler's *The Negro Press in the United States* (1922); Vishnu V. Oak's *The Negro Newspaper* (1948); Roland E. Wolseley's *The Black Press, U.S.A.* (1971, 1990); Andrew Buni, *Robert L. Vann of the Pittsburgh Courier: Politics and Black Journalism* (1974); Lawrence D. Hogan, *A Black National News Service: The Associated Negro Press and Claude Barnett, 1919–1945* (1984); and Henry Lewis Suggs, *P.B. Young, Newspaperman: Race, Politics, and Journalism in the New South, 1910–1962* (1988). My work helps to fill a void in black historiography, representing the only published book-length state study on the American black press.

I have visited many institutions in Mississippi and throughout the United States while working on this study. I am grateful to the staffs of the following libraries: Jackson State University; Alcorn State University; Tougaloo College; Florida Memorial College; Utica Junior College; Mississippi Valley State University; Rust College; Prentiss Institute; Natchez Public Library; Jackson Public Library; Greenville Public Library; Vicksburg Public Library; Cleveland Public Library; Detroit Public Library; Meridian Public Library; Indianapolis Public Library; New York Public Library; Mississippi College Library; Millsaps College Library; University of Mississippi Library; Mississippi State University Library; University of Southern Mississippi Library; University of Miami Library; Princeton University Library; Atlanta University Library; Howard University Library; State University of New York at Albany Library; University of Pennsylvania Library; and the Department of Archives and History, Jackson, Mississippi.

A 1975 Research and Publication Committee grant from Jackson State University greatly aided the early research efforts of this study, as did a 1979 National Endowment for the Humanities summer stipend at Atlanta University. My work was also supported by a 1982–83 research grant from Florida Memorial College and by a 1985 grant from New York State/United University Professions, State University of New York at Albany. This support was immeasurably helpful in the conclusion of the study. Greenwood Press graciously permitted the use of copyright materials.

I am thankful for the help of many individuals who aided this study, including Deborah LeSure, Curtis Franks, Colia LaFayette Clark, Jerry W. Ward, Jr., Wendell P. Holbrook, James Conyers, Rev. Jefferson Rogers, Mary Grace Rogers, Barbara S. Ricks, Henry Lewis Suggs, Robert Obudho, Gloria Shepherd, Yaw Oheneba-Saky, James M. McPherson,

and David Gerber. To Mississippi journalists, I owe a debt that words
cannot adequately express—thank you.

Abbreviations

CORE	Congress of Racial Equality
NAACP	National Association for the Advancement of Colored People
NNPA	National Newspaper Publishers Association
RNA	Republic of New Africa
SCLC	Southern Christian Leadership Conference
SNCC	Student Nonviolent Coordinating Committee
UNIA	Universal Negro Improvement Association

CHAPTER 1

Historical Development

1865–1939

The black press in Mississippi began in the eighteenth and nineteenth centuries during the era of slavery. These first efforts at mass communication were expressed through music, songs, religion, language, myths, legends, and stories. In these ways, blacks could pass along vital information and knowledge from generation to generation. Mississippi's slavery system sought to prevent communication among slaves, and in the nineteenth century the Mississippi legislature enacted a number of legal measures to prevent the successful development of such a communication network. For example, Mississippi law and custom held that slaves could not learn to read and write; whites must be present at any black assembly, including religious services; and blacks could not legally be trained as typesetters.[1]

Nevertheless, in spite of these restrictions, blacks communicated with each other. A grapevine system emerged through which slaves exchanged information and news of their own communities and of the white world. It was especially evident during Mississippi's major slave revolts of 1835 and 1841 and during various rumors of revolt from 1800 to 1860.[2] To plan an uprising, people needed to communicate information; in Mississippi, as elsewhere in the slave South, blacks succeeded in sharing information with distant and nearby communities by developing their own underground codes. Spirituals, language, visual and hand signals, preaching, and other symbols communicated news of births, deaths, secret meetings, plans of escape, and hopes and prayers for freedom.

1

Some white slaveowners, in spite of the slave codes, taught blacks to read and write, so written communication remained a possibility, however small, for some blacks striving for human expression under slavery.[3]

The small free black population in Mississippi during slavery had no significant impact on the development of black communication networks. The group's population never topped 1,375 during any decade between 1800 and 1860.[4] Slavemasters closely watched and supervised the free community for fear that they might offer assistance to the slaves.[5] Thus, slaves, not free blacks, planted the seed that led to the development of a medium of communication.

During the Civil War, the problem of giving and securing information became profound for blacks in Mississippi. Their population had increased from 3,454 in 1800 to 437,406 in 1860. Black concerns were made even more immediate by the fact that Mississippi constituted one of the main battlegrounds of the war, especially the region around Vicksburg. In addition, 18,000 blacks from Mississippi fought on the side of the Union during the war.[6] The movement and safety of the black troops concerned blacks at home, many of whom had escaped the plantations and settled in areas under federal control. The war's conclusion in April 1865 enabled Mississippi blacks to focus on the need for a medium that would allow public expression of their concerns and interests to the general community and outside world. A striking example of these early efforts took place in Natchez, Mississippi. During May 1865, blacks in that city published a circular calling for a state convention in Natchez on June 5, its purpose to express past grievances and to demand that the legislature grant suffrage for blacks.[7] This publication represents one of the first known attempts by blacks in Mississippi to address their needs through print.

The creation of black lodges or secret societies in Mississippi after 1867 also aided the development of black newspapers. Many of the local lodges established their own newspapers during the 1880s and 1890s to advertise their organizations and to share information on matters of interest to their members and to the black community.[8] The first successful black newspaper in Mississippi began in 1867, when Henry Mason of Vicksburg established the *Colored Citizen*. Mason was a political leader during the late 1860s and the 1870s. In 1870 he served in the Mississippi House of Representatives, as a delegate from Warren County. No known copy of Mason's paper survives; however, judging from contemporary papers in Arkansas and Louisiana, an average edition of the *Colored Cit-*

izen probably ran four pages and yearly subscriptions cost from one to two dollars, with advertisements appearing in each issue.[9]

In November 1868, James D. Lynch established the *Colored Citizen's Monthly* in Jackson. It published for three years. Lynch, a free black before the Civil War who migrated to Mississippi from Philadelphia in 1867, served as one of the state's leading religious figures during Reconstruction and as Mississippi's secretary of state from 1869 to 1872.[10]

A third black newspaper, the Canton *Citizen*, was established in 1869 at Canton. The Vicksburg *Colored Citizen* and the Canton *Citizen* survived only for a short period of time, however—probably less than a year. They lacked economic strength and did not yet have a successful public following in the black community, the latter problem exacerbated by the illiteracy rates of blacks. As in the North, however, these first efforts demonstrated that black Mississippians could produce a paper, and in the following decade a number of other individuals and groups in the state carried the challenge forward. Unlike its contemporaries, the *Colored Citizen's Monthly* managed to develop a consistent following that supported it for at least thirty-six months. Other institutions producing black press materials during this period included Rust College, established in 1866 as Shaw University by the United Methodist Church at Holly Springs, and Tougaloo College, established in 1869 at Tougaloo, by the American Missionary Association.[11]

Throughout Reconstruction, five topics greatly concerned blacks in Mississippi: the church, education, farming, government, and the emerging press. The movement to strengthen the press as an institution in Mississippi's black community was reflected in the continuation of the *Colored Citizen's Monthly* of Jackson and the creation of five new black newspapers during the 1870s.

James Lynch was joined in 1870 by J.J. Spelman as an editor of the *Colored Citizen's Monthly*. Spelman was a local black leader in Hinds County. Because Lynch was a Methodist minister, the paper was affiliated with the Methodist Church. Religion sometimes cannot easily be separated from the political, social, and economic affairs of nineteenth-century American black publications. Like Lynch, many editors were ministers; most black readers were church members so they expected a deep religious emphasis in the press, the church providing the centerpiece of black life and survival.

The black church's interest in the press was first expressed on July 12, 1870, by the Baptist Missionary Convention (black Baptists of Mississippi and Louisiana) at Vicksburg, Mississippi. The convention's constitution called for the establishment of a committee to organize a newspaper, which would become the official organ of the body. Nine years later, with the separation of the Louisiana and Mississippi conventions, the black Baptists of Mississippi passed a resolution in July 1879 that called for the purchase of a printing press for the convention. This focus on printing soon found expression in the formation of a newspaper, the *Baptist Signal*.[12]

In 1870, the *People's Journal* was established in Jackson; in 1877 the paper became the *People's Advisor* and later the *People's Defender*. Between 1873 and 1874, the *Reflector* was published in Jackson by the General Missionary Baptist Association. In addition to these papers in the 1870s, J. Garrett Johnson served as editor of the Jackson *Field Hand*. Blanche K. Bruce, a leading black political figure, edited the *Floreyville Star* in 1874 in Rosedale. At Vicksburg, the *Mississippi Republican* was produced from 1877 into the 1880s.[13]

Blacks established newspapers in Mississippi, as elsewhere in the United States, because of a need for what I. Garland Penn termed "a more direct means of communication" among the Afro-American people. The papers viewed their role as part of the black defense strategy and as a medium for relaying the interests and needs of the Afro-American community. The papers' complexity lay in the fact that a wide variety of different individuals and groups, usually of the black elite, established them; the differing shades of opinion indicated in the black press throughout its history often reflect this fact.

The *Colored Citizen's Monthly* typified the other six black papers published in Mississippi during the 1870s. Published at Jackson, the state capital, as were three of the other black papers of the 1870s, the *Colored Citizen's Monthly* had an average edition of four pages, each a standard size of 22 by 32 inches. Subscription rates reflected those of many black newspapers of the time, usually one to two dollars yearly.[14] The paper championed Republican politics, as did most black newspapers of the period, because the Republican party supported black political and civil rights, which the Democrats had generally opposed.

Jackson emerged as the economic, political, and social center of activities for both blacks and whites in Mississippi, especially as it related to press interests in the state. In the 1860s, the average life of a black paper in Mississippi was short—the Vicksburg *Colored Citizen* and the Canton *Citizen* survived for only a few months. However, unlike the 1860s, most papers in the 1870s existed for a year or more. Scholars have been unable to locate any copies of a black Mississippi paper from the 1870s, so we know little about content and format.

Press activity increased in the 1870s with the establishment of three additional black colleges. Alcorn University was created in 1871 as a public-supported land-grant institution for black youth. In 1875, the Christian Women's Board of Missions established the Southern Christian Institute, at Edwards, Mississippi. Two years later the American Baptist Home Mission Society founded Natchez Seminary for Freedmen, later reorganized at Jackson in 1883 as Jackson College. Along with Rust College and Tougaloo University, both founded in the late 1860s, these institutions promoted educational press development among blacks, especially in the production of newsletters about the work of the various institutions and in their annual college catalogues.[15]

Illiteracy among blacks of the era constituted a major problem plaguing the early black press in Mississippi. Although college attendance provided a new body of readers to diminish the problem somewhat, the poor economic condition of blacks after the Civil War and a weak, almost nonexistent advertising base posed two other significant problems.[16] In spite of these problems, however, the black press prevailed and grew in the face of great hardships suffered by blacks after the end of Reconstruction in 1877. In I. Garland Penn's observation, black journalists saw their work as "advocating Afro-American advancement."[17] Service to black people represented the black newspapers' main concern in the nineteenth century.

Many of the editors and publishers of this era had been born in slavery; others had escaped from slavery, and still others had been born free. By the 1860s and 1870s, their efforts for self-improvement and promotion of black interests had paid off. Black people in Mississippi, by voting and electing officials for the local, state, and national governments, changed the old state order and formed a new movement for a better society.

Five of the most outstanding black leaders in Mississippi from 1860 to 1879 had significant experience as working journalists. Henry Mason was a member of the Mississippi House of Representatives and editor of the Vicksburg *Colored Citizen*. James J. Spelman also served as a representative and coedited the Jackson *Colored Citizen's Monthly* with James D. Lynch, secretary of state. Two of the most noted black leaders during Reconstruction were Mississippi's U.S. senators, Blanche K. Bruce, editor of the *Floreyville Star* (Bolivar County), and Hiram R. Revels, editor of

Hiram Rhodes Revels (1827–1901), the first Afro-American senator in U.S. history, served in Congress in 1870–71, during Reconstruction. He was a noted journalist and religious and educational leader during his lifetime and the first president of Alcorn University, created in 1871 at Lorman, Mississippi. Courtesy Clark–Atlanta University Library.

the New Orleans *Southwestern Advocate,* which was subsidized by the Methodist Episcopal Church, North. Their backgrounds as journalists perhaps account for their intense articulation of social, economic, and political problems. In fact, their journalistic skills probably aided their efforts to promote universal suffrage, federal support to protect black rights, the establishment of free public school systems in the South, land for blacks, and an end to racial discrimination against all groups in the United States.[18]

The role of John Roy Lynch as a journalist of this period is unclear. Lynch (no relation to James D. Lynch) represented one of the three most important black leaders in Mississippi during Reconstruction (the others were Revels and Bruce). He was also one of the earliest black photographers in Mississippi, working in a studio shop in Natchez in 1866. Disagreement over his role as a journalist centers on whether he or James Lynch served as editor of the *Colored Citizen's Monthly* with the coeditorship of J.J. Spelman. Penn credited John Roy Lynch with the paper; Wharton selected James Lynch, as did William J. Simmons. I am inclined to accept the last two because James Lynch's base was Jackson, whereas John Roy Lynch came from Natchez. In addition, the latter made no mention of the *Colored Citizen's Monthly* in his autobiography.[19]

Unlike the largely Republican black press during Reconstruction, the white press of Mississippi consisted primarily of Democratic papers, such as the *Clarion* (also known as the Meridian *Clarion,* Jackson *Clarion,* Jackson *Clarion and Standard,* and the Jackson *Clarion-Ledger*) and the *Vicksburg Commercial.* Generally, the Democratic papers were antiblack and conservative, especially on matters concerning black rights and Republican politics. A small, independent white press was also active during this period. Wharton notes that the *Hinds County Gazette* fits this description because the paper was "critical of the methods of both the Republicans and the Democrats." Another segment of the white press in Mississippi during this era comprised the moderate and radical Republican papers, such as the *Mississippi Pilot* and the *Vicksburg Times.*[20]

By 1879, only two black newspapers were being published in Mississippi, the *People's Advisor* at Jackson and the Vicksburg *Mississippi Republican.* The economic, social, and political position of blacks in Mississippi had also reached a low point by this date. The overthrow of Radical Reconstruction by the old guard between 1875 and 1877 created general depression—perhaps even panic—among many blacks by 1879. Beginning at that time, many blacks expressed interest in migrating from Mississippi to Kansas or to other areas of the United States.[21] The issue of black migration away from the South would provide a major concern far into the future for the black press in Mississippi and elsewhere. At that time the black press had to struggle to establish its place in the black community and to safeguard its position in the general Mississippi community.

Mississippi boasted seventeen black newspapers during the 1880s, for the most part religious-oriented journals.[22] This growth reflected, in part, the hardening economic, political, and social conditions after the Civil War, when the state's Confederates had attempted by whatever means possible to deny black progress and humanity. By the 1880s, they had successfully overthrown Radical Reconstruction in Mississippi, and through law and custom they created a new system of deprivation, one that sought to compel the segregation and powerlessness of the Afro-American people in the state. Thus, the 1880s resulted in the proliferation of religious journals as one avenue by which blacks might overcome the objections of whites to the standard black commercial newspapers. Nonreligious black papers were, however, produced in significant numbers by blacks in the North and elsewhere in the South during this period.

Ida B. Wells-Barnett must be included in any list of Mississippi journalists. Although based in Memphis, Tennessee, where she published *Free*

Speech, in the late 1880s and early 1890s, her writing had a wide following and impact in Mississippi, especially in the northern parts of the state. Her work on lynching had a special impact because this subject constituted one of the major concerns of blacks in the state during that time.[23]

Papers published in the 1880s remained similar to those of earlier periods, with four pages in each edition and usually published weekly. Subscription rates generally ranged from one to two dollars per year. Individual issues cost five cents each. Circulation figures for most of the black press in the state varied between five hundred and one thousand copies per issue.[24] The Republican party still held the political loyalties of most black journals in Mississippi; however, a number of black publications expressed their affiliations only in terms of a religious group, such as the Baptist or Methodist church, or as independents without political affiliations.

Forty-six black papers published during the 1890s in Mississippi, consisting of commercial, religious, fraternal, educational, and organizational organs. As with earlier periods, no copy of a paper from this era is known to exist today. Much of the general data on the papers of the 1890s follows the patterns of the 1870s and 1880s.

In fact, the vast majority of black newspapers in Mississippi came into being during the thirty-two years from 1867 to 1899, but most were journals in operation from one to two years. A few lasted five years or longer, particularly the Jackson *People's Journal*, which survived into the 1890s under several different names. The longevity rate in the 1880s and 1890s improved somewhat, but the month-to-month struggle remained a burden for the black press. The growth of Mississippi's black press corresponds with that of the black press nationwide during that time. In 1870 ten black newspapers existed across the United States; by 1880, the number had risen to thirty-one, and by 1890 it reached 154.[25]

The black press in Mississippi closely parallels the general experience of the black press in other Southern states, particularly during the period 1865–99.

In Mississippi, the increase in the number of papers from six in the 1870s to seventeen in the 1880s to forty-six in the 1890s resulted from a variety of factors, including increased black interest in self-help businesses; an expanding array of black organizations, such as lodges, educational institutions, and religious-interest groups; many black individuals' and organizations' desire to possess their own publication outlets; and

Dr. A.A. Cosey (1874–1942), pastor of the Greene Grove Baptist Church, Mound Bayou, was a leader of the black press for over thirty years, serving as an editor at the *Journal* (Clarksdale, 1899–1907), the *Advance Dispatch* (1914–33, Mound Bayou, later at Vicksburg to 1942), and the *Baptist Echo* (1909, also at Mound Bayou). Courtesy *Multum in Parvo*, 1912.

awareness of the need for better communication systems among blacks. Black newspapers in nineteenth-century Mississippi could be secured in all parts of the state, especially in towns such as Jackson, Vicksburg, Natchez, and Greenville. In all, black papers were published in more than thirty-seven locations throughout the state during this period.

The number of black editors and publishers in Mississippi between 1865 and 1900 never reached more than one hundred. As a group they appear to have been primarily moderates, although a large number of conservatives also were involved. Given the harsh realities of the period, a militant stance would have been dangerous, if not deadly.[26] The development of the Jim Crow system in Mississippi and the rest of the South in the 1880s and 1890s affected all of these journalists. In fact, the Mississippi Plan, a product of the 1890 Mississippi Constitutional Convention, placed strong restraints on black civil rights in Mississippi; Isaiah Montgomery, a black leader from Mound Bayou and the only black present at the convention, voted with the majority of whites, thus solidifying the antiblack attitude in the state.[27]

Blacks produced a wide variety of newspapers in the period 1867–99, largely as a result of the willingness of many individual blacks and their religious and social organizations to finance the operations of local newspapers. Although a moderate amount of advertising appeared in Mississippi's nineteenth-century black newspapers, black businesses remained too small to support fully the needs of black papers, and most white businessmen did not want to support the black press. Consequently, unlike the white press, which could depend on local and even state advertisement dollars, the black press relied largely on the resources of the editor and publisher—and whatever else the paper could scrounge up—to secure its survival.[28]

The *Baptist Signal* illustrates the economic problems that plagued the Mississippi's black press during this era. First proposed as an organ for black Baptists as early as 1870, this paper did not appear until 1880. Thereafter, its existence remained stormy; even with the support of a major black religious body, the paper only appeared monthly, with a circulation of 1,000, between 1880 and 1883, when it changed to a weekly.[29] In 1882, the general expenses for the *Baptist Signal* included an annual salary of $300 for the editor, $211 for type and paper, $73 for office rent, and $584 for office expenses—a total of $1,168. The *Signal* does not appear to have had a large volume of advertisements, and subscriptions for 1882 amounted to only $127.75, leaving a balance of

$1,040.25 for payment by the Mississippi Conference.[30] This sum represented an enormous subsidy for any group under the conditions faced by black Mississippians in the 1880s and 1890s.

Between 1900 and 1950, a vicious system of segregation prevailed in Mississippi and the rest of the South. As mentioned earlier, Mississippi led the segregation movement with its 1890 Constitutional Convention and the Mississippi Plan,[31] the first official segregation laws. During the next fifty years, the state acquired a reputation as the least attractive place for blacks in the United States. Jim Crow affected all aspects of black life, including black newspapers. The period 1900–1950 represented a time of despair as a result of a system that sought to oppress, demoralize, and control an entire people.

The first two decades of the twentieth century offer an opportunity to view the black press in Mississippi as it reached its apex[32]—a total of ninety-seven publications existed during those years. After 1920, the number of black papers declined steadily for twenty years, so that only thirty-three papers operated from 1921 to 1940. From 1941 to 1949, the number began to grow, reaching thirty-nine. Commercial newspapers represented the most numerous sector of the press. Between 1900 and 1919, fifty-one such papers existed. At the same time, twenty-one fraternal organs appeared, along with fifteen religious newspapers and ten educational journals.[33]

These papers most commonly operated in urban centers, but many small towns and even villages also had newspapers. Location in or near a large concentration of black people always aided a paper's survival. For example, most commercial papers during 1900–1919 operated near large Afro-American communities. Vicksburg (four black papers), Greenville (four), Jackson (three), Meridian (three), Moss Point (two), Aberdeen (two), Holly Springs (two), and Mound Bayou (two) had the most black papers during this era.[34]

During this period, the circulation of the typical black paper usually ranged between five hundred and one thousand copies per week. The actual number of readers probably remained much higher as a result of the traditional information sharing in the black community—one copy of a paper would pass through several hands.[35]

Most black papers in Mississippi faced financial difficulties from 1900 to 1919. Although similar to the white weekly press in design and make-up, the black press vastly differed from the white press in that many white papers enjoyed general economic strength (once they had secured a solid foundation in a white community). The difference lay in the volume of advertisements upon which white papers could depend for their survival. Despite their greater economic security compared to most black papers, the huge number of white papers produced during this period diluted the resources available to them, and thus many of them also enjoyed only short lives. Still, one should be careful in comparing the black and white presses, as the central theme in the survival of the black press lay in individual support for papers, followed by black community group interests. White papers that survived for a long time generally depended on advertisement support from white businesses. Thus, the growth and development of black journalism in Mississippi must be viewed as a community's financial, labor, and creative sacrifices to support communication efforts and needs of black people. Profit never provided a major incentive for the black press during the early decades of its existence in Mississippi. At the close of the nineteenth century, blacks in the state had wealth in business and property in the amount of $13,400,213. In 1907, blacks in Jackson held wealth estimated at less than $2,000,000; seven individual blacks held more than $200,000 each.[36] The black press depended on smaller and weaker black businesses. Few black papers of this era received white advertising; those that did got it in amounts too small to aid their growth and development.

As in the nineteenth century, the success or failure of many black papers depended upon the personality and resourcefulness of their editors and publishers. Furthermore, because the black press rarely proved profitable, the editors generally combined journalism with other fields of interest. They worked as doctors, ministers, printers, and teachers, among other occupations. Many of Mississippi's editors were born in the state or elsewhere in the South and spent most of their lives in the region. They had received good educations, usually as far as high school or college level; many attended Alcorn College, Natchez Junior College, Rust University, Jackson College, or Tougaloo College. Schools outside Mississippi that produced black editors included Morehouse College and Tuskegee Institute. Most of the editors were men.[37]

The increased publishing activities of the growing black fraternal, religious, organizational, and educational institutions in Mississippi strengthened the black press during this period. Stronger financial bases and increased membership enabled them to offer more aid to a variety of press interests for longer periods of time than had been possible earlier. Racial solidarity emphasis and self-help ideals promoted throughout black America, especially under the influence of Booker T. Washington, black educators, ministers, and businessmen, also influenced the black press's development.

Black editors and journalists confronted not only their own local concerns but national and international race issues as well. Marcus Garvey's Universal Negro Improvement Association (UNIA), the National Association for the Advancement of Colored People (NAACP), the National Urban League, and the Niagara Movement all stood at the forefront of the fight against racial injustice; Mississippi's black press reported these developments from a somewhat guarded perspective because of threats to their lives.

A number of black press agencies, such as the Associated Negro Press (Chicago), the R.W. Thompson News Agency (Washington, D.C.), Allen's News Agency (New York), the Hampton Institute Press Service (Virginia), the Tuskegee Institute Press Service (Alabama), the Capital News Service of the NAACP (New York), and the Crusader News Service (New York), served Mississippi and the rest of the nation between 1900 and 1939. The Colored Press Association, later named the Negro Press Association, which had a Mississippi branch in 1910–19,[38] also served the national black press during this era.

During this heated period, the vast majority of Mississippi's white press continued to support segregation and oppose black rights. Examples of papers in this mold included the *Greenwood Commonwealth* and the Jackson *Issue*, both edited at one time by one of Mississippi's most famous demagogues, James K. Vardaman, the *Clarion-Leader*, and the *Jackson Daily News*. In 1907, white Mississippians produced 241 periodicals and newspapers, including 203 weekly papers, sixteen dailies, eight semi-weeklies, six semimonthlies, and eight monthly journals. They operated in 144 locations in seventy-nine of Mississippi's eighty-two counties.[39]

Black readers and journalists endured great hardships for their efforts, including negative portrayals in the white press and threats of violence and economic reprisals for reading and circulating black newspapers produced outside the South, such as the *Chicago Defender*, the *New York Age*, the *Afro-American*, and the *Crisis*. Nonetheless, information and news continued to reach black people in Mississippi, as it had during the slavery era. An example of the intimidation of a black editor in Mississippi occurred in 1904, when Rev. C.S. Buchanan, editor of a Baptist newspaper, the *Preacher and Teacher*, was forced to flee with his family

E.B. Topp (ca. 1912), a graduate of Jackson College, was a significant editor in Mississippi for more than twenty-five years at such papers as the *New Light*, a Baptist organ in Jackson. He also served as the Grand Secretary of the Grand Lodge of Odd Fellows of Mississippi district number ten (a fraternal organization). In the first decade of this century he spent three years in Africa as a religious teacher and missionary. Courtesy *Multum in Parvo*, 1912.

from West Point, Clay County, after a meeting of 100 whites who objected to his printing activities and economic position in the community.[40]

Black journalists had an impressive impact on black life in Mississippi between 1900 and 1919, particularly by providing the opportunity for people to understand themselves and the world better. Because Mississippi was primarily a rural state, blacks had limited avenues for obtaining information, entertainment, and news; the black press during this period filled part of the void in black communication needs and interests.[41]

The 1920s constituted a period of intense white supremacist activity in Mississippi, as evidenced by the continued expansion of the Ku Klux Klan, the increased volume of black migration from Mississippi, the tragedy of lynching, and the depressed economic, political, and social conditions of blacks in the state. Other significant events during the decade included passage of the Nineteenth Amendment, ensuring voting rights for women in 1920, the Mississippi floods of 1927, and the stock market crash of October 1929. The Harlem Renaissance, a flowering of black cultural talents throughout the United States, especially in New York City, came about during this time.[42]

During the 1920s the Mississippi black press changed little in terms of general circulation, distribution, cost, background of editors, and so forth. Few copies of black Mississippi papers from that era have survived, with the exception of educational journals. In addition, Duke University has one copy of the June 25, 1923, issue of the Mound Bayou[43] *Advance Dispatch*.

In addition to other concerns, black journalists in Mississippi faced a disturbing decline in the number of black papers. Only thirty-one major black publications appeared in the 1920s, down from a total of sixty-six papers during the years 1910–19. This number included nine commercial papers, eight fraternal organs, five religious journals, and eight educational publications. The decline of the press resulted from the strengthening of racist ideals in Mississippi, where white citizens viewed much of the black press as an attempt to act independently. The economic position of most black readers and publishers also caused declining readership. Although most of the black papers remained weeklies between four and twelve pages in length, general expenses of putting newspapers out still required more than the available financial resources. If a paper could not raise advertising dollars, and if the editor's and publisher's personal resources had limits, such financial restraints could spell the end for the journal. Finally, the outward migration of tens of thousands of blacks from Mississippi during the 1920s also diminished readership. Taken together, these factors created an atmosphere of hopelessness for much of

Office of the Excelsior Grand Court of Calanthe, ca. 1911. The *Calanthian Journal* of this fraternal organizaiton was published weekly at Edwards between 1904 and 1917, by W. A. Scott, publisher and editor. Courtesy *Multum in Parvo*, 1912.

the black press in the state, an atmosphere that would persist for decades.

If the 1920s proved a difficult time for blacks in Mississippi, the 1930s constituted a disaster. In addition to the oppressive Jim Crow system, blacks had to contend with the massive economic crisis of the Great Depression and the related social and political matters.[44] The continued decline of Mississippi's black papers highlights the significance of these issues. Between 1930 and 1939, only thirty-three black publications existed in Mississippi, including fifteen commercial, six religious, two fraternal, and ten educational journals. These figures compare to sixty-six papers produced in the period 1910–19 and forty-six in the 1890s. Jackson remained the leading center for black journals, with seven, followed by Mound Bayou with three and Vicksburg with two.[45]

Out of the vast array of events, movements, and individuals of the period emerged three major themes: segregation and its impact upon life in

Mississippi; lynching and the fear and terror associated with it; and the blacks' quest for voting and political rights.

Fear and intimidation prevented many editors from seriously examining important issues; yet many reprinted stories from the wire services or from accounts given in other papers throughout the country.

Many black newspapers focused a great deal of attention on soft news. Critics have noted that they devoted a disproportionate amount of space to sex, fillers, sports, pictures, and entertainment news. The editorial page received little serious attention. An earlier study of black American newspapers confirms most of this assessment.[46] Individual papers differed on this point, however.

Two papers from the Delta region of northwest Mississippi exemplify black journalism during this period: the *Southern Advocate*, established at Mound Bayou in 1933 and edited by B. A. Wade and two associate editors, Isaac Peterson and P. A. Smith, and the *Delta Leader*, published at Greenville, and purchased in 1938 by Rev. H. H. Humes.

The *Southern Advocate* was a local weekly, heavily emphasizing religious matters. Many Delta blacks supported this focus, as Rev. J. H. Kyles of Shelby, Mississippi, suggested in a comment to *Southern Advocate* readers: supporting the paper would "keep them in touch with the news of our churches and inform them of what the colored people are doing."[47] An examination of the *Southern Advocate* for 1938–39 reveals that Rev. Kyles correctly assessed the religious nature of the paper, but somewhat incorrectly praised the journal's coverage of the black world.

The *Southern Advocate* was a medium-size paper with five columns and four pages. It appeared on Saturday and contained local news, with a religious focus on Mound Bayou and the surrounding black communities, such as Benoit, Shelby, Rosedale, Mile Community, and Symonds, among others. In addition, the paper printed popular news of the Mound Bayou area (entertainment, travel, society, church, and educational news, announcements, and local advertising), and state news. The paper offered little focus on national and international affairs and events.

Generally, the *Southern Advocate* did not print an editorial in each issue, reflecting its editorial weaknesses. On special occasions, however, the paper commanded the strength to speak on local matters, such as a religious event; the anniversary of the founding of Mound Bayou; the death of a noted citizen; a picnic; problems in the city, such as fire prevention and crime; local politics (suggesting that local blacks vote and support the Democratic party because their "ballot . . . would . . . mean much in gaining political and economic freedom"); and unfair attacks by the white press on Mound Bayou. The *Southern Advocate* rarely spoke out on national events. The paper noted in 1938 that Afro-Americans should place top priority on effective use of the U.S. judicial system to further black rights. The paper suggested that much of the black legal struggle would take place before the U.S. Supreme Court. The publication of the autobiography of Dr. Adam Clayton Powell, Sr., also interested the paper. The *Southern Advocate* had high praise for this literary work of the late 1930s.[48]

The *Southern Advocate* followed the economic tradition of earlier black weeklies. Its advertising base consisted largely of small black businesses in Mound Bayou, Bolivar County, and the surrounding Delta counties. In the four-page issue of May 28, 1938, eleven ads appeared on page two, three appeared on page three, and two appeared on page four, for a total of sixteen ads for that week. On October 14, 1939, twenty ads appeared in an issue of six pages.[49]

The *Southern Advocate* resembled the vast majority of black papers in that it did not receive adequate operating funds. The paper sought money through subscription drives, by operating a printing press for community needs in Mound Bayou and the Delta, and by frugality wherever possible. Such methods included receiving community-based news free of charge from local reporters in different Delta communities. Editor Wade advertised another unusual method to save money and to attract readers: "Used envelopes wanted . . . save the envelopes you get in the mail everyday. We will accept 100 clean used envelopes with canceled stamps attached for one month's subscription to the Southern Advocate" ran a 1938 announcement in the paper.[50]

Rev. H.H. Humes, a Greenville Baptist minister, assumed control of the *Delta Leader* in 1938. He viewed the policy of the paper as "a brave attempt to preach with the dominant idea of elevating the minds to higher planes of thought, educating the mind to cleaner and clearer thought; the hands to love the creations of honest toil. The young Negro must realize that the future of the race rests upon his shoulders and that a sane, sober, and sound future cannot be built upon the shoulders of a 'gitterbugging generation' a scant 75 years removed from bondage."

During the late 1930s, the *Delta Leader* was a standard-size newspaper, issued on Saturday, with a subscription rate of two dollars per year, or five cents an issue. The paper's weekly circulation stood at five hundred copies in 1938, but Rev. Humes claimed that this figure reached a high of 4,300 copies, with 20,000 readers, in 1939. The *Leader* was a politically Democratic paper.[51]

A follower in the tradition of Booker T. Washington, Rev. Humes viewed the Mississippi black press as an accommodationist medium that could pull and push for black rights, but without anything that might be termed radicalism by the controlling whites. Therefore, to reach a moderate balance, the *Delta Leader* covered local, state, regional, national, and international news, especially those items of particular interest to blacks. The paper belonged to the Associated Negro Press (ANP), and a variety of ANP news items appeared in the paper. Thus, unlike the *Southern Advocate*, which paid little attention to national and international news coverage, the *Delta Leader* offered its readers a wider range of information.

The paper had a fairly well-developed editorial page, especially in contrast to the underdeveloped page in the *Southern Advocate*. Rev. Humes cared deeply about local matters in Greenville, Washington County, and the Delta. He campaigned to promote the idea of black progress in the Delta, but he also offered advice to outsiders, whom he criticized as unfair whenever they completed "short studies" of the Delta region.[52] Yet the tone of editorial columns of the *Delta Leader* always remained moderate.

The *Delta Leader* secured good advertisements from both black and white businesses in the area. The paper might have been aided by the fact that Greenville had a more moderate history of race relations than most other cities in Mississippi. The strong black educational, religious, and business community in Greenville, which could trace its origins to the late nineteenth century, provided another factor in the paper's success. Furthermore, blacks in Greenville had successfully published a series of black papers since the 1880s.

Advertisements in the *Delta Leader* ranged from the Greyhound Bus Company to the black-owned Hotel Montrose. A November 1938 issue of the paper carried forty-three ads; by October 1939, a weekly issue contained fifty-seven ads. This variety of advertisement sources enabled the paper to survive the depression years. Nonetheless, the *Delta Leader* also hired out its presses for standard printing business to make ends meet.[53]

Both David Cohn and James W. Silver concluded that in the 1930s Mississippi presented "a hopeless situation" in which blacks were politically "as dead as the Indian" and "racial problems were without hope of solution in the present and without direction in the future." The *Crisis* told its readers in 1936 that Mississippi constituted "the worst" state "so far as general American standards go." The *Crisis* noted that the state had "nearly two million in population, but the largest daily paper has only 33,040 circulation. The state pays the smallest amount—$4.45—per capita for the education of Negro children and only $45.34 per capita for whites as compared to the national average of $99 per capita."[54]

Such was the state of affairs in the seventeenth territory to join the Union. Racist would not be too harsh a word to describe the view of the vast majority of the white press in Mississippi toward blacks during this period. The Jackson *Clarion-Ledger* continued its leadership role as a major voice against black equality in Mississippi. In this paper's view, blacks had no political, economic, or social rights except those bestowed by white Mississippi.[55]

Yet Laurence C. Jones, founder of Piney Woods School for blacks in Brandon in 1903, could write of the white press in Mississippi, "Throughout the state, the press is found solidly standing for uplift and opportunity for the members of our race. The *Jackson Daily News*, edited by Major Frederick Sullens, and numerous county papers are outspoken in encouraging industrial, economic, and educational development on behalf of the colored people of Mississippi."[56] Jones's opinion may have been influenced by his desire to secure additional white support for the school rather than by sharp and clear analysis of the white press in Mississippi. His interpretations of the black situation and the press certainly differ sharply from George S. Schuyler's analysis during his 1936 visit to the state.

Schuyler found that segregation held a tight grip on life for blacks as well as for many poor whites. The white press cast in print the codes of white Mississippi, which included keeping blacks in their place. At the top of this list stood black Mississippi editors and black newspapers, which could do no good but would only stir up trouble. Therefore, the editors were caught in a no-man's-land, where they dared not criticize local whites and where they followed a policy of "generally avoiding nine-tenths of the real news and practically all of the possible topics crying for comment."[57] Such was the fate, Schuyler suggested, of many black editors in Mississippi.

Free State, Brandon, January 20, 1900, was a four-page weekly from 1898 to 1905. *Golden Rule*, Vicksburg, January 27, 1900, a four-page weekly from 1898 to 1907 edited by W.E. Mollison and H.L. Slaughter, had a circulation ranging between 400 and 650 copies. Both courtesy Library of Congress.

Worst of all for black editors was to be forced out of business or to have their lives threatened for publishing a black newspaper. White Mississippians took both actions against blacks during the Great Depression years. Schuyler describes several such cases. One editor explained to him that when he was told to cease publishing a paper, he did so at once, for, he said, "I didn't want to die, so I stopped."

Some blacks and whites in Mississippi saw a hopeful sign for race relations in 1938 when the all-white Mississippi Education Association created a committee to suggest approaches whereby students might study black life and culture. Although a small step, it represented an example of a moderate solution in terms of the Mississippi experience and the problems of that era. The New Deal programs may have influenced this effort.[58]

The 1930s represented crisis years for Mississippi's black press as a result of the economic crisis that gripped all of the United States during the decade. Yet blacks in Mississippi faced far worse conditions because of the region's white supremacy system. This modern form of slavery and exploitation would carry over into the 1940s and would continue to have a negative impact on black life and institutions. This clearly was the case for the black press in Mississippi, which continued to decline in terms of real numbers and distribution during World War II. Nevertheless, a few papers survived even those terrible days, and the voice of the black press, weak as it was in so many ways, continued to carry the message of the black Mississippi experience to the world.

CHAPTER 2

World War II and After

1940–1949

For the black press in Mississippi, the tragic decade of the 1940s meant great distress. After World War II, which America fought to save freedom abroad, black Americans hoped for a truer sense of freedom in the United States. In addition to all of the troubling questions and problems of the earlier decades, many new themes and issues emerged to capture the interest of black Mississippians and their press. First, they considered World War II, the blacks' role in the war, the treatment of black soldiers, and the status of blacks in the postwar period. Second, the cold war conflict erupted between the United States and the Soviet Union, creating the "West" versus "East" paradigm. Third, race relations in Mississippi and the rest of the nation and the related problems of racism and segregation concerned Mississippi's blacks, as did the emigration of blacks from Mississippi and elsewhere in the South during the war years. The black press also pondered the economic, political, and social status of blacks in Mississippi, as well as lynching and other violence against blacks. Next, blacks expressed interest in the goals and programs of black organizations, such as the NAACP, in Mississippi and in Richard Wright as a leading black writer and thinker of the era. Finally, black interest in the Democratic party increased, and with it concern about Strom Thurmond, Dixiecrat candidate in the 1948 presidential election, about lingering problems of the Great Depression, and about discrimination by New Deal relief agencies.[1]

Thirty-nine black journals published during this period, a slight increase over the thirty-three papers published during the Great Depression of the 1930s. Religious and fraternal groups still played a major role in black papers during the 1940s; however, many of these journals had folded by 1949. In their place, commercial papers, although few in number, took command of black journalism during the war years. The age-old problems still remained, so perhaps economic problems forced most of the fraternal and religious organs to close. Consequently, a few individuals remained to direct five or six important papers for a black population in Mississippi of 1,074,578 in 1940.[2] With fewer and fewer active papers, the few remaining journals sought out advertising dollars from both black and white businesses. Although a few survived, many more papers closed during the next decade.

Black journalists in Mississippi worked at thirteen commercial papers during the 1940s, including the *Jackson Advocate*; the Jackson *Weekly Recorder*; the Mound Bayou *Southern Advocate*; the Greenville *Delta Leader*; the Jackson *Mississippi Enterprise*; the *Vicksburg Tribune*; the Vicksburg *Black Man*; the Jackson *Herald*; the Jackson *Eagle Eye*; the *Mound Bayou Digest*; *Progressing Together* (Tupelo); the New Albany *Community Citizen*; the *Vicksburg Tribune*; and the *Greenville Mississippian*.

The six religious journals active during this period included the Vicksburg *Advance Dispatch*; *Soldiers of Faith* (Brandon), Anselm J. Finch, editor; *Mississippi Snaps* (Brandon); the Coffeeville *Colored Messenger*; the Yazoo City *Central Voice*; and *Saint Augustine's Messenger* (Bay Saint Louis).

Active fraternal organs consisted of the Meridian *Echo* and the Mound Bayou *Taborian Star*. Eighteen historically black educational institutions in Mississippi published educational journals during the decade: Alcorn A&M College, Jackson State College, Mississippi Valley State College, Mississippi Industrial College, Natchez College, Rust College, Tougaloo College, Coahoma Junior College, Utica Junior College, Campbell College, Mary Holmes Junior College, Okolona College, Piney Woods School, Prentiss Institute, Saints Junior College, Southern Christian Institute, and West Point Ministerial Institute. The *Mississippi Educational Journal*, an official organ of the Mississippi Association of Teachers in Colored Schools, also published throughout the 1940s.[3]

The state of Mississippi's black press during the 1940s indicates that a continuous decline occurred in all areas of black journalism except for educational organs. Educational institutions maintained at least one active publication throughout the decade, while the commercial, religious, and fraternal organs did not succeed as well in keeping their journals going from year to year. For the most part, black papers still remained under the control of black male editors. In fact, few black women served as journalists during this period except for occasional religious publications of interest to black women or newsletters of black women's organizations such as the Mississippi State Federation of Colored Women's Clubs.[4]

As in previous decades, most black editors only engaged in part-time journalism, with full-time careers as ministers, businessmen, or teachers. Percy Greene represented a departure from this pattern when he became full-time editor of the *Jackson Advocate*. Yet few others followed his example.[5]

In the 1940s Mississippi's black papers published weekly rather than daily. An average journal ranged from four to eight pages, reaching six to eight pages for most papers by 1949. This increase in length from previous decades aided in the struggle for advertisement dollars by providing additional space for advertisements.

Journals of the decade sold for between one and two dollars for a one-year subscription; by 1949, however, many of the rates had increased, as in the case of the *Jackson Advocate*, which charged $3.50 annually. Single issues of most journals cost five cents each in 1940 and remained at that price for the rest of the decade. On average, circulation stood at one to two thousand copies; however, major black papers, such as the *Jackson Advocate* and the Greenville *Delta Leader*, had much higher circulation, with editions of three thousand or more common.[6] Wider news coverage perhaps accounts for the greater popularity of these two organs.

Two major factors appear to have led to a major upheaval in the political affiliations of the black press in Mississippi during the 1940s, affecting their character and their news coverage. First, segregation discouraged effective black politics, including support for the Republican party. Second, black attraction to Franklin D. Roosevelt and the early New Deal programs resulted in a national black movement from the Republican to the Democratic party. Both developments affected the black press in Mississippi, resulting in a switch to become Democratic or independent, or to concentrate more on religious matters. The 1940s witnessed an end to an active black Republican press in Mississippi but not, however, to black Republican activity.

Gunnar Myrdal, quoting Edwin Mims, author of *The Advancing South* (1926), noted in 1944 that of the institutions that blacks have created in the United States, the press has had "the greatest single power" among them.[7] Two other institutions, the church and black night-life, have greatly influenced through their spheres of influence the ways in which the black community has viewed the world. In many respects, these power bases all can claim an equal place as sources of information for black people. The press's special place in terms of written communication rested, of course, on its ability to address itself to the complexities of American black life. Through the 1940s, Mississippi's black press took a variety of positions on the social, economic, and political concerns of the day. The editorial page often served as the battleground for the intellectual argument over black strategy and direction in Mississippi and the rest of the nation. In Mississippi, the early 1940s represented a critical period for black journalists, especially during 1941, when the United States entered World War II.

An exploration of four newspapers during 1941 provides some understanding of the varying editorial positions, approaches to news, and working patterns of the black press in a segregated environment.[8] Two of the papers—the Mound Bayou *Southern Advocate* and the Greenville *Delta Leader*—were located in the Mississippi Delta. The other two, the *Jackson Advocate* and the *Mississippi Enterprise*, were based in Jackson, in central Mississippi. The papers had much in common. Each had begun publishing during the Great Depression—the *Delta Leader* in 1929, the *Southern Advocate* in 1933, the *Jackson Advocate* in 1938, and the *Mississippi Enterprise* in 1939. All were located in major black population centers, and each had a small but solid circulation—5,300 copies for the *Leader* in 1948, 3,000 for the *Jackson Advocate* in the same year, and 3,000 for the *Mississippi Enterprise* in 1947. The exact figures for the *Southern Advocate* are not available for this period, but given the average circulation figures for the state, it may have ranged between 500 and 1,500 copies each week.[9]

The *Leader*, *Enterprise*, and *Jackson Advocate* all published standard-size weekly newspapers, averaging six to eight pages long. The *Southern Advocate* ran four pages in each issue. Each paper cost five cents per issue, two dollars per yearly subscription. These papers espoused conservative politics, except for the *Jackson Advocate*, which was considered "radical" because of its support of black civil and voting rights.

In general, each paper's editorial coverage could be defined as follows: the *Mississippi Enterprise* and *Delta Leader* provided local and state news and disproportionate coverage of religious items; the *Southern Advocate* gave an endless attention to religious questions and some local news; and the *Jackson Advocate* expressed concern for local, state, national, and international news. The editors (Willie J. Miller at the *Enterprise*, B.A. Wade at the *Southern Advocate*, Rev. H.H. Humes at the *Delta Leader*, and Percy Greene at the *Jackson Advocate*) all had years of experience in Mississippi. Both Greene and Humes attended Jackson College during the 1920s. Greene's influence extended from 1927, when he served as editor of the *Colored Veteran*, an organ devoted to the cause of black veterans in Mississippi, who were not allowed to join the American Legion at that time.[10]

In 1941 these papers subscribed to the Booker T. Washington's philosophy of black self-help, racial uplift, and economic advancement.[11] Greene could be perceived as a moderate or, in the eyes of some whites, a radical, on some issues, especially his insistence on black voting rights.

Wade focused on local matters in the *Southern Advocate* from January 11 to September 13, 1941. The paper showed concern about events in Mound Bayou, especially a disastrous fire in early January, church affairs, and gambling.[12]

A summary of editorials in the *Delta Leader* for January 4 through December 27, 1941, shows that Humes considered blacks in Greenville and the entire Delta area as part of his paper's domain, devoting much space to black problems and achievements. Humes also took the position that blacks caused many of their own problems. He considered himself a disciple of Booker T. Washington and rarely criticized whites, except Germans and Italians for their role in World War II; he also attacked Japan in this regard. Humes took pride in the Delta's prosperity (as he interpreted it) without pointing out that such prosperity did not exist for the black masses. He called for close cooperation between tenants and landlords in the region and urged blacks not to leave the farm for the city. Finally he expressed absolute support for the United States and its World War II allies.[13]

Greene and the *Jackson Advocate* concerned themselves particularly with local and state affairs from August to December 1941. His editorials fall into four major categories. First, the paper criticized blacks for some of their problems, for example health issues (such as poor hygiene, high alcohol consumption, and irregular medical checkups) and police matters (such as a high murder rate among blacks), which did nothing, in the *Advocate*'s view, to improve the image of blacks in society. The *Advocate* also called for an "equalization" of society under the segregation system, particularly for black teachers, whose incomes were much lower than white teachers in the state. Second, the paper highlighted black achievements, with special attention to black business leaders, and called for a better economic position (especially in terms of jobs) for blacks. Third, the *Advocate* strongly supported the war effort, with hard-hitting attacks on Germany and Japan and a call for expanded democracy at home. The paper noted the greatness of America and its institutions. Finally, the paper placed an importance on world faith in Christianity as the only solution for the problems of mankind. The editorials suggest that Greene was caught between Booker T. Washington's position that blacks should stress economic development rather than publicly fighting for political and social rights and the view that discrimination should end at once and that blacks should receive their political rights (i.e., the vote).[14]

The *Mississippi Enterprise*'s tone for eight months in 1941 remained basically local, with Jackson and Hinds counties at the top of the list, and some state news. Miller was enthusiastic about the "unlimited opportunities for qualified Negro men and women" in Mississippi and elsewhere in America. His editorials also stressed the black loyalty to America as war approached. The paper took pride in "Negro History Week," but criticized the high homicide rate among blacks in Mississippi.[15]

An extended study of the World War II era (1938–49) and the four papers reveals eight dominant themes of their editorial positions: the goals, aims, and role of the black newspaper; the meaning of World War II and blacks' role in the conflict; suffrage, politics, and the American system of government; race relations; economic freedom (employment, business opportunities, better education, and equal pay); racial pride (blacks' past, religion, advancement, and future); crime (both blacks killing other blacks and lynching of blacks by whites); and the black migration to the North.

All four papers believed that they had a mission to serve as leaders, speakers, and servants and to offer news, information, and direction to the black community. For example, the *Jackson Advocate*'s motto stated

Percy Greene (ca. 1944), publisher and editor of the *Jackson Advocate*, casting the first ballot by a black in a Democratic primary in Mississippi history. Greene (1897–1977), born in Jackson, was educated at Jackson College. During the 1940s he was one of the most effective black journalists working in Mississippi. Courtesy *Jackson Advocate*.

Jackson Advocate, June 8, 1946. Greene created the *Advocate* in 1938 and served as publisher until 1977. Because of his conservative views in the 1950s and 1960s, he became the most controversial black journalist in twentieth-century Mississippi. Courtesy *Jackson Advocate*.

sharply that "We stand with the people, by the people and for the people," and the *Delta Leader* believed it must rally blacks "to the realization of the debt Negroes owe to God, to our fellowman, to ourselves; for a better relationship between Mankind."[16]

The *Mississippi Enterprise* saw itself filling the information needs of Mississippi's blacks. "What we have tried to do is give Jacksonians and Mississippians a paper in which there is plenty of space to give accurate accounts of news, in the religious, educational, business, professional, civic, fraternal and social fields—a privilege denied them in the daily papers and most of the foreign papers sent into the state." Equally important to the *Enterprise* and the other papers as well was the obligation to reflect in its pages "the better side of Negro life." But this did not include discriminating against white Mississippians, for the *Enterprise* "often found it necessary to go to our good white friends, not only for financial support but often for moral support." The *Enterprise* always clearly expressed that black newspapers (and black leaders) should not make a lot of noise; indeed, the paper noted in 1948 that "both the Negro newspaper and Negro leaders should exercise such great care and judgment, should be so honest and unselfish in making statements to be thought about and acted upon by the masses." The *Enterprise* also assumed that many negative aspects of black life would simply not be addressed in public.[17]

Philosophically, the four papers continued to support Washington's goals. The *Jackson Advocate* quoted Washington's famous 1895 "Atlanta Compromise Address" in every issue.[18] Although black conservatism generally prevailed throughout this period, differences existed among the papers in this regard.

The dominant themes in the national black press included Nazism and fascism in Europe, World War II and the Soviet Union's postwar struggle to become a world power, and the role of the United States and Western nations.[19] The *Delta Leader, Mississippi Enterprise,* and *Jackson Advocate* called on blacks to view the war as an effort to bring about "the defeat of Hitler and all that Nazi Germany stands for." Special concern for black editors in Mississippi included black loyalty (financial, moral, and physical) to the Allies and the black press's responsibility to stress this loyalty, concern about discrimination against black soldiers, the need for national unity to overcome the forces of Germany, Italy, and Japan, and a need for American power to prevent Communist expansion from, as the *Enterprise* expressed it, destroying "our way of life."[20]

The black press in Mississippi saw the war as a struggle to save democracy. Surprisingly, only the *Southern Advocate* paid little attention to the conflict. Its first mention of World War II involved a January 1941 story about the formation of an all-black air unit at Tuskegee, Alabama, to which some white pilots objected. Another six months passed before a second war-related news item appeared.[21] Perhaps this paper believed its limited resources (news space, staff, and so on) should be devoted to purely black local matters. Furthermore, two white dailies, the Memphis, Tennessee, *Commercial Appeal* and the Greenville *Delta Democrat-Times*, supplied the area with day-to-day war news.

Percy Greene's leadership of the *Jackson Advocate* made it the most significant black political paper in Mississippi during the war years. He took radical positions for black rights, especially for suffrage and political participation in Mississippi. Yet even Greene felt compelled to tell the white political establishment that blacks would in no way threaten their power or influence. During the 1948 election, Greene proposed a fifteen-point program to the state legislature in which he urged members to deal with black problems and race relations. He noted that the "only purpose" of black political activity in Mississippi was "to join with [the Democratic party] in the spirit of the Constitution in Democracy in making Mississippi a better place for both its White and Negro citizens to live." The white press in Jackson thought that Greene had "power" and influence in bringing out the black vote in Mississippi for Harry Truman. However, as Luther P. Jackson pointed out in 1948, of Mississippi's 563,754 qualified black voters, only 5,000 had registered, only 0.9 percent of the possible total.[22] Thus Greene represented a paradox—he spoke out vigorously for black political rights when it was assumed that blacks had no rights, yet failed to advocate overturning the conservative forces that had ruled in Mississippi since Reconstruction ended. Instead, he sought a union of these interests with black concerns. Only the *Jackson Advocate* dared to suggest this option.[23]

Greene's rival in Jackson, the *Mississippi Enterprise*, took a much more conservative stance on black political rights. The paper said very little, if anything, about this issue during the war years, politically Democratic in its outlook and not questioning the status quo. After the war, the paper noted the importance of the American system, with its "framework of the law," and of the fact that in the United States "man controls the state—and the state does not control the man." All of America's achievements and values resulted from the "spiritual" nature of the society "based as they are upon the dignity and rights of man."[24] Thus, the *Enterprise* seemed to say that blacks had rights because they too were Americans. The paper, however, refrained from taking a strong editorial position on this issue.

In the Delta, neither the *Southern Advocate* nor the *Delta Leader* focused seriously on black voting and political rights. The *Southern Advocate*, however, viewed the American judicial system, especially the Supreme Court, as an important source for change in the South. This paper's only interest in politics occurred in its support of white Democratic candidates. If blacks did not support the Democrats, the paper argued, their ballot would not "mean much in gaining . . . political and economic freedom." Nothing was ever said about how black interests could be secured or protected by the same system that had sought to keep them powerless. Conversely, the *Delta Leader* elected to say nothing.[25]

In the 1930s and 1940s, the four papers supported Booker T. Washington's contention that blacks and whites in the South could, and should, remain separate on social matters but that on economic questions their interests coincided. Thus, the papers stressed the positive role that they could play in both areas. They believed that an alliance among the upper classes could aid both goals. The *Delta Leader* advocated the "better element" among both blacks and whites "working together" to improve better relations between the races.[26]

Another major concern of the black press during this period was the need, as the *Mississippi Enterprise* saw it, for blacks "in the South who have the courage to truthfully give to the world a true picture of existing conditions." The *Delta Leader* expressed this idea in terms of blacks needing to be "guilty of . . . selling the idea of racial improvement . . . racial progress . . . and better relations between the white and the black than now exists in the Delta."[27] The press always emphasized blacks' responsibilities but rarely stated whites' burden in improving race relations.

The press showed deep concern for the economic situation of black Mississippians. Black businesses, the *Enterprise* stressed, would lead to "becoming self-respecting, self-supporting citizens."[28] The press also called for "better jobs with better pay" for blacks employed on farms, in factories, and by other white business concerns. In 1948 the *Jackson Advocate* observed that without economic opportunity for blacks and for many poor whites, Mississippi, which in the 1940s had the lowest per capita income in the United States, would remain at the bottom.[29]

Other issues connected to the theme of jobs and economic security included calls for equal distribution of state funds among white and black schools and for better housing and health-care services and opposition to unions and strikes, which the *Delta Leader* described as anti-American in their "drastic demands" on American business. This antilabor mood reflected the general white Southern position on this issue.[30]

Finally, other significant themes during and after World War II include race pride, achievement, and advancement; crime; and black migration to the North. Closely related to pride and achievement (the historical heritage of black survival from slavery through the Civil War and the political, social, economic, and cultural movement from 1865 onward) were the special place of the black church, minister, school, and teacher. All of the papers highlighted the importance of "Negro History Week," an annual observation in February.[31]

The press viewed crimes committed by blacks against other blacks, especially murders, as a serious problem. The *Delta Leader* expressed its outrage by noting that "at one time we thought that Negroes were beginning to get murder and violence out of their systems and learning how to settle their differences without thought of taking a life."[32] The black press also viewed with interest the fact that many blacks escaped the severe penalties for murder because intervention on their behalf by influential white business leaders or politicians. In addition to spotlighting these problems, the press also noted the injustice of many local police departments—stiffer sentences for cases involving blacks accused of crimes against whites and racketeering. The late 1948 disappearance of J.E. Conic, a black Jackson barber and distributor of the *Chicago Defender* and *Pittsburgh Courier* became a major case. Despite a large reward for information raised by local blacks, he was never seen alive again. His body was discovered in a pond outside the Jackson city limits. Lynching continued to be a problem; cases of interest to the *Enterprise* in 1942 included the lynchings of two fourteen-year-old black youths in Shubuta, Clarke County, and of Howard Wash, a farmhand near Laurel.[33]

The black press viewed migration from the South to the North as "a serious and sad mistake." Despite problems in the South, many editors described the urban environment as worse than anything on the farm. The *Delta Leader* invited blacks who had migrated to the cities to move "back to the farm," if they could not make a living in Chicago or Detroit. They saw the South as the historical home base for blacks in the United States with the most promise for the race.[34]

The black press confronted the white press, which intertwined with Mississippi's political machine and secret organizations from 1900 to 1950. The *Fayette Chronicle* expressed this state of solidarity as "the preservation of white supremacy in the south."[35] This translated into a policy of making the white newspaper the first line of defense for the segregation system. News reporting and comments sought always to portray blacks as inferior to whites and therefore unworthy of full citizenship rights. The leading segregationist paper of the era was the morning *Clarion-Ledger* (with the later addition of the afternoon *Jackson Daily News*). The Hederman family of Jackson controlled these papers from the 1920s onward, making them the most powerful publishing family in the history of the state.[36]

Although the overall focus of the white press (between the two world wars and after) remained antiblack, some white newspapers rose above this irrational behavior by calling for moderation and change in Mississippi. The most significant papers in this group were the Greenville *Delta Democrat-Times* and the *Pascagoula Chronicle*. Both papers supported the cause of racial moderation and justice for blacks, considered heresy by many white Mississippians.[37]

The economic demands on the black press in Mississippi during the 1940s did not differ from previous periods. As one scholar has noted, nationally and locally, "The major financial problem faced by these papers, as business organizations, is the inability to obtain large advertising support. The future of the press, however, will only to a very slight degree be influenced by its success in overcoming this obstacle; as a social institution, and not as a business, it will have to be judged."[38]

This certainly held true for Mississippi's black journalists. To survive, black papers had to keep costs as low as possible, in part by securing the free services of black reporters, especially for church, social, and local news, and by maintaining a small office, staff, and general budget. The staff usually consisted of one or two people—the editor and a family member or friend. Black papers also needed dependable sources of advertising dollars or other funds (from printing work, for example). Advertising, especially from both black and white businesses with many black customers, remained critical.

A study of advertisements in five black Mississippi papers for the early period of World War II reveals that general advertisements came from both black and white sources. In Mound Bayou, the *Southern Advocate*, a commercial paper, and the *Taborian Star*, a fraternal organ, depended on black advertising revenue in 1940 and 1941. However, a small number of white advertisements did appear in the *Southern Advocate*.

In Greenville, on the other hand, the *Delta Leader*, also a commercial paper, based its operating expenses on black, white, and Chinese advertising. These included funeral homes, laundries, taxi companies, Wong Ben's Grocery, local physicians, and the Pepsi-Cola Company. The *Leader* had a much larger advertising base than the *Southern Advocate* and the *Taborian Star*, which were located in the all-black township of Mound Bayou.

This pattern held true for the *Mississippi Enterprise* and the *Jackson Advocate*. Like the *Delta Leader*, they attracted a small number of white advertisements, but the largest volume of advertising dollars clearly came from black businesses. Table 2-1 illustrates the total number of advertisements for two separate issues of each of these papers. For the larger papers (the *Leader*, the *Enterprise*, and the *Advocate*), the number of advertisements for a weekly issue during the early 1940s stayed above forty-five. This volume of advertisements aided the papers in meeting their publication costs. The small range of advertisements for the *Southern Advocate* and the *Taborian Star* during this period indicates that both organs received large subsidies, the *Southern Advocate* from the publisher and editor, the *Taborian Star* from the Knights and Daughters of Tabor.[39]

During the 1940s blacks failed to gain a control of any radio stations in Mississippi. Blacks did appear on black-oriented programs during the decade, however, on stations managed and owned by whites. Vicksburg represented one of the early centers of black radio interest in Mississippi.

TABLE 2-1. Advertisements for Two Separate Issues of Black Papers, 1939–45

Paper	Date of issue	No. ads	Date of issue	No. ads
Southern Advocate	Oct. 12, 1940	10	Sept. 13, 1941	12
Taborian Star	Nov. 1941	7	Dec. 1944	9
Delta Leader	June 22, 1940	62	Jan. 4, 1941	45
Jackson Advocate	Aug. 2, 1941	43	Dec. 5, 1942	60
Mississippi Enterprise	Sept. 23, 1939	61	Sept. 8, 1945	89

Jerome W. Stampley, a black educator, developed a radio program on black life at station WQBC. His work was significant, according to Bruce Payne, another early black radio pioneer, because "his weekly program was devoted to presenting Black accomplishments. He presented the Alcorn, Jackson State and Tougaloo College choirs; thirty minutes of culture, classical, semi-classical music and spirituals. He also presented the top Black bands of the day when they came through town. . . . His program was well respected for the quality of culture and entertainment that it presented."[40]

Bruce Payne also began his radio career in Vicksburg at WVIM (now defunct) in 1948. He hosted a black teenage—oriented show geared toward talent and local news. Choirs, bands, and drama comprised the meat of his radio program. But Payne, like Stampley, also felt a need to do something else. Payne said he always tried to "present some Black news," because "there were not a lot of Blacks in radio at that time."

Many barriers to blacks in broadcasting existed during the 1940s. Payne notes that in Vicksburg there existed "Gross discrimination—there were some white station operators/owners . . . who felt that Blacks had no place—traditional roles were expected; being on the radio was like being out of the Black race. There was a lot of discrimination by the white populace. Many just wouldn't listen to Blacks on the radio."[41]

In Greenville, blacks sponsored programs on radio station WJPR. A typical program there resembled black radio activities in Vicksburg. For example, the Knights and Daughters of Tabor, a black Masonic organization in Mississippi, committed its resources to hosting an eight o'clock Sunday morning program: the Delta-Mello-Tone Singers supplied the music and a guest spoke each week on a topic of interest to blacks and the general public. Another leading disc jockey of the period was Early Wright of WROX in Clarksdale. He began his career in 1947 and reached listeners throughout the Delta.[42]

Blacks in Jackson felt it represented an example of better race relations when radio station WJXN broadcast the speech of Washington, D.C., attorney Belford W. Lawson in 1949. Lawson, national president of Alpha Phi Alpha Fraternity, Inc., addressed the graduate chapter of the fraternity at Jackson, Alpha Epsilon Lambda, calling "for the total abolition of segregation and discrimination everywhere."[43] While these were indeed courageous words at the time, the question lingered: Who would speak out in the future?

Nevertheless, in spite of efforts by people like Stampley and Payne, blacks remained powerless in terms of radio communication during and after the war. As a group, they did not control a single radio station, and they had little airtime on white-owned stations. Black-oriented radio programs generally lasted from fifteen to thirty minutes. Because these programs contained mostly music (singing and instrumental), the remaining time consisted of announcing the performers and of advertisements. Blacks had to take care when appearing on radio programs to abide by the segregation codes of the white South.[44] Thus, newspapers remained the major vehicles of black communications in Mississippi.

W. E. B. Du Bois stated in 1943 that the black press "must be looked upon not simply as a business enterprise but as real institutions which the Negro race has created and is using for its advancement. They must, therefore, fill in the future a higher and higher function." This higher development included the effective use of columnists, blacks who had received training at schools of journalism, and a commitment to use black newspapers "for the education of youth and the direction of adults."[45]

The situation in Mississippi resembled the national mood described by Du Bois; however, another generation would come and go before trained black journalists could assume a major position on newspapers in the state. In Mississippi, as elsewhere, the press could not afford an adequate salary for holders of bachelor's degrees. Consequently, for this period the vast majority of black journalists in Mississippi had either taught themselves, received training in printing shops, or worked in other occupations, such as the ministry or teaching.

The black press received severe criticism during the 1940s. Some blacks believed that black press organs were too conservative, and some whites alleged that black papers promoted radical thinking. Du Bois viewed this criticism as unfair to most of the black press. He observed that the black press, "was not guilty of stirring up Negroes to revolt. Negro public opinion has stirred the newspapers to voice revolt." Furthermore, the black press was "not guilty of misrepresenting the condition" of black people; and although it did "play up crime and scandal" this news focus was "not nearly as much as the white press." Finally, although the black press did "emphasize, and often exaggerates" the actual accomplishments of blacks, Du Bois viewed this as much less than "the boastfulness of the national press."[46]

Too often, both white and black critics took black newspapers to task for what they viewed as its greatest shortcoming, dealing "single-mindedly with the problems of being a Negro in the United States, the prospects, the triumphs, and the despairs of all those for whom the fact of being a Negro outweighs, for a part of the time at least, all other concerns."[47] Such an analysis, as was too often the case in segregated America in the 1940s, did not take into consideration the vast complexities of the black press and of the Afro-American people. The range and the variety of the black press, even in Mississippi, remained large enough to cover the interests, needs, and concerns of a vast portion of the Afro-American news market. This range included religious, educational, fraternal, and commercial journals, from Mississippi and from other parts of the world.

The key to understanding the black press in Mississippi and elsewhere in the 1940s lies in assessing the term "responsibility," which has constituted a watchword for black journalists from 1827 to the present. Roscoe Dangee, editor of the *Black Dispatch* (Oklahoma City), argued in 1946 that the true measurement of the black press and of black editors lay in whether the press met four criteria, including integrity and honor, courage, vision and understanding, and conviction.[48] For oppressed people the questions remain how they can achieve freedom and a sense of self-determination, how they can protect their culture and historical memory, and how they can communicate their needs to other members of the group. This has represented the true task of the black press in America. A problem emerges when the interpretation of this task is addressed by the individual components of the black press throughout the United States. The black press must promote its continued development and seek to defend the economic, political, and social freedom of blacks throughout the world.

In many ways the role of the black press in Mississippi from 1900 to 1950 can be likened to an unfulfilled dream. It often proved difficult for the press to record, analyze, critique, or offer remedies for social ills in an atmosphere of hatred. Submission to the system was the watchword, although some black organizations, such as the NAACP and the Committee of One Hundred for the General Improvement of the Condition of the Colored People in Mississippi supported political and social rights for all.[49] Other individuals, such as teachers, ministers, community leaders, and doctors, remained vigilant in their efforts to keep a wholesome atmosphere alive within their communities. Success was hard to achieve. The heavy hand of Jim Crow took its toll, and the black papers of Mississippi disappeared one after another. By 1949 only a few black journalists remained to carry the struggle into another decade of pain and challenge.

CHAPTER 3

The Conservative Mood

1950–1959

The 1950s constituted a terror-filled decade for blacks in Mississippi. With the intensification of the national and regional struggle against segregation and discrimination, Jim Crow's supporters consolidated their efforts to protect the old order. Part of this response consisted of a series of violent terroristic acts against blacks. Mississippi represented the heart of the segregationist campaign to keep blacks degraded.

In addition to these pressures, Mississippi's blacks faced the harsh reality of everyday tragedy that life held for them in terms of their social, economic, and political conditions. The black population continued to decline, from 1,077,469 in 1940 to 986,707 in 1950 to 915,743 by 1960, a loss of 161,726 people over the period. For the first time, blacks had become a minority. Mississippi's white population numbered 1,188,429 in 1950, and the state had 3,778 of other ethnicities, including Native Americans and Chinese Americans. Mississippi had in 1950 a total population of 2,178,914 people.[1]

A rash of lynchings occurred during the 1950s—whites killed black males for a variety of alleged crimes against the segregation system or for just being black. Blacks endured an educational system in which the state provided yearly $35.27 per black student versus $117.43 per white pupil for 1952.[2] Health care represented another problem. A 1951 study noted that as late as the end of World War II "there were, in 1944–45, 2,785 hospital beds available for whites, 1,275 for Negroes; and 1,360 white doctors as against 57 Negro doctors."[3]

It appears that most white Mississippians viewed segregation as a system worth fighting and even dying for. To do so, they had to prevent blacks from registering to vote or from voting if they had somehow managed to register. By 1951, as many as 20,000 blacks had registered but only about 5,600 actually voted. Mississippi's black voting potential numbered 500,000 during the 1950s but fear kept most blacks far away from the polls. By 1958, only 3.4 percent of eligible blacks had registered to vote. Steven F. Lawson notes that in Forrest County, white clerks asked black registrants such questions as "How many bubbles are in a bar of soap?"[4]

Mississippi still suffered from economic depression. The number of farm jobs declined during the decade as a result of the introduction of new machinery. This loss had a tremendous impact on blacks, as more of them left the farm for the city. The problem for blacks and many poor whites was Mississippi's dubious distinction of having the lowest per capita income and median family income ($1,198 in 1950) in the United States. In 1950, 300,000 Mississippians worked on farms; by 1960, this figure shrank to 142,000. In 1960, only 2,123 families in the state had a yearly income of $25,000 or more. In such a climate, Ross Barnett, gubernatorial candidate in 1959, proclaimed, "The Negro is different because God made him different to punish him. His forehead slants back; his nose is different. His lips are different, and his color is sure different. . . . We will not drink from the cup of genocide.[5] The psychological and physical terror spread during the 1950s had a major impact on all aspects of black existence. Of all Mississippi's institutions, white terror had perhaps its greatest impact on the black press.

Segregation created a period of fear and silence for many in the black press during the 1950s. In fact, by 1954 only five black commercial papers published in Mississippi—four conservative (pro-segregation, white-dominated) sheets that made niggardly responses to conditions and one radical journal of resistance. The former consisted of the *Delta Leader*, the *Jackson Advocate*, the *Mississippi Enterprise*, and the New Albany *Community Citizen*. The fifth paper was the underground Jackson *Eagle Eye*.

During the 1950s, two additional commercial papers—the Natchez *City Bulletin* and the *Meridian Morning Sun*—appeared in Mississippi. Religious journals of the decade included the *Saint Augustine's Messenger* (Catholic), published at Bay Saint Louis, and the *Central Voice* (Baptist), published at Yazoo City. Fraternal organs active during this period included the Meridian *Echo* and the Mound Bayou *Taborian Star*. Black organizations publishing newsletters included the Jackson Progressive Voters League, the Mississippi State NAACP, the Jackson Urban League, the Mississippi chapter of the National Business League, the Civic Club of Mound Bayou, and the Mississippi State Federation of Colored Women's Clubs. Educational journals existed at such predominately black institutions as Alcorn A&M College (the *Alcorn Herald* newspaper and the *Alcornite*), Piney Woods School (the *Pine Torch*), Prentiss Institute (the *Prentissite*), Okolona Industrial Institute (the *Mississippi Letter*), Rust College (the *Sentinel* and the *Bearcat*), Utica Junior College (the *Bulldog Growl* and the *Uticanite*), Tougaloo College (the *Tougaloo News* and the *Eagle Queen*), Jackson State College (*Blue and White Flash* and the *Jacksonian*), and Mississippi Valley State College (the *Valley Voice* and the *Delvian*). The *Mississippi Educational Journal*, a professional organ active since the 1920s, also continued to publish.[6]

The U.S. Supreme Court's May 1954 *Brown vs. Board of Education of Topeka* decision horrified white Mississippians. Massive resistance to school desegregation took place for the remainder of the 1950s and throughout the 1960s. This movement had widespread effects on all aspects of black life, especially in terms of political organization, educational advancement, economic opportunities, and a general apprehension regarding blacks' physical safety.[7]

Mississippi's black masses welcomed the *Brown* decision, and many hoped that at long last the nightmare of racial segregation would soon be over. Except for the *Eagle Eye*, the black press adopted a passive attitude. This stance, despite good intentions, led to the decline of the black newspaper. Many readers assumed that black editors had been bought off by the establishment to abandon the struggle for black advancement.

The black press in Mississippi during the 1950s operated in an intense environment in which, as Dr. T.R.M. Howard of Mound Bayou noted, "You have got to be a black man in Mississippi at least 24 hours to understand what it means to be a Negro in Mississippi."[8] Many events of the era—both inside and outside of the state—had a profound impact on life and institutions. National issues affecting the black masses and press included the Korean War (1950–53), the aforementioned *Brown* decision and white resistance to it, the Montgomery bus boycott (1955–56), Martin Luther King, Jr.'s emerging leadership, the civil rights movement, the selection of Dr. Ralph J. Bunche as the first black to receive the Nobel Peace Prize (1950), the operatic career of Leontyne Price, Autherine

Lucy's admission to and suspension from the University of Alabama (1955–56), the Little Rock school crisis (1957), the Civil Rights Act of 1957, and the creation of Ghana (1957). The old issue of lynching and the murders of a number of black men—for example, Willie McGee (1950), Rev. George Lee (1955), Emmett Till (1955), Lamar Smith (1957), and Mack Charles Parker (1959)—remained concerns.

On the state level, blacks watched Medgar Evers's application for admission to the University of Mississippi (1954), the formation of the White Citizens' Council, with its first chapter at Indianola (July 11, 1954), the murder of Clinton Melton at Glendora (1955), the shooting of Gus Courts at Belzoni (1955), Clyde Kennard's attempt to enter the University of Southern Mississippi (1957–59), Clennon King's attempt to enter the University of Mississippi (1957–59), and a series of actions by the Mississippi legislature, including the 1956 enactment of several anti-integration laws and establishment of the State Sovereignty Commission and the passage of a law to investigate the NAACP in 1958.[9]

Jackson remained the center of black publishing in Mississippi during the 1950s; however, activity continued in the old strongholds of Greenville and Mound Bayou. Black publications appeared in all parts of the state, including the *Meridian Morning Sun* and *Echo* in east Mississippi; the New Albany *Community Citizen* in north Mississippi; the *Saint Augustine's Messenger* on the Mississippi Gulf Coast; the *Jackson Advocate*, the Jackson *Mississippi Enterprise*, the Jackson *Eagle Eye*, and the Yazoo City *Central Voice*, in central Mississippi; the Greenville *Delta Leader* and the Mound Bayou *Sentinel* in the Delta region; and the Natchez *City Bulletin* in the southwestern part of the state.

The major papers maintained moderate circulation rates, ranging in 1958 from a high of 55,000 for the *Saint Augustine's Messenger*, a Catholic organ with a national audience, to 7,805 for the *Delta Leader*, 5,309 for the *Jackson Advocate*, and 2,575 for the New Albany *Community Citizen*.[10]

Economic, political, and social factors converged during the 1950s to decrease the number and variety of black papers in Mississippi. Although the black press had begun to decline before the Great Depression, by the 1950s the crisis generated by the black struggle against segregation and white opposition, black migration from Mississippi, and the cruel forms of the state's racism, including censorship, created general black disinterest in the media. Thus, the fact that only eleven major papers existed signals the deathblow for positive black journalism in Mississippi during this period. As many blacks knew only too well, the white power structure had bought off many black newspapers either to aid in the destruction of the civil rights movement or to slow the progress of blacks' demands for a new direction for society.

The tragedy of the 1950s lies in the segregationists' success in securing control of so much of the Mississippi's black press. Their ability to secure such a hold is not surprising, given whites' economic and political power, their success at dividing and conquering, and the exodus of tens of thousands of blacks from the state. With them went their talents as editors, printers, reporters, businessmen, and so forth, weakening the remainder as a force against segregation.

The vast majority of the white press remained pro-segregationist during the 1950s, led by the Jackson *Clarion-Ledger* and the *Jackson Daily News*. Other Jackson journals espousing this position included the *State Times*, an afternoon paper, and the *Citizens' Council*, a monthly tabloid newspaper of the Citizens' Councils of America. Organized in 1954 the latter group represented a major effort by Mississippians and other Southerners to fight desegregation. In the towns and rural areas, a variety of white dailies and weeklies followed the example of the Jackson white press, and a policy of firm commitment to segregation and white supremacy held command in more than 90 percent of the white papers.[11]

Four white Mississippi editors of the 1950s constitute outstanding examples of the very best traditions in American journalism: Ira Harkey, copublisher of the *Pascagoula Chronicle*, Hazel Brannon Smith, editor and publisher of the *Lexington Advertiser*; Hodding Carter, Jr., editor of the Greenville *Delta Democrat-Times*, and P.D. East, editor and publisher of the *Petal Paper*, in Petal, located near Hattiesburg. As moderates, perhaps even radicals in Mississippi's frame of reference, they at least attempted to examine rationally the conditions of both whites and blacks in Mississippi and suggested that Mississippi needed change, growth, and development for its future. At the center of their arguments stood black men and women; life in Mississippi would never really improve until white Mississippians' view of black people had changed. As a group, these white editors suffered economic reprisals and social ostracism, but they withstood the bombardment of the segregationists and succeeded in keeping freedom of the press alive during a decade of doubt.[12]

Although based in Jackson, the *Jackson Advocate*, the *Mississippi Enterprise*, and the *Eagle Eye* differed greatly in their interest in news and events. With the rural Mound Bayou *Sentinel*, these four papers reflect the era and offer a good overview of the black press.[13]

Among the Jackson papers, the *Jackson Advocate* stood out. For years, most notably during the 1940s, the *Advocate* had represented the major black voice against the dismal state of affairs for both blacks and whites. At the time, most blacks supported the journal's efforts to bring about social change. In the 1950s, however, the paper developed a distorted worldview.[14] Many black Mississippians abandoned the paper and it suffered greatly. In spite of these setbacks, the paper's full-time editor, Percy Greene, seldom missed an issue.

A summary of Greene's positions during the 1950s indicated that he was conservative on social relations between blacks and whites, moderate on economic questions (except for labor unions), and a supporter of the status quo on political issues, except on black voting rights. On many issues, he followed the traditionalist style of Booker T. Washington. On one hand, he was the antisegregationist calling for change and a new direction in Mississippi; but on the other, he advocated strong, independent black institutions (schools, churches, businesses, and so on).

On international issues, the *Advocate* feared that attitudes about white supremacy could spell disaster for American foreign policy in Korea and among black, yellow, and brown people. However, Greene carefully noted "the courage, bravery, sacrifice, loyalty, patriotism and conduct of the Mississippi Negro soldier in the Korean war." He observed that as in World Wars I and II, blacks fought abroad "for the same and identical kind of Democracy for which all other soldiers of Mississippi are fighting."[15] For blacks this meant an effort to secure equal justice and opportunity in the United States.

The *Brown* decision occupied a major place in the thoughts of the *Advocate* from 1954 through the 1960s. The paper agreed that segregation should be abolished. But the *Advocate* lamented the court's failure to realize "that no matter what kind of decision the United States Supreme Court makes, government in the United States starts at the local level, the law is enforced by the elected officials at the local level, and that no decision by any court is stronger than the public opinion, for or against it, at the local level."[16] Greene believed that Southern white goodwill toward blacks had a much bigger role than court decisions. The South could work out its racial problems if only the right leaders could devise solutions to the problems.[17]

The *Advocate* viewed the *Brown* decision as the stimulus for the problems that grew out of the Montgomery bus boycott of 1956 and the civil rights movement. The *Advocate* believed that the boycott only "succeeded in making matters worse for the masses of Montgomery Negroes." This theme runs through the paper from 1954 to 1959. The paper also decried President Dwight Eisenhower's order to send federal troops to Little Rock to enforce a court order involving the admission of black students to Central High School. This action, observed the *Advocate*, created "a deepening of the animosities towards the Negro and a widening of the gulf between responsible Negroes and Whites."[18] Greene had little to say on the significance of the 1957 Civil Rights Act, the first since Reconstruction.

Although he supported black voting, suffrage had a limited purpose for Greene: "The only sound reason for Negroes in the state wanting the right to vote is so that they will be able to join with the better class white people in bringing about whatever is best in the state, and in their local communities."[19]

On the international scene, the *Advocate* expressed interest in the problems growing out of colonialism in Asia, Africa, and the Caribbean, with a special emphasis on Africa. Africa had particular importance to Americans, Greene wrote in 1959, because "the world race relations picture and demands are changing rapidly and Africa, and the Africans and their leaders are exerting a profound influence in bringing about the change." As the ancestral homeland of American blacks, attention to African issues reflected racial pride. Although the paper viewed Africa as a continent with a major role in world affairs, it also believed that much of the African past came from "primitive cultures." Yet the *Advocate* wrote on the comparative condition of "extremes in racial segregation and discrimination" in Mississippi and Africa and the problems that this caused in the economic development of both areas.[20]

Segregation and the related social, economic, and political situation constituted the major issue in Mississippi during the 1950s. The *Jackson Advocate*'s solution was simple: blacks had nothing to fear from whites, and the best class of whites and blacks could work things out if outside forces would stay away. The paper argued that black businesses should strengthen and grow, because they represented part of black progress. Still, the *Advocate* acknowledged that "the white people control all the money, all the jobs, all the instruments of power, the police, and the jury."[21] The *Advocate* supported black voting rights but did not support the efforts of any of the civil rights organizations, including the NAACP, the strongest statewide organization. The paper labeled the movement for educational desegregation after the *Brown* decision and the NAACP's efforts as "the greatest mistake in the entire history of the struggles of the American Negro."[22] Although the *Advocate* supported an end to segregation, it saw nothing wrong with blacks and whites following Booker T. Washington's program.

To promote this work, the *Jackson Advocate* saw its task as that of "telling [blacks] the truth about [their] conditions and surroundings instead of telling [them] what [they] want to hear."[23] Unfortunately, this approach did not include a serious treatment of the problem of lynching and black assassinations. These atrocities only appeared in the news pages—without commentary. The case of Emmett Louis Till, the fourteen-year-old black youth killed in Mississippi for allegedly whistling at a white woman, provides one example. While the violent murder of Till saddened the *Advocate*, the central issue for the paper remained blacks' continued maintenance of the "good will of the people." The paper told blacks that Mississippi had "thousands of fine white people in the state who wholeheartedly condemn the slaying of the Till boy, who still are friendly towards the Negroes' desire and right to equality under the law, while at the same time totally rejecting the NAACP drive for integration of the races in the state."[24] Other papers remained silent. The black public could only conclude that the paper regretted that some blacks had to face unjust deaths, but the desire for better race relations required that blacks not retaliate or protest too loudly.

By the end of the 1950s, the influence of Percy Greene and the *Jackson Advocate* had died. The public viewed the *Advocate* as a conservative, pro-segregationist organ, a view reinforced by the financial help the *Advocate* received from the Mississippi State Sovereignty Commission, an antiblack state agency established in the mid-1950s to counter the civil rights activities in the state. Greene, on the other hand, saw nothing wrong in accepting the funds. He accused blacks who charged him with selling out as displaying "a totally naive view of the nature of politics, and the work of politically created commissions."[25] In Greene's view, the *Advocate* needed funds, so he secured them. He maintained this state of mind throughout the 1960s, when he and the *Advocate* continued to face the scorn of many blacks, particularly members of the Ministers' Improvement Association of Mississippi, civil rights leaders such as Medgar Evers, and others.

Like the *Jackson Advocate*, the *Mississippi Enterprise* had operated in

Jackson since the 1930s. But unlike most other black papers of that period, the *Enterprise* espoused Democratic politics.[26] Its Democratic sympathies set it on an early course of accommodationism with white Mississippi. In 1950, a staff of three operated the paper: Willie J. Miller, managing editor, Sarah M. Harvey, associate editor, and her son, William Harvey, who served as circulation manager. By 1954, Miller had assumed the title of publisher-owner, and Sarah Harvey became the editor. An eight-page weekly, in 1950 the *Enterprise* charged its readers $1.50 for a six-month subscription to the paper ($3.00 per year) or seven cents for a single issue. By 1954, these rates had increased to $2.50, $4.00, and ten cents. The paper in 1950 and 1955 claimed a weekly circulation of three thousand copies.[27]

The *Enterprise* viewed its role during the 1950s as one of offering its "readers a news service dedicated to reflecting the better side of Negro life" and of "achieving a society in which there will be no unimportant people." The paper argued that there would "always be a need for a Negro newspaper because . . . when it comes to the overall interests of Negroes in our society, only the Negro press can be counted upon as a Negro voice and champion." Therefore, there was a need for the black press to express "its voice in America's fight for truth, freedom and justice."[28] This represented the general tone of the black press of the period.

Putting these words into action, however, was another matter. The *Enterprise* felt it important to stress local, state, and regional news. International news only became important when it touched directly on blacks. The Korean War represented one such event—the paper had to cover the conflict because blacks, as Americans, served in the war. For the *Enterprise*, then, the blacks' glory in the Korean War meant that they had successfully demonstrated "a record of bravery that is in full accord with the record made by American Negro soldiers in other wars."[29] The paper's major international concern was the communist threat. Blacks, the *Enterprise* suggested, should aid in the fight "against aggression" by the communists in Korea and work to end the influence of the American Communist party.[30] On affairs in Africa, Latin America, and other parts of the world, the paper said little.

Although accommodationist in its general political outlook, the paper, like Booker T. Washington, believed that blacks had political rights, especially the right to vote. Consequently, the *Enterprise* gave extensive editorial support in 1953 and 1954 to the Progressive Voters' League, a local organization devoted to securing black voting privileges, but only before reactionaries took hold of white public opinion in response to *Brown*.[31] Nonetheless, the *Enterprise* stood its ground—as American citizens, blacks had the right to register and to vote. On who they would vote for, the paper remained dead silent.

On the issue of taxes, the *Enterprise* connected taxes with "good citizenship" and wrote that taxes represented "one of the few ways in which every citizen" could "participate in the government." But the paper never demonstrated how, when, and under what circumstances black taxes would aid and contribute to freeing blacks from segregation and oppression. The *Enterprise* believed taxes constituted "an insurance against slavery," but the paper apparently did not include the 1950s in this analysis of the situation.

The *Enterprise* also took on the problem of peonage, running a front-page story on four white Winston County farmers whom a federal grand jury charged with holding a black man in peonage in 1954. Like most of the white press in the South the *Enterprise* espoused an antilabor position. In response to labor organizers in Mississippi, in 1950 the paper noted that the "Negroes in Jackson and Mississippi in many instances are to be congratulated for their wisdom in refusing to allow outside agitators to come in and make trouble between them and their present employers." The *Enterprise* concluded that blacks were "here in Mississippi to live and die, to leave for our children a heritage of better homes, better schools, and better economic and social conditions." Blacks could only do this "by making friends of those people around us, by completely ignoring outside agitators."[32]

The *Enterprise* did not take an editorial position on the political implications of the Willie McGee case, in which a black man allegedly raped the white woman who lived with him; McGee was electrocuted by the state of Mississippi, in spite of an international outcry about the affair. The paper instead ran a page-one story that quoted Governor Fielding L. Wright as saying that he believed "that the Communists had interceded in the case in order to convince Mississippi's Negro population that it could not obtain justice in the courts and should turn to communism." Furthermore, the governor continued, "I honestly believe that at least 90 percent—I'd even say 95 percent of the Negroes in this state are good Negroes. They don't want anything more than they are entitled to."[33] Willie McGee was lost in white supremacist attitudes about the "proper" place of blacks in Mississippi life. One can only conclude that the *Enterprise* too often joined the camp of the "good Negroes."

The *Enterprise*'s attitude, like the *Jackson Advocate*'s, extended to the realm of segregated social relations. For the *Enterprise*, Mississippi represented "the Promised Land" because "No where on earth may we find more beautiful homes and palaces for lesser or minority groups, than in America."[34] The *Enterprise* failed to point out that this social paradise did not extend to the vast majority of blacks, who faced discrimination and housing restrictions. The paper never examined the general black condition or the social implications of segregation. Instead, the *Enterprise* praised the efforts of white official Mississippi: "We commend all efforts being made to improve the educational system of our state. . . . It has come a long way and for this we can all be thankful."[35] Despite progress, black life remained separate and unequal. To overcome prejudice, discrimination and racism, the *Enterprise* called on black Mississippians to have "an open mind, a willingness to take all factors into consideration, an attitude of understanding and goodwill, a prayerful seeking of the Divine will. Even then there will be vast differences of opinion, which is not unhealthy; but there will be a lessening of tensions, and more approachable method of solving our differences in a Christian atmosphere."[36]

The complexity of the *Mississippi Enterprise* and the *Jackson Advocate* during the 1950s centered on the need, as both papers saw it, for "the spirit of working together," as Percy Greene suggested, with "the better class white people" to increase the opportunities open to black people, a goal that included an improved economic position for blacks but did not require a change in the political and social life. Progress and change would come, both papers assumed, if blacks remained patient, struggled (with white support) to improve their educational position, and expressed an interest in politics, but only to support Mississippi's Democratic power structure and white supremacy.

Most black Mississippians rejected such attitudes, and during the 1950s the *Enterprise* and the *Advocate* began to lose black public support, resulting in a declining number of black subscriptions. Both papers, however, survived because of white support from advertising and from funds supplied by the Mississippi State Sovereignty Commission. Advertisement support continued to come from black businesses during and after the 1950s as a result of the traditional support for the black press; however, black businesses directed their efforts primarily toward conservative and moderate papers.[37]

A third black journal in Jackson during the 1950s was the *Eagle Eye*, published by Arrington W. High. An underground paper, the *Eagle Eye* usually consisted of a single 14-by-8½-inch typed mimeographed sheet that High produced at home. Individual issues sold for ten cents each or a one-year subscription price of $5.40; however, many people probably received the paper free.[38] The paper must have intrigued its readers, for High did not hold back his tongue in expressing his outrage at segregation and racism. Then, too, the paper represented an at-home effort with little regard for the higher art forms of journalism. The *Eagle Eye* aimed solely to express a personal message against segregation.

The *Eagle Eye*'s purpose differed somewhat from that of the *Mississippi Enterprise* and the *Jackson Advocate*, seeing itself as "America's Greatest Newspaper Bombarding Segregation and Discrimination."[39] In the struggle to conquer segregation, High emphasized certain targets: segregated education; myths of white supremacy; white leaders ("hoodlums"); the Mississippi Constitution of 1890; the state legislature; Jackson's banks; Mississippi's governors; certain black leaders; white men who raped black women; religious leaders who did not attack segregation; the Jackson school board; the white press; lower-class white segregationists; black editors such as Percy Greene; the Jackson Police Department; the Jackson City Council; and the Citizens' Council.

The paper's good graces included such freedom-fighting organizations as the NAACP, national institutions like the U.S. Supreme Court, labor groups, and individuals such as Dr. T.R.M. Howard of Mound Bayou— the very organizations and institutions most hated by white Mississippians. Central to the *Eagle Eye*'s campaign to end segregation was the question of equality in public education. The paper lashed out at white Mississippi and its leaders (especially the governor) for perpetuating segregated schools and for their attempts to strengthen the old system by a plan to "equalize white and black educational institutions and personnel." The *Eagle Eye* considered this approach wrong. Editor High wrote in early 1955 that

the ignorant state of Mississippi's so-called educational equalization program for Negroes never was intended to give the Negro justice but was only a fake to by-pass the ruling of the U.S. Supreme Court of last May 17, 1954; which said that segregation in education was unconstitutional. However, on the local level, the Negro teachers are being swindled on this so-called equalization of teacher's salaries right in Jackson, Mississippi. Negro teachers with higher scholastic rating as well as experience today, in some instances, are receiving way less pay than some white teachers who barely were able to get their diplomas. Yet, Hugh L. White, Governor—tells the people of this country to let us alone—we will settle our problems. Hugh, this won't work today because we Negroes are going to demand that education in Mississippi will be for Mississippians in one school room for all children regardless of race, creed or color.[40]

High designed the *Eagle Eye*'s to bring anger from its adversaries and to encourage blacks to stop fearing Southern whites. The paper certainly succeeded in the former, but questions remain about the latter. Simply put, it seems that few blacks in Jackson read the paper with any degree of seriousness. The underground sheet was just that—underground—and because blacks could turn to other papers with radical views, such as the *Chicago Defender* and the *Pittsburgh Courier*, they had little or no interest in the *Eagle Eye*. Although some might have enjoyed the editor's figurative language mocking Mississippi whites, blacks knew that laughter alone could not address their burdens. To many blacks, the *Eagle Eye* did not constitute an effective weapon in the struggle against segregation.

The Jackson Police Department did not approve of the *Eagle Eye*'s words, and "Arrington W. High, Editor-Publisher of the *Eagle Eye* was picked up and charged with the distribution of literature." Such was the punishment for calling Mississippi "the most ignorant, undemocratic, unholy place and a honeynest for finding the lowest form of white hoodlumism." In fact, the *Eagle Eye* called most white Mississippians hoodlums because of their mistreatment of black people and because of their role in keeping Mississippi underdeveloped. But like his counterparts at the *Jackson Advocate* and the *Mississippi Enterprise*, High also had a great deal of faith in the white upper classes. He argued that they could make a difference in the long run because Mississippi's problems did not originate with them but rather with the poor whites: "Regardless how the turn may go the peckerwoods in ignorant Mississippi must face the fact, the *Eagle Eye* is fighting wrong and not fighting the white man or white woman of the better class, but is fighting the lowdown dirty white hoodlums who are in authority."[41]

A fourth black paper of the 1950s was the *Sentinel*, located in Mound Bayou, second only to Jackson as a black publishing center. Established in 1952 by Isaac Peterson, the *Sentinel* resembled earlier papers in Mound Bayou in its reasonable price (a one-year subscription cost $1.25 for service in Mound Bayou, $1.75 for areas outside of the town) and in its local focus. The tabloid-size paper published semimonthly, with an average edition of four to six pages.[42]

The paper maintained a moderate tone on political, economic, and social matters. It did not attack the white establishment but defended the rights of blacks in the state, especially on the issue of the franchise. The *Sentinel* saw itself as "a medium of getting the current events over to the populace, molding public sentiment and rendering a great service to both the advertisers and the buyers," striving to "publish news that is news, while it is news." Although a small paper, the *Sentinel* sought to provide a "service" to Mound Bayou "and the readers throughout the nation."[43]

A survey of the paper from 1952 to 1954 reveals a newspaper very much in the tradition of the *Mississippi Enterprise*. The central difference lay, however, in the *Sentinel's* interest only in Mound Bayou and the surrounding areas, versus the *Enterprise's* local, state, and regional focus. For the *Sentinel*, the social problems of Mound Bayou and Delta blacks required attention. The paper concerned itself particularly with the inconveniences black customers faced when denied the use of restrooms at service stations and the abuse of black drivers by some elements of the Mississippi Highway Patrol.[44] The paper reminded blacks in early 1953 that to vote their poll taxes had "to be paid on or before January 31, 1953. Don't forget." Although white election officials never counted Mound Bayou's black ballots in state elections, the *Sentinel* nonetheless did its duty by stating the obvious right of blacks to vote in all elections.[45]

Besides espousing black self-help, the paper said little on economic issues during the period, failing to offer advice or comments on the various available economic options. The paper focused on local matters, including church activities, the need for public support of the *Sentinel*, the desire for close relations with Winstonville, another nearby all-black town, support for local black businesses, "race progress" exemplified by Mound Bayou, support for the local Boy Scouts, encouragement for education, praise for the (black) Montgomery Green Post of the American Legion at Mound Bayou, and support for various local drives and community efforts.

The *Sentinel* took special pride in a visit to the historically black town by Governor White in 1953, the first such visit by an active governor of the state. For the *Sentinel*, this represented a grand occasion because Mound Bayou blacks had "waited long for the opportunity to entertain a governor of our great state." This had a special significance, because blacks would now know that White was "governor of all the people of Mississippi."[46]

The *Sentinel's* location in Mound Bayou—an all-black town—offered it a small measure of protection from the direct hostilities of whites; however, security ceased to exist outside the town limits. The *Sentinel* took the middle course—it did not anger whites with radical editorials denouncing segregation and demanding equality. Like the mainstream Jackson black press, it chose to suggest moderate change over time. The *Sentinel* best expressed its feelings on these matters when it noted the kindness a group of Mound Bayou blacks had received after a visit to the Delta Electric Plant at Cleveland, Mississippi, in the summer of 1953. "The group was highly pleased with the courtesies shown by the Light Company," the *Sentinel* recalled. At that particular critical point in history, the paper concluded that "All of this helps to establish better relations."[47]

The economics of black publishing during the 1950s remained very much the same as in the 1930s and 1940s. The few papers that survived into the 1950s attracted the advertisement dollars of black and white businesses, especially of the former. Because so few black commercial papers remained active in the state, such journals as the *Jackson Advocate*, the *Mississippi Enterprise*, and the Mound Bayou *Sentinel* pulled most black newspaper advertising. To reach the black market, many black merchants did not care whether a paper had moderate or conservative views. Such a laissez-faire attitude kept several mediocre black papers going through the decade. The survival of these papers, such as the *Mississippi Enterprise*, did not constitute an altogether encouraging sign for the black masses.

In its September 13, 1952, issue, the Mound Bayou *Sentinel* contained sixteen advertisements, from black businesses in Bolivar County. Two years later, this pattern continued as the February 27 issue contained nineteen advertisements. The range of local advertisements included the

Knights and Daughters of Tabor, the Advocate Print Shop, OK Cafe, and Liddell's Garage and Service Station.

Conversely, the *Jackson Advocate*, a much larger paper that had angered much of the black community by 1959 had a roster of fifty-eight advertisements in its September 26, 1959, issue. The *Advocate*'s supporters included such black businesses as Dotty Cab Company, Knights and Daughters of Tabor, Denton Funeral Home, Zebra Motel, Gerri's Palm Tavern, and Sweet's Hotel. Ninety percent of the advertisements, however, came from white merchants in Hinds County and elsewhere, including Friendly Finance Company, Coca-Cola, and Tillman Finance Company (all from Columbia, Mississippi), the Gravel Company and the Stallings Company (Houston, Mississippi), the *Christian Science Monitor* (Boston), Dumas Milner Chevrolet Company, Jackson Typewriter Company, Mississippi Power and Light Company, and Jitney Jungle (Jackson). Despite its philosophy and policies, the *Advocate* continued to publish, largely as a result of white support and the stubborn persistence of its editor, Percy Greene.[48]

To direct public opinion on the issues of segregation, descgregation, and the Southern way of life, the Mississippi legislature in 1956 established the State Sovereignty Commission to serve as an official body to maintain the status quo in Mississippi and to destroy the civil rights movement. To do so, the commission worked to maintain a "network of Negro informers blanketing Mississippi."[49] Unfortunately, this network also included segments of the black press that received funds for their continued operation. When the black community discovered these connections, however, black support for these journals generally evaporated.[50]

Other black papers survived through the personal income of individual editors, such as Arrington High at the *Eagle Eye*. Still others had the backing of black organizations, like the Knights and Daughters of Tabor, who continued to support the *Taborian Star*. Educational institutions published the largest number of black journals, but as such they faced the direct threat of economic censure from white Mississippians. Because these papers generally could only address items of "school interest," they had limited ability, and in many cases their circulation did not reach the masses.

The economic hardships of black publishing also extended to the media interests of Afro-Americans in radio and television. Blacks in Mississippi did not own a single radio or television station during the decade.

As in the 1940s, however, whites encouraged fifteen- to thirty-minute black religious or musical programs on white-owned stations in such Mississippi cities as Cleveland, Vicksburg, and Hattiesburg.[51] A few cases, however, followed a different pattern.

White interest in the new format of black-oriented radio stations resulted in the creation of WOKJ in Jackson on September 13, 1954.[52] Under the ownership of the Dixieland Broadcasting Company, blacks assumed major staff positions at the station, among them Rev. L.H. Newsome, religious director and advertising salesman, Bill Spencer, host of popular musical shows, Bill Jackson and Wade Graves ("Pappa Rock"), disc jockeys, James Rundles, assistant program director and news director, and Bruce Payne, also host of musical shows. Although blacks hosted musical programs and conducted short news segments, WOKJ always had a white manager during the 1950s.

Bruce Payne credits William Harvey (also of the *Mississippi Enterprise*) as the first black disc jockey in Jackson. Payne suggests that the significance of WOKJ lay in its early history as "Mississippi's first radio station programming 100 percent Black appeal features with an all-Black program staff."[53]

The medium of television remained tragically closed to blacks, who could not appear in commercials or on other programs—they remained invisible to Mississippi's television audiences. Because of the small number of television stations in the state, blacks had little opportunity to view diverse white programs. (Mississippi's rural nature and extreme conservatism did not encourage cultural diversity, even among whites.) Jackson, the center of state media interests, had three stations, Meridian had two, Columbus, Gulfport, Hattiesburg, and McComb also had broadcasters. Other communities had to tune into stations located in other states, especially in such cities as New Orleans and Memphis.[54] It took black Mississippians another generation to break segregation's hold on television.

By the end of the 1950s, the economics of the free black press had reached a crisis point. The black press had severely declined for twenty years, and the intensified massive resistance campaign against desegregation had also taken a heavy toll on the community. But blacks in Mississippi had a resource in the black press from other states, receiving copies of such papers as the Baltimore *Afro-American* and the *Chicago Defender*. They also received encouragement from the national civil rights movement. The Montgomery bus boycott and the work of Martin

Luther King, Jr., and others provided a special sense of hope and faith because those struggles occurred in neighboring Alabama.

Yet by 1959 only five major commercial black papers remained active in Mississippi, including the *Jackson Advocate*, the *Mississippi Enterprise*, and the *Eagle Eye* (all located in Jackson), the New Albany *Community Citizen*, and the Greenville *Delta Leader*. Several religious and fraternal papers also published, but they had marginal influence. Also, more than a dozen black educational journals existed in the state.

Thus, in spite of a black press that did not successfully address the total black historical predicament, Mississippi's blacks could at least point to the possibilities of a long struggle ahead for justice and equality in the poorest state of the Union. They could also demand a new direction for the state's black press and a new commitment from black journalists to fight, a commitment that would serve as one of the guides in the coming struggle for black freedom.

CHAPTER 4

The Civil Rights Movement

1960–1969

The decade between 1960 and 1969 remains one of the watershed periods of American history. Not since the Civil War of the early 1860s had economic, political, and social events burst all at once into a national movement to drastically change the American system. This movement, although it had many parts, received its impetus from the struggles of black people. It began in the South, with the Montgomery bus boycott of 1955–56, gathered strength with the 1957 educational crisis in Little Rock, and found renewed resolve from the killings of numerous blacks during the 1950s in Mississippi.

The freedom struggle—the nonviolent movement for justice and social change—increased its activities during the 1960s, remaining focused on the South because of its intensive racism and segregation. Between 1960 and 1965, a series of freedom movements took place, including the sit-in movement, which began in Greensboro, North Carolina, in 1960 when four black college students from North Carolina A&T sought to desegregate a Woolworth's lunch counter; the establishment in 1960 of the Student Nonviolent Coordinating Committee (SNCC), a student activist organization at Shaw University in Raleigh, North Carolina; the Freedom Rides campaign of 1961, which sought to break segregation on public transportation in the South; James Meredith's attempt to register at the University of Mississippi in 1962; the August 1963 March on Washington to focus attention on the plight of blacks and the poor (Native Americans, whites, Chicanos) in the United States; the campaign to break segregation's hold on Birmingham; Mississippi's Freedom Summer campaign in 1964 to encourage black voter registration and to combat the fear of the system of segregation; and similar campaigns in Albany, Georgia (1961–62) and Selma, Alabama (1965).

After 1965, Northern blacks assumed a major portion of the civil rights movement's attention, although events and campaigns in the South continued to significantly affect the general movement for black freedom. A turning point came in 1966, with James Meredith's march in Mississippi and when Stokeley Carmichael demanded "Black Power," which led to a stronger emphasis on black nationalism in the movement. The Northern campaigns centered on strengthening black economic and social positions and on ending to de facto segregation in that region. Although all of the major civil rights organizations took part in this work, the NAACP, the Congress of Racial Equality (CORE), SNCC, and the Urban League played key roles. The major struggles raged in such cities as Chicago; Detroit; Newark, New Jersey; New York; Philadelphia; and Washington, D.C. Much of the Northern response to black conditions appeared in a series of public disturbances through the late 1960s.[1]

The 1968 assassination of Martin Luther King, Jr., at Memphis represented another turning point in that it signaled an abandonment of many aspects of the nonviolent philosophy of the early 1960s movement. However, the Poor People's Campaign, a movement to bring national attention to the problems of poverty, continued, and its followers set up a tent city in Washington, D.C., in 1968. Yet the vigor demonstrated during the early movement days had dissipated in the last years of the 1960s. The Kerner Commission's 1968 report seemed to sum up the state of affairs for the period. This presidential body found that American society was "moving toward two societies, one black, one white—separate and unequal . . . where discrimination and segregation have long permeated much of American life and now threaten the future of every American."[2]

The plight of poor Mississippi blacks continued as a major concern. The state's black population declined by 11 percent during this period, from 920,595 in 1960 to 815,770 in 1970. By 1970, blacks constituted 37 percent of the total population, a decrease of 5 percent from the 1960 figure of 42 percent. From 1865 to 1970, more than 700,000 black Mississippians emigrated. Seventy-one percent of Mississippi's black families had incomes of less than $5,000 in 1969, whereas 71 percent of white families had incomes higher than $5,000. By 1960, black Mississippians had a median of 6.0 years of education, while whites had a median of 11.0 years. The median black family income in 1969 was $3,865 for urban dwellers and $2,407 in rural areas, compared to $8,883 and $5,890 respectively for whites.[3]

In Mississippi, the black press of the 1960s had a variety of voices, highlighted by the conservative commercial journals from the earlier periods, such as the *Delta Leader*, the *Mississippi Enterprise*, the *Jackson Advocate*, and the New Albany *Community Citizen*. The decade also witnessed the development of a freedom movement press as an arm of civil rights organizations and as an effort to attack the segregation system and to promote the cultural, economic, political, and social development of blacks. Religious and fraternal groups and other black social organizations also constituted another component of the black press.

Mississippi's black press walked a tightrope during the 1960s. If it appeared too conservative or pro-segregationist, then the black community and the freedom movement would attack or denounce it. Conversely, a radical or freedom movement journal faced abuse from white segregationists such as the Ku Klux Klan, the White Citizens' Council, police departments, and other antiblack groups and individuals. All black journals had reason to fear the state government and its agent, the Sovereignty Commission, which had the power to curb the press's effectiveness or to coerce it outright through direct payments to editors. The religious, fraternal, social, and educational organs occupied a middle position. The educational publications had a particularly precarious position, because the Mississippi legislature and the Mississippi College Board could cut their budgets.[4] Thus, as the freedom movement substantially intensified its attacks on segregation, the black press was forced to support one side or the other. One thing was clear: the movement needed a strong black press to overcome the centuries of oppression blacks had suffered. Some papers answered this call, others did not.

Many major themes dominated the pages of Mississippi's black press during the 1960s, including the black press's role in the freedom struggle; segregation and the denial of black economic, political, and social rights; desegregation and the influence of the U.S. Congress and the U.S. Supreme Court; black boycotts; the Mississippi Freedom Democratic party; movement divisions over strategy; black social concerns such as poverty, health care, family issues, employment, and education; black migration out of Mississippi; conditions in Parchman Prison, in Sunflower County; black political activity in the state, such as the Charles Evers's 1969 election as the mayor of Fayette, the first black elected to this office in a bi-racial town since Reconstruction; and Hurricane Camille, which ravaged Mississippi in 1969.

The press also addressed issues of wider concern, such as black land ownership in the South; the goals of civil rights campaigns including the 1963 March on Washington and the Freedom Summer of 1964; fear of a "white backlash" against black demands; black separatists and national-ists like Black Muslims and the Black Panther party; the Black Power movement; de facto segregation in the North; the impact of Northern black rebellions; police brutality and white violence against individual blacks, for example, the bombing of a Birmingham church in 1963; the murders of Medgar Evers (1963), John F. Kennedy (1963), Michael Schwerner, Andrew Goodman, and James Chaney (1964), Robert F. Kennedy (1968), and Martin Luther King, Jr. (1968); James Meredith's at-tempt to enter the University of Mississippi, in 1962; Meredith's role as an activist, and his march and shooting in 1966; Lyndon Baines John-son's War on Poverty; the Vietnam War; the Poor People's Campaign; the Nixon administration's hostility toward integration and black prog-ress; the independence movement and the struggles of black people in Africa; and black culture, including the death of Richard Wright on No-vember 28, 1960, in Paris.[5]

Black Mississippians had ten commercial newspapers to read during the 1960s, an increase of three from the 1950s. These papers published in the following cities: Greenville (the *Delta Leader*; the *Negro Leader*, Al-bert Jenkins, editor; and the *Mississippi News*, Levye Chapple, Jr., Wal-ter Wilson, Mrs. H.H. Humes and R.L. Chandler, editors and publishers), Jackson (*Close-Up Magazine*, the *Jackson Advocate*, and the *Mississippi Enterprise*), Meridian (*Memo Digest*, Robert E. Williams, editor), Mound Bayou (*Mound Bayou Weekly*, Fred Miller, editor), New Albany (*Community Citizen*), and Vicksburg (*Citizens' Appeal*, Dilla E. Irwin and Ollye Brown Shirley, editors). Three Mississippi cities continued to dominate the black press—Jackson, with at least eight publications not counting educational and social organs, Greenville, with four, and Mound Bayou, with three.[6] A sharp decline in the number of religious and fra-ternal papers continued during this period, although the black Catholic *Saint Augustine's Messenger* of Bay Saint Louis continued to publish, and a fraternal organ continued to appear at Mound Bayou—the *Taborian Bulletin* (successor to the *Taborian Star*).

Several dozen freedom movement organs provided communication

Mississippi Free Press, Jackson, October 12, 1963. A weekly, the *Free Press* was established to promote "Good Government, Higher Living Standards, Better Educational Opportunities, and Social Justice in Mississippi." It was active between 1961 and 1973 and was priced at $3.00 for a subscription in Mississippi and $4.00 elsewhere. Its circulation totaled 2,000 copies in the early 1960s. Courtesy *Mississippi Free Press*. *Community Citizen*, New Albany, June 8, 1961. This organ was created in 1947 and remained active until 1977. Like the *Jackson Advocate*, it received major support from the Mississippi Sovereignty Commission (a state agency) during the 1950s and 1960s for its attack on the civil rights movement in Mississippi and the South. Courtesy *Community Citizen*.

among the disparate segments of the civil rights movement and offered a more progressive source of news and information for blacks in Mississippi and for other individuals with an interest in Mississippi's struggle for justice and equality. These papers appeared throughout the state. In Jackson such journals included the *Mississippi Free Press*, which had three editors between 1961 and 1967, Henry J. Kirksey, Paul E. Brooks, and Charles Butt; the *North Jackson Action* (NAACP), edited by Colia Liddell (1960–61); *Mississippi Freedom Democratic Party Newsletter* (1965–69?), and the *Hinds County Freedom Democratic Party Newsletter* (1966–69?). In Greenville appeared such organs as the *Freedom Village Progress Report* (1974–   ), the *Delta Ministry Newsletter* (1963–   ), and the *Delta Ministry Reports* (mid 1960s–   ). The *Freedom Journal* (1964) published at McComb, the *Voice of the Black Youth* at Mayersville (1968–   ), and the *Voice*, edited by Johnny Magee (1970) and Milburn Crowe (1971), at Mound Bayou. The freedom movement journals ushered in a period of intensive questioning of all aspects of segregation, resulting in the demand for total equality for Afro-Americans. These papers also raised new issues and challenges for the black press, demanding that all parts of the media act to secure the people's freedom from economic, social, and political oppression. Furthermore, they demanded that the black press support black freedom struggles outside the United States.

Tensions developed between the conservative-commercial papers and the radical-freedom movement organs as the civil rights movement became more effective and successful in attacking segregation. The movement's supporters constantly attacked the editors of papers such as the *Jackson Advocate* who accepted direct payments from the Sovereignty Commission, which aided the state's efforts in blocking the civil rights movement. Without the Sovereignty Commission's support, some black papers clearly would have disappeared. (The *Advocate* gave away free copies during this period.)

Dozens of black educational organs published during the 1960s at historically black senior colleges, junior colleges, high schools, junior high schools, and elementary schools. Although effective as local school-interest publications, fear of white anger (and budget cuts) prevented any student or faculty publication from appearing too radical or progressive. Black fraternal and organizational press interests also remained active during this period.

Black commercial papers reported circulations averaging between

2,000 and 6,000 copies. The Greenville *Negro Leader* printed 6,000 copies per issue in 1966; the Meridian *Memo Digest* issued 4,000 copies per week in 1969; the *Mississippi Enterprise* had an edition of 5,000 copies in 1962; *Mound Bayou Weekly*, 1966, 10,000 issues; the *Saint Augustine's Messenger* printed 5,000 copies per issue in 1966; and the *Mississippi Free Press* numbered 2,000 per issue in 1967. Most black papers had an actual weekly circulation of 2,000 to 3,000 copies, and many editors would increase their circulation figures when outsiders asked for them. Many believed that larger reported circulations extended the life of the newspapers. Although circulation figures are not available on the freedom movement organs, the actual numbers probably ranged from 250 to 500 copies up to 1,000 or more for the papers' weekly or monthly issues—the organizations almost never had the money for larger print runs. But freedom paper editors always expected that people would pass their papers along to other readers.

Black women assumed a greater role in black press activities in the 1960s. Dilla E. Irwin and Ollye Brown Shirley represented the creative forces behind the Vicksburg *Citizens' Appeal*. In the Delta region, Mrs. H. H. Humes actively worked with *New*, a black Greenville journal. At Jackson, Sarah Stevens continued her work as editor of the *Mississippi Enterprise*, while Frances Reed Greene served as the society editor of the *Jackson Advocate*. A number of women served as editors and staff members for the freedom movement organs of the period, including Susie B. Ruffin, editor of the *Mississippi Freedom Democratic Party Newsletter*.[7] The increased activity by black women helped to promote a more humanistic perspective in the press's treatment of social, political, and economic issues, especially as they related to black children, families, and women. This contribution had a lasting impact on future black press efforts in Mississippi, as black women became unwilling to let black men dominate as they had in earlier periods. This attitude had a liberating effect, for both black women and men and resulted in a freer black press for all. Black men largely staffed and headed black papers and other media activities because they controlled the funding sources.[8]

During this time, the white press fell into three groups. The first group consisted of extreme conservative papers, such as the *Clarion-Ledger* and the *Jackson Daily News*, both controlled by the Hederman family of Jackson. This group also included the *Woman Constitutionalist*, a monthly tabloid published at Summit; the *Citizen*, a monthly that served as the official organ of the Citizens' Councils of America; and newspa-

Freedom's Journal, McComb, 1964, grew out of the work of the Mississippi Freedom Summer Project under the editorship of Barbara JoAnn Lea. Published weekly, its major goal was to promote self-expression, education, and political awareness among the black youth of Pike County. Courtesy *Freedom's Journal*. *Vicksburg Citizens' Appeal*, July 5, 1965. A civil rights organ in its focus, the *Citizens' Appeal*, edited by Ollye Brown Shirley and Dilla E. Irwin, was published between 1964 and 1966. It was established to "print full news of events in the Vicksburg area Negro community—social and club activities, sporting events, and political and civic news." Courtesy *Vicksburg Citizens' Appeal*.

pers such as the *Natchez Democrat*, the *Hattiesburg American*, the *Fayette Chronicle*, the *Tunica Times-Democrat*, and the *Pike County Summit Sun*. In 1969, Pat Watters wrote that Mississippi papers like the *Clarion-Ledger* and the *Jackson Daily News* were "likely to be among the worst newspapers in the world."[9] This statement holds true for much of the white Mississippi press of this period, because the papers were dishonest in their treatment of—or refusal to treat—blacks; were racist and prejudiced against minorities, non-Christian religious groups, and women; and were very weak in terms of journalistic standards, ethics, fairness, and goodwill toward other human beings. But such papers represented the leading press voices in Mississippi, and as such they helped to support totally the system of segregation and oppression.

Moderate papers formed a second category of the white press—most notably, Hazel Brannon Smith's *Lexington Advertiser*, Hodding Carter, Jr.'s Greenville *Delta Democrat-Times*, and P.D. East's *Petal Paper*. Other constructive journals of the 1960s included the McComb *Enterprise Journal*, edited by Oliver Emmerich, the *Tupelo Journal*, the *Batesville Panolian*, the *Clarksdale Press-Register*, and the *Tylertown Times*.[10] As occurred earlier, segregationists often abused moderate editors, but most withstood the pressure and sought to offer guidance toward a better future through their papers.[11]

Finally, several small, radical white organs constituted the third segment of the white press of this era, offering a progressive press voice. *Kudzu—Subterranean News from the Heart of Ole Dixie*, established at Jackson in 1968, represents among the best-known of these papers. An eight- to twelve-page tabloid, *Kudzu* had "a moderate New Left point of view." In Mississippi, this represented a radical, even subversive, orientation. The paper sought the "cultural and political liberation of all people" as one of its major goals. For its efforts local authorities often harassed the paper. White students at historically white universities also published underground papers, like *Descant*, circulated during 1967–68 at the University of Mississippi.[12]

The contents of different black papers—conservative, freedom movement, and community—sharply reveal divisions among black papers. On economic, social, and political concerns the papers opposed each other, and they used the press to present their philosophies to the black public and to influence white public opinion. The papers rarely agreed, especially when it came to the goals and programs of the civil rights movement and segregation. The conservative editors also feared the consequences of a black challenge to the white segregationist power structure. The freedom movement organs disavowed the go-slow approach and demanded an immediate end to segregation and full economic, political, and social rights for blacks. They looked to the ideals and examples of such black freedom fighters as Harriet Tubman, Nat Turner, Frederick Douglass, Sojourner Truth, Marcus Garvey, and W.E.B. Du Bois for guidance in the search for black liberation. After a 400-year history in North America, they felt that blacks had suffered enough and that the time had come to face the white segregationists.

Four of the conservative organs of the era exemplify this element of the black press in Mississippi for the 1960s: the Walls *Mid-South Informer*, the New Albany *Community Citizen*, the Jackson *Mississippi Enterprise*, and the *Jackson Advocate*, the last three active for all of the 1960s and perhaps the best known of the conservative sheets.

Jessie Gillespie, publisher of the *Mid-South Informer*, expressed his point of view and, by allusion, that of his paper as well, in 1965. In a letter to the editor of the *Natchez Democrat*, he gave this assessment on the condition of Mississippi's blacks: "It is deplorable to note how truths have been twisted in regard to the racial situation here in our state. When one reads some of our national magazines he would think that the Negro is living as he did 100 years ago. I will admit that some are living as we were in that age, but that is because we have not taken advantage of the opportunities that have been open to us."[13] Black poverty in the Delta region remained overwhelming, but Gillespie did not see it. His solution (for those blacks with problems) consisted of a request that Martin Luther King, Jr., the NAACP, CORE, and the Southern Christian Leadership Conference (SCLC) turn their attention to business. He preferred this approach to trying to take away what whites had "worked for centuries to acquire. Let us tell these agitators and extremists to pack their carpetbags and return to their respective states and try to solve their own problems and return the leadership of the Negro community back to the local people and let us strive to build our own communities to the level that other races have attained."[14]

Northeast of Walls, another editor expressed the same sentiment. Rev. J.W. Jones of New Albany, publisher of an antifreedom paper, the *Community Citizen*, editorialized that wise blacks should support the status quo—a long-running theme in the four-page paper established in 1947 as "A Negro paper dedicated to the maintenance of peace, goodwill, order, and domestic tranquility in our state." To preserve Mississippi's segregated system, Jones offered his paper's arch-conservative support as "a paper of character, education and information" for use in the campaign to promote segregation.[15]

Published semi-monthly, the *Community Citizen's* staff consisted solely of Rev. Jones; however, local reporters such as Mrs. Rufus Owens of Corinth helped with local news and distribution. In 1961, a one-year subscription to the paper cost two dollars, $1.25 for six months. Single issues cost ten cents each.[16] The *Community Citizen's* circulation during the 1960s ranged from a high of 1,437 in 1960 down to 670 in 1969.[17] As a supporter of official Mississippi, the paper had a Democratic political affiliation.

An average issue of the *Community Citizen* generally contained editorial support for white segregation; reprints from conservative newspapers and magazines, such as *U.S. News and World Report*, the *Augusta* (Georgia) *Courier* and the *Clarion-Ledger/Jackson Daily News*; a column on news events; reprinted letters supporting segregation; church and local news; tidbits; reprinted news from black colleges; and religious poetry.[18] Little hard news appeared in the paper, especially regarding New Albany, its home base. A conservative paper did not want to anger anyone at home, if possible.

For economic support, Rev. Jones turned to the State Sovereignty Commission, and he received handsome rewards—seventy-five dollars per month. A recent study of the commission notes that "Throughout the 1960s the Reverend J.W. Jones . . . apparently wrote editorials in line with Sovereignty Commission views."[19]

The *Community Citizen* criticized the freedom movement. The paper's negative comments included special attacks on the NAACP, Martin Luther King, Jr., James Meredith, and local and regional blacks who used various movement strategies (sit-ins, boycotts, and demonstrations) to attack segregation. In the view of the *Community Citizen*, the movement should not attempt to change Southern society through radical means. The paper summed up its position in 1964:

> Demonstrations have drifted into race riots. So-called ministers and other fake leaders are responsible for the drift and disaster which the country has experienced in three years. The sit-ins, stall-ins, and boycotts have become obnoxious. . . . A minority is getting out of control. . . . It is divinely right that Negroes and those rabble-rousers who are leading demonstrations be lawfully stopped. We

know that the white people have done more for us than we have
done for ourselves with access to available opportunities. It is di-
vinely right that we show our gratitude for the knowledge and other
intelligent phases of welfare which we have inherited from the
white people of this country. . . . Believe it or not—a majority of
our race are not trustworthy. . . . We cannot depend on members
of our race until he has finished what he has promised. . . . Demonstrators and Negroes are trying to pull them [white people] down
to the Negro level.[20]

To keep black demonstrators in line, the paper supported laws
enacted by the Mississippi legislature in 1964 to punish blacks and other
activists. The new laws, the paper suggested, would "achieve the purpose of peace for which [they were] designed."[21] The paper also expressed official Mississippi's fear of foreign influence in the civil rights
movement, labeling American blacks active in the movement "nothing
more than tools used to complete a job begun by the Communists."[22]

The *Community Citizen* appreciated the work of Governor Ross Barnett and of other government officials. Unlike white officials in Montgomery, New Orleans, Little Rock and elsewhere, Jones suggested in an
editorial that Mississippi "State officials made preparation to handle the
Freedom-Rider agitators without the aid of any outside help." Thus,
Mississippi had been spared "a disgrace" suffered by other Southern
states.

The paper believed that blacks remained politically behind whites,
and blacks had to decide whether they would represent "an asset or a li-
ability" to the country. The *Community Citizen* concluded that blacks
had "nothing to contribute to society." As a result, blacks needed to learn
"that color is no barrier to any race; second that class is the means of
promotion for any individual or race." Furthermore, Afro-Americans, he
suggested, had "the same opportunity to receive God's blessings as does
the white man. . . . And we receive just what we deserve. . . . No
man ever goes higher than his aims." But the matter did not end there.
According to Jones, before blacks could assume their place in Southern
political life, they had to grow and develop. For him, the central theme
lay in the fact that "since slavery, the white man has led us [blacks] to a
degree of intelligence which he knows enables us to shoulder the moral
responsibility of our race. In this we are lacking."[23] The *Citizen* carefully
followed the segregationist line in its editorial policy. But the paper

could on occasion outdo the work of the late Senator Bilbo. It concluded that the freedom movement and organizations such as the NAACP believed that "if we succeed in pulling other races down to our own level, then we will be satisfied."[24]

The solution to the problem of social relations in Mississippi, according to the *Citizen*, lay in segregation. This system produced a low crime rate, the paper believed, because "Segregation demands respect for right principles. Segregation was the method that God used to defeat an ambitious imagination."[25] For Rev. Jones, the segregated South and the de facto segregated North contained "the largest public school system on earth, the most expensive college buildings, the most extensive curriculum, but nowhere else has a minority advanced as slowly in culture as we have. . . . The white race is above the colored race."[26]

Rev. Jones suggested in 1962 that the admission of James Meredith to the University of Mississippi provided the clearest evidence of this phenomenon by upsetting the balance of segregation, a system that had "served to the Negro's best advantage . . . a system which has worked." "Meredith's enrollment has proven a natural misfit at the University at Oxford. . . . He allowed the NAACP to push him into a situation which he has not the ability to fit in. . . . By nature, which there is no remedy for, Negroes are slower, or less active, than white people. . . . The southern white man is more accommodating to us than we are to each other."[27]

The paper's coverage of economic issues also focused on the civil rights movements' threat to black economic well-being. The *Citizen* believed that civil rights could not create jobs for blacks and that unemployment could only end by "the advancement of scientific production." Jones feared that the "vote-thirsty" John F. Kennedy "Administration will succeed in leading illiterates [blacks] to believe that prejudice is the main cause of unemployment." For black economic health, blacks should ally with whites against communists and should remember "that 95 percent of Negroes employed in this country are employed by white people. And many of the previous Negro employees have forced themselves out of jobs through their arrogant and hostile attitudes." Furthermore, the paper noted, protest and economic requests by black leaders "not only offends man, but it is against the teaching of God."[28]

Politically, socially, and economically, the *Community Citizen* and the *Mid-South Informer* represented twisted viewpoints during the height of the civil rights movement. A third conservative black paper, the *Jackson*

Advocate, proved the most significant of the pro-segregationist organs of the decade. Its editor, Percy Greene, became the leading black journalist spokesman for the white segregationist position in Mississippi.

Greene and the *Jackson Advocate* followed what many believed an extreme pro–status quo stance on major issues affecting blacks. John Salter, Jr., noted that because Greene and the paper assumed and promoted a pro-segregation position, no blacks paid "any attention" to the observations of either.[29]

Greene received thousands of dollars from the Sovereignty Commission to be one of its ambassadors, traveling to New York City, Washington, D.C., and Los Angeles, "to attend governmental and nongovernmental conferences and conventions."

At home, the commission expected Greene to use the *Advocate* to support segregation. One example of this special work of the paper occurred in 1965, when the *Advocate* published a special industrial supplement, intended to highlight Mississippi's economic strength and the blacks' role in it. Greene received $750 for advertising, promotion, and distribution of the supplement and sent five hundred copies to the Sovereignty Commission.[30]

During the 1960s, the *Advocate*'s staff consisted of Greene and his wife, Frances Reed Greene. A standard-size newspaper, the paper consisted of eight pages published every Thursday. Individual issues cost at ten cents, and one-year subscriptions between 1965 and 1968 cost five dollars. Throughout the early 1960s, the *Advocate* indicated on its editorial page that it was a member of the Audit Bureau of Circulation, a national accreditation agency that confirms circulation figures.

In addition to the large number of reprints in an average weekly issue, the *Advocate* focused on wire service news (ranging from local to international) for pages one and two of the paper; cartoons, home needs, fillers for page three; pro-segregation editorials on page four; sports and cartoons on page five; health and cartoons on page six; and stories continued from page one on pages seven and eight. Pictures appeared on pages one, three, and eight. Advertisements generally appeared on all pages except one and four.[31]

Like many similar black papers, the *Advocate* reprinted many editorials and other information from other Southern newspapers and other voices of the American press, including the *Christian Science Monitor*, the *New York Times*, and *Time* magazine. Politically, the paper continued its affiliation with the Democratic party. It claimed a weekly circulation rate of 4,500 in 1960 and 6,000 in 1968,[32] but these rates seem excessive given the paper's extremely low standing in the black community.

The *Advocate*'s basic social, political, and economic positions remained largely unchanged from the 1950s, extending support to the old themes of interracial conferences and improved race relations, all linked to the creation of a better image for Mississippi. It continued to stress the need for black cooperation with whites and called for increased industrialization and for improvements in the economic position of blacks in the South. The *Advocate* encouraged the continued operation of black public elementary and secondary schools and colleges but applauded the U.S. Fifth Circuit Court's 1962 decision that ordered the University of Mississippi to admit James Meredith. When riots broke out at Ole Miss following Meredith's appearance on campus, however, the paper quickly switched to the support for law and order.

The *Advocate* praised the Civil Rights acts of 1964 and 1965 for extending citizenship rights in the area of public accommodations to blacks, especially for making travel among states much easier. The paper cherished freedom of the press and pointedly noted any attempts to block its rights, especially "unfair" criticism from civil rights leaders, which Greene felt brought black economic boycotts (or the threat thereof) and thereby constituted censorship. Only one civil rights organization, the National Urban League, received a "high achievement" rating from the *Advocate*.

On foreign affairs, the paper criticized events in the Congo (Zaire) and supported United Nations efforts there; however, it noted that Africa's future lay in a "black-white partnership."[33]

The *Advocate* had numerous misgivings during the decade, most notably on the civil rights movement and any kind of "agitation, protests, and demonstrations" in the South. These activities, the paper repeatedly argued, represented the wrong methods to bring about change, suggesting that "the future hopes of Negroes for enjoying freedom and citizenship in accordance with the high American ideals, without resorting to revolutionary techniques can best await the inevitable actions of the Congress of the United States, and the development of American public opinion." Therefore, the *Advocate* viewed its role as one of pointing out the unproductive path that nonviolent philosophy offered. Thus, it disagreed with organizations such as CORE, the NAACP, SNCC, SCLC, and the Freedom Democratic party. Other than offering its support for open public accommodations and the Civil Rights acts of 1964 and 1965 (which were consistent with the paper's goals), the *Advocate* said nothing positive about the major events of the decade, including sit-ins, Freedom Rides, the March on Washington, the Freedom Summer, the march in Selma, the 1966 Civil Rights Act (which represented too much of an extension of civil rights for the paper's views), Martin Luther King's work in Chicago, Stokeley Carmichael and Black Power, and James Meredith's march. Although the *Advocate* spoke against the murders of Medgar Evers, John F. Kennedy, Michael Schwerner, James Chaney, Andrew Goodman, Martin Luther King, Jr., and Robert F. Kennedy, it placed the blame on the activities of the civil rights movement. To the *Advocate*, the blacks could secure salvation through a "new leadership, a new dialogue, a new formula" outside of the civil rights movement. The paper continued to find wisdom in the program of Booker T. Washington.[34]

In contrast to these conservative papers, freedom movement organs such as the McComb *Freedom's Journal*, the Jackson *Mississippi Freedom Democratic Party Newsletter*, and progressive community newspapers like the Jackson *Mississippi Free Press* and the Vicksburg *Citizens' Appeal* took a much different tack. Established during the civil rights movement, these journals advanced black journalism, offering critical voices that challenged perceptions about blacks. Heir to the tradition of a black fighting press, they urged a forward-looking policy of struggle for black people and encouraged equality and human rights for all people.

Established in 1964, and edited by Barbara JoAnn Lea, *Freedom's Journal* was a six-page weekly that worked to inform the public about the excesses of the segregation system. The journal encouraged and promoted the creative work of the civil rights workers, stressed unity and cooperation, and sustained the interests of the black masses in the struggle. The journal published short essays in history, economics, politics, and social matters, as well as poetry, short stories, and other creative works.[35]

The *Mississippi Free Press* similarly expressed its philosophy:

Our purpose is to promote education and enlightenment in the principles of democracy to encourage all citizens to participate fully in their government. Until Negroes in Mississippi gain the power of the ballot and until all the people exercise the rights of citizenship, the needs of Mississippi will continue to go unmet; legislation to promote the social welfare and encourage economic growth will continue to be non-existent. In Mississippi, the fear of economic reprisal and the lack of vital knowledge make even registering to vote an extremely difficult task.[36]

Thus, the *Free Press* served as a major vehicle for "communication and interpretation in Mississippi." John Salter, a teacher and activist in Mississippi during the early 1960s, noted the importance of the *Mississippi Free Press*: "It was a blend of social news and civil rights, with the latter paramount, and because of this, the power structure condemned it vigorously." The paper experienced many problems, including police interference with the distribution of the journal and surveillance of the staff by the Sovereignty Commission. The paper's supporters included Medgar Evers, Jackson's black youth, white lawyers William Higgs of Jackson and Tom Johnson of Canton, activists Charles Butt and Salter, and Hazel Brannon Smith, the white editor of the Lexington *Advertiser*, whose plant printed the *Free Press*. For this support, the Sovereignty Commission and the Citizens' Council threatened her.[37]

A four- to eight-page weekly tabloid, the *Free Press* cost four dollars for a one-year subscription, ten cents per single issue. Its weekly circulation ranged from 2,000 to 3,000 copies in the early 1960s; by 1966 this figure stood at 5,340.[38] The paper had several editors during the decade, including Butt, Henry Kirksey, Lucy Komisar, and Paul E. Brooks. In reviewing the history of the *Free Press*, Kirksey observed in 1981 that Butt, the first editor of the paper and a Caucasian, "built up a clientele of concerned middle class whites from the North. He wrote letters asking them for donations to pay for subscriptions for poor Blacks in Mississippi. Using that technique, they built up circulation (and it should have been larger) to 10,000 at one time. The problem with that was that the subscription price was $1 per year, so when a person sent in $20, that was supposed to be for 20 subscriptions, and $1 was just not a realistic cost."[39] Still, the *Free Press* offered Mississippi readers a more progressive voice than the *Jackson Advocate*, the *Mississippi Enterprise*, or the *Clarion-Ledger*.

Jackson also served as the headquarters for the *Mississippi Freedom Democratic Party Newsletter*, the official organ of the political group established on April 26, 1964, seeking to challenge the official state Democratic party. A contemporary scholar noted that "In direct contrast to the state Democratic party, the MFDP was open to all citizens of voting age, regardless of race, creed, or color, and advocated a coalition of poor whites and blacks to bring substantive change to Mississippi. The MFDP from the beginning pledged loyalty to the national Democratic party."[40] The national Democratic party did not fully appreciate the organization's struggle to achieve political equality for all Mississippians, upholding the regular segregationist slate of delegates at the 1964 Democratic National Convention.[41]

The tabloid-size *Freedom Democratic Party Newsletter* ranged in length from three to six pages and published twice monthly. Subscriptions cost five dollars for twenty-four issues, or ten cents per copy. In 1965, Susie B. Ruffin served as editor; however, by 1967, Estell Thomas assumed the role of editor, and the newsletter's base of operations moved to Sunflower County, in the Delta region.[42]

The Vicksburg *Citizens' Appeal* was established in August 1964, by the Warren County Freedom Democratic party, the local branch of the Mississippi Freedom Democratic party, "to help close the information gap. The gap is, of course, far too wide and too historic to ever be closed by this newspaper alone. But we are sure we can help. We are sure we can provide Vicksburgers with what we feel they do not now get: civil rights news impartially reported, coverage of the Negro community, and journalism of high standards."[43]

The *Appeal* began as a weekly in 1964 but by 1965 had become a bi-weekly, published by the Hill City Publishing Corporation. An eight-page tabloid, the *Appeal* appeared on Saturdays during its first year of operation and later on Mondays. One-year subscriptions cost $3.50, and single issues sold for ten cents. Two local black women, Ollye Brown Shirley and Dilla E. Irwin, served as editors of the *Appeal* between 1964 and 1967.[44] The circulation usually ranged between 300 and 500 copies, but this number did reach 3,000 during this period.[45]

Irwin found that in Vicksburg "Blacks were at first enthusiastic about" the *Appeal*, "but they just wouldn't support its continuation." She believed that the difficulty lay in the poverty of local blacks: "So many would say they just didn't have the dime." Yet local black businessmen supported the paper: "They would buy advertisements but they were only about $2.00 or so. That does not go very far, $1 or $2 or $2.50." Still, their support helped the paper survive for four years. Vicksburg's white press felt differently. The *Appeal*'s staff found that their "little paper just made the white press frantic. They were jealous and afraid of us. They had nothing to do with us. It seemed like they were frightened to death, and a big paper like that [the *Vicksburg Evening Post*], and this little thing. It was amazing their response, which was all negative. They didn't do anything in particular to destroy us; and we just printed everything that happened."[46]

The contents of the *Appeal* centered on freedom movement news, but Irwin viewed the paper as also covering "a lot of political, community, church, and club news. . . . We received news releases through the mail. Some of the freedom workers knew people from various places, and these people would send in news, like Ralph McGill [white editor and publisher of the *Atlanta Constitution*], we'd get stuff like that. We got quite a bit through the mail, and then we would just get it ourselves."[47]

The *Appeal's* editorials defended the poor and blacks and called for a new society where "fear and lawlessness" would not control the base of human life. The *Appeal's* central message demanded that American segregation and discrimination had to end at once, or the country would continue as a society characterized by "violence and hatred."[48]

Irwin described the *Appeal's* economic crisis: "We just couldn't get any financial support at all."[49] The *Appeal* faced the same fate as most Mississippi black papers during the 1960s, but the freedom movement journals had especially acute problems. Although they had the support and encouragement of black and white liberal activists in the South and financial and moral aid from supporters in other parts of the country, such aid had limits. Most found that they had to depend on local black resources for advertisements and sales of the papers for survival. The papers also greatly depended on the services—often free—of key individuals who served as editors and other staff members. The strains of such efforts meant that many of the movement papers published only for three or four years, on average, or that they published erratically.

The black conservative press organs of the state fared somewhat better because they could generally call on the State Sovereignty Commission for aid. They also received income from advertisements by both white and black businessmen. This support resulted in the continuous publication of such papers as the *Mississippi Enterprise*, the *Community Citizen*, and the *Jackson Advocate* for the entire 1960s.

The range of advertisements that appeared in two movement papers (the *Citizens' Appeal* and the *Mississippi Free Press*) and in two conservative organs (the *Community Citizen* and the *Jackson Advocate*) indicates the degree of business support for the black press during this period. A sample of the advertisements in each of the four papers clearly reveals a striking amount of support for the conservative journals by Mississippi businessmen: in the March 6, 1965, eight-page issue of the *Jackson Advocate*, fifty-six advertisements appeared and the *Community Citizen* for June 8, 1961, contained forty-one ads. Broken down by race, forty-six advertisements (84 percent) in the *Advocate* represented white businesses and ten advertisements (16 percent) came from blacks. The *Community Citizen* had thirty-nine white advertisements (95 percent) and two black advertisements (5 percent). In contrast, judging from the August 22, 1964, issue of the *Citizens' Appeal* and the October 12, 1963, *Mississippi Free Press*, the movement papers received their entire advertisement support from black or black-oriented businesses.

The white business advertisements that ran in the *Advocate* included such companies as Colonial Bread, the Office Supply Company, Walker Farms Dairy, Tillman Finance Company, H & R Block Company, Ora-Jel, Werlein's for Music, Craigs Motors, Inc., Pepsi-Cola, Friendly Finance Company, Jitney Jungle, and Terry Furniture Company. Black advertisements in the *Advocate* included Denton Funeral Home, Dotty Cab, Mississippi Negro Citizenship Association, and S & S Grocery and Cafe. The *Community Citizen*'s advertising came from businesses such as Coca-Cola, Union Lumber Company, Harrison Motor Company, Hamilton Hardware Company, City Furniture, and Fred's Discount Store. Many of the *Community Citizen*'s advertisements came from white businesses outside of New Albany (a small town of 5,151 people in 1960, 6,335 in 1970), such cities as Tupelo, West Point, Corinth, and Columbus. The *Appeal*'s ads came from such black businesses as Dillon Burial Association and Funeral Home, Johnson's (Auto) Repair Shop, Pal's Barber Shop, Mary Lou's Beauty Salon, Thomas Repair Shop, Ebony Variety Shop, Walnut Lounge, Blue Room Nite Club, Reather's Grocery, O.K. Cleaners, and Bill Gray's Barber Shop. The *Free Press* received advertising from businesses such as Denton Funeral Home, Summers Hotel, Jenkins Gulf Service, Collins Funeral Home, Taylor's Cleaners, Peaches Cafe, Joe's Little Grocery, Conic's Beauty and Barber Supply, MLS Drug Store, Smith's Super Market, People's Funeral Home, Penguin Drive-In and Chinn's Grocery Market.[50]

In Vicksburg, Irwin found that black businesses appreciated the *Appeal* and "thought it was viable, and everybody was sick," when the paper ceased publication.[51] Such sentiments expressed the condition of the black press in Mississippi. Readers in black communities wanted newspapers, but the problem remained of how poverty-stricken groups could produce a paper with such meager resources.

The area of radio and television posed more difficulties for black ownership and programming. Fourteen Mississippi radio stations during the 1960s offered partial or total black-oriented programming. The central problem remained the lack of black ownership of radio companies. As in the 1950s, whites controlled all radio stations; however, blacks served as announcers, disc jockeys, and in other staff positions for stations in black areas. Three of the better known black-oriented stations of this period were: WOKJ-AM, Jackson, WQIC, Meridian, and WESY-AM, Greenville. Black ownership of radio stations remained low nationally as well: Out of the 310 black-oriented stations in 1969, blacks owned only sixteen.[52]

Many black Mississippians viewed the stations as avenues for receiving entertainment, especially black religious music, rock and roll, and rhythm and blues. The stations also served as sources of news, most notably in the early morning, at noon, and in the evening. Most newscasts only lasted for five minutes, and such a time frame could not adequately treat local, state, regional, national, and international news. The absence of a focus on black news posed an equally serious problem for the average black listener.[53] As a source of news, radios could not match the depth and fullness of treatment offered by black newspapers. They did offer a quick way to receive a summary of the day's events. The communications revolution through radio and television had a major impact on black Mississippians during the 1960s and attracted a huge segment of the black population for its message of short news, information, and entertainment. Nonetheless, the fact remained that blacks did not own or control a single radio or television station in Mississippi.

The civil rights movement also used radio and television media to bring about social change. Black Mississippians could witness the movement through the media, which helped to raise their group consciousness and to lift their fears of white power. The media also exposed Mississippi's blacks to the quest for freedom by blacks and others in foreign lands.[54]

Mississippi television remained closed to blacks during the decade. The state's dozen or so stations, located in a half dozen cities, devoted themselves to segregation and white supremacy. Black news and the movement penetrated Southern television stations largely through the national news networks. But white broadcast managers often censored such news and information from outside Mississippi, interrupting civil rights news or other broadcasts involving blacks or related topics.

The major case in Mississippi involving black interest in television occurred in 1964, when the United Church of Christ, Aaron Henry (an NAACP leader) and businessman Robert L.T. Smith challenged Lamar Life's renewal of WLBT-TV's license, in Jackson. They argued against WLBT to the Federal Communications Commission (FCC) based on the station's history of racist programming under white management. Its negative and unfair practices included denying blacks airtime to discuss controversial issues, interruptions of national news programs such as the Huntley-Brinkley Report whenever the civil rights movement was discussed, constant pro-segregationist propaganda, especially during the 1962 enrollment of James Meredith at the University of Mississippi, attacks against Tougaloo College without the opportunity for school officials to respond, and references to blacks as "niggers" and "nigras."[55]

Such violations of the Fairness Doctrine, however, did not convince the FCC to revoke WLBT's license, and the case was appealed to the court of appeals, which finally revoked the station's license in 1969. A nonprofit group, Communications Improvement, received a temporary license to operate the station in 1971.[56]

The freedom movement years of the 1960s produced a watershed period in the history of Mississippi's black press. Not since the early twentieth century had the number, range, and distribution of black papers reached such a level. By 1968, however, many of the movement organs had begun to decline. Eight years of constant struggle under severe conditions had taken their toll, and funds from outside Mississippi became scarce. Many early movement activists had also either left Mississippi or entered into other concerns and careers; consequently, they no longer lent their talents to local black press efforts. Finally, by the late 1960s, the movement's focus had shifted from Mississippi and the South to the cities of the East, Midwest, and the West. This new decline for Mississippi's black press did not accurately reflect the total achievements of the civil rights movement, however. For if the freedom movement achieved anything, it broke down the racist barriers of segregation and discrimination in Mississippi and the South and strengthened black consciousness in the United States and abroad. This focus of the movement served as a base for part of the Mississippi black press's future work. The black press in Mississippi had had two voices during the 1960s, one demanding immediate freedom, equality, and justice for blacks, another pressing for gradual changes in black progress. Both had an audience among blacks and whites. For the mass of black Mississippians, burdened for centuries under slavery, oppression, and Jim Crowism—full freedom was still a dream to be secured at some distant date regardless of the struggles waged by the freedom movement. Many blacks supported the movement press, but some remained afraid of a system that did not hesitate to kill blacks or whites who did not obey the laws and customs of white supremacy. White supremacists viewed the work of progressive black newspapers as an offense punishable by beatings, burning of property, forced emigration, or death. Still, many blacks contributed their ten cents to purchase copies of movement papers; others gave time and energy to produce and distribute them. But over the years this support in itself could not save the papers from their financial plight.

The conservative black papers strove to stay in print and to disseminate Booker T. Washington's traditional message: "In all things that are purely social, we can be as separate as the five fingers, yet one as the hand in all things essential to mutual progress."[57] The conservative papers also enjoyed the support, goodwill, and encouragement of white supremacists in Mississippi, including financial rewards for the most cooperative ones. They constituted the real paradoxes of the age: journalists who sold their publishing operations for the money of Jim Crow yet remained journalists. The shame of their positions lies in the confusion they caused the freedom movement, in the divisions they helped to create, and in the information they supplied to the segregationists. They did not aid the struggle for black freedom at its most critical stage; instead, they helped to diminish the movement's longevity.

By 1969, only six commercial papers remained continuously active in Mississippi: the *Jackson Advocate*, the *Mississippi Enterprise*, the *Memo Digest*, the *Community Citizen*, the *Negro Leader*, and *Close-Up*, a quarterly magazine that sold for thirty-five cents per copy.[58]

The occupation of black journalist in Mississippi during the decade of the 1960s remained a dangerous one. Extremist organizations such as the Ku Klux Klan and the White Citizens' Councils attacked progressive black editors, publishers, and staff members with beatings, arson, and murder. But they endured and left for succeeding black and progressive journalists a lasting legacy of humanism and courage to publish the truth as they saw and lived it.

CHAPTER 5

The Postmovement Era

1970–1979

The 1970s represented a period of disillusionment for the black masses in Mississippi. The mood was created by the death of Martin Luther King, Jr., in 1968, the negative response of Richard Nixon's administration to black aspirations, and the civil rights movement's failure to radically change the nature of black existence in the United States. Indeed, such a situation existed in spite of the bright promise the movement had given poor blacks and others during the 1960s. Thus, although a number of changes had occurred, especially in the arena of politics, the general black condition remained dismal.

The movement's emphasis on political rights is reflected in the fact that in 1960 only 5.2 percent of the Mississippi's black voting-age population had registered to vote, whereas by 1970 the percentage stood at 67.5 percent. Black political clout had also become impressive—by 1975 blacks held four seats in the Mississippi legislature and a total of 225 offices statewide, a number that increased to 295 in 1977, including fifteen black mayors, the largest number of any state.[1] All was not well for blacks in Mississippi, however. Politically, they remained underrepresented in political offices in the state, and no black held statewide office in Mississippi during the 1970s.[2]

A number of social changes also took place during the decade. The state's overall system of reactionary segregation and extreme racism generally disintegrated and what appeared to be a more open society took its place, particularly with the desegregation of the public educational system and with the end of Jim Crow practices in public accommodations, libraries, restaurants, movie theaters, health centers, and other areas of public interest. Yet the centuries-old problem of racism and discrimination could not disappear overnight, and many blacks discovered that desegregated schools did not necessarily mean that the number of black principals and teachers would remain the same. They found that control of the schools too often remained in the hands of white Mississippians and that public schools were seriously weakened by the creation of private all-white academies. More subtle forms of racism became a keynote feature of the 1970s.

Mississippi's black population continued to decline during this period, from 50 percent of the state's population in 1930 to 49 percent in 1940, to 45 percent in 1950, to only 42 percent in 1960, to 37 percent in 1970 and only 36 percent in 1975, when Mississippi's total population stood at 2,389,000. Between 1960 and 1970, 100,000 blacks left Mississippi for other states. A smaller number left during the 1970s, but black emigration continued to have a major impact on black institutions and life.

Other blacks found themselves in Mississippi's prisons. In 1978, 66.9 percent (1,860) of the 2,785 male prisoners in Mississippi were black males. Many white Mississippians also faced difficult conditions during this period. In fact, one study found that large numbers of whites in northwestern Mississippi lacked many basic human rights, such as health care and jobs, suffered because of the social, economic, and political problems produced by widespread poverty.[3]

In spite of all the new advances, blacks in Mississippi found their greatest disappointment in the economic arena of the 1970s. In fact, 59 percent of all black families in Mississippi were classified as living below the poverty line at the beginning of the decade.[4] Although the black middle class grew during this period and for the first time a small number of blacks acquired high-paying state government jobs, most black Mississippians faced an economic crisis.[5]

While the political, social, and economic status of blacks in Mississippi remained complex, the black press also endured a series of ups and downs. In general, however, the 1970s witnessed a regeneration of and renewed interest in the black press. To some extent, part of the black press atoned for the shameful divisions created during the civil rights movement by papers such as the *Jackson Advocate*, the *Mid-South Informer*, and the New Albany *Community Citizen*.

Sixteen significant black newspapers published between 1970 and 1979 in Mississippi: the *Jackson Advocate*; the *Mississippi Enterprise*; the Meridian *Memo Digest*; *Pas-Point Journal* (established in Moss Point in 1976 by Bernard Barnes and E. V. Cole); the Jackson *Reconciler*, a religiously oriented paper established by John Jenkins in 1977; the Natchez *Bluff City Post*; *Tutwiler Whirlwind*, founded in 1979 and edited by J. D. Rayford during that year; the Greenville *Negro Leader*, established in 1962 by Albert Jenkins; the *Mississippi Free Press*; the *Natchez News Leader*, established in 1971 by W. H. Terrell and T. C. Johnson; the Jackson *New African*, edited by President Imari A. Obadele I, Republic of New Africa; the Greenville *Mississippi News*, founded in 1974 by Katie M. Johnson and David Johnson; the Jackson *Weekly Communicator*, established in 1975 by James Meredith and Louis Armstrong; the Jackson *Highlighter*, founded by Gene L. Mosley in 1975; *Brotherhood*, established in Columbus in 1976; and the Jackson *Metropolitan Observer*, established in 1976 by Lee Dilworth. The Emergency Land Fund published *Forty Acres and a Mule*, an important organizational journal. Edited by Jessie Morris, this publication addressed issues regarding black farmers, land, and the loss of black property in the South. As in the past, black journalists continued to focus their activities in the urban areas of Mississippi; half of the papers' readership in Jackson was a result of the high concentration of black professional and higher-income groups in Hinds County.

Several magazines also published during this time: *Close-Up Magazine* continued to appear during the early 1970s. Four new monthly magazines, all published in Jackson, were *Outlook Magazine*, established in 1974 by James Meredith; *Reaction Magazine*, created by R. T. Sanders, Rufus Rawls, and Theodore Bozeman, Jr., in 1976; *Street Talk*, founded in 1978 by Jerry Sutton, Jai Barnes, and Harold Gater; and *Sunbelt*, established in 1979 by Thomas H. Espy. Out of this group of four, *Reaction* and *Sunbelt* published the most developed journals while the other two magazines emphasized sensationalism, crime, and sex.[6]

An average black newspaper in Mississippi during the 1970s had a subscription rate of between six and ten dollars for one year and single issues averaged fifteen to twenty-five cents a copy. As late as 1970, 59 percent of blacks in Mississippi still lived in rural areas, making it diffi-

William Terrell, copublisher (with Theodore C. Johnson) of the *Bluff City Post*, Natchez, 1978–. In the late 1970s the *Post* had a circulation between 500 and 1000 copies per week and cost $7.00 a year or twenty-five cents an issue. Courtesy William Terrell.

TABLE 5-1.   New Weekly Black Mississippi Newspapers during the 1970s

Paper	Years of publication	No. staff	No. pages	Price
Natchez News Leader	1971–74	3–5	26	15¢/$6
Bluff City Post	1978	4	8	15¢
Mississippi News	1974–76	3–8	8	10¢/$7.50
Brotherhood	1975–76	1–2	8	15¢
Pas-Point Journal	1977–80	2	8	25¢
Metropolitan Observer	1976	1–2	8	25¢

cult for the black press to reach them. In addition to this problem, the median family income for blacks in the state was $3,209 per year. Although the rate for Hinds County was higher ($4,277), it remained much lower than that of the average white family in the county, $10,702. With such poverty, few black families could afford one dollar each month for a weekly newspaper.[7]

Only three of the ten active black Mississippi commercial papers of the 1960s survived into the 1970s—the Meridian *Memo Digest* and two Jackson papers, the *Jackson Advocate* and the *Mississippi Enterprise*. At Bay Saint Louis, the Catholic *Saint Augustine's Messenger* also continued to publish. None of the major freedom movement organs survived into the 1970s except the Greenville *Delta Ministry Newsletter*, the Mound Bayou *Voice*, and occasional newsletters from branches of national organizations such as the NAACP and the Urban League.[8] Therefore, thirteen of the sixteen commercial papers of the 1970s were new organs. As in the 1960s, all of them had difficulty in securing the economic support necessary for prosperity. In fact, most of them survived for only a short time. Yet, as in the previous periods of the black Mississippi experience, a variety of individuals or groups always remained willing to invest their funds. Such efforts kept the black press afloat during the 1970s.

Ten major themes occupied the attention of the black press in Mississippi during the 1970s: concerns about discrimination against blacks and other minorities; emphasis on political activity, especially the election and appointment of blacks to public offices; the quality of education and the survival of black colleges; crime; the criminal justice system and police brutality; the civil rights movement, especially the work of Skip Robinson and the United League of Mississippi; the economic plight of blacks and the loss of black land throughout the South; Klan activity and

TABLE 5-2. Weekly Black Mississippi Community Newspapers during the 1970s

Paper	Established	No. staff	No. pages	Price
Community Citizen	1947–72	1	4	Free/10¢/$2
50/50	1979	1	12	Free/$4 yr.
Tutwiler Whirlwind	1979	1	12	Free/50¢/$24
Mississippi Enterprise	1933	3	8	Free/25¢
Weekly Communicator	1976–77	2	8–24	Free/$13 yr.
Highlighter	1974–76	1	16–24	Free/25¢/$10

the conservative mood of white America; the end of the second Reconstruction; and events abroad, especially the struggle in Vietnam and southern Africa.

The major news items of special interest for this period included the Jackson State University student protests and the deaths of two black youths at the hands of the Jackson police and the Mississippi highway patrolmen (1970); the Republic of New Africa's plan to build a black nation in the South using Mississippi as a base of operations and the shootout between the group and the Federal Bureau of Investigation and the Jackson police (1971); the leadership and career of Charles Evers; the Watergate crisis; and the violent beatings and deaths of blacks at the hands of policemen, Ku Klux Klan members, and other antiblack groups. Examples of the latter include the 1975 killings of four black youths in Picayune; the 1977 murder of James Calhoun, a fifteen-year-old black male, by the Klan in Sunflower County; the 1979 wounding of Melvin Brown and Stanford Young by the police in Jackson; the NAACP's financial problems caused by a court decision ordering the organization to pay more than $1 million to Port Gibson merchants for damages they suffered during a long boycott in the 1960s; the case of Robert Earl May, a fourteen-year-old youth who was sent to Parchman Prison; the U.S. Supreme Court's *Bakke* decision (1978) and *Weber* decision (1979) and the issue of affirmative action; and the deaths of hundreds of blacks, including some Mississippians, at Jonestown, Guyana, in 1978.[9]

Black journalists nationwide viewed Mississippi's black press with continued interest and concern during the seventies. Because Mississippi blacks sat on the front lines of U.S. oppression of the African-American people, the national black press supported many of the avenues of black protest in the state, including the use of all media to express the black point of view and to defend black rights. Aid for Mississippi's black press came from black newspapers in Northern, Western, and Southern states, especially in the form of liberal reprint policies, subscriptions to journals, and cooperation on projects sponsored by the predominantly black National Newspapers Publishers Association.[10] Such support helped the black press in Mississippi survive during this period.

Twenty-four daily and 119 weekly white newspapers published in Mississippi during the 1970s. Hinds County remained the center of white publishing during the decade, and the *Clarion-Ledger* and the *Jackson Daily News* continued as the leading newspapers in terms of circulation and distribution. The total circulation of daily white Mississippi newspapers reached 378,000 in 1975.[11]

In general, much of the white press remained conservative, but the extreme antiblack racism of the 1960s moderated in most papers. The new style called for a calmer approach in dealing with black people. Many white papers took a middle-of-the-road position, neither damning Afro-Americans nor offering support for black progress. At last, black Mississippians could at least read white papers without finding the reactionary treatment of black people that appeared earlier.

The white moderate journalists continued to press for changes. Influential in this regard were old voices such as Hazel Brannon Smith of the *Lexington Advertiser*; John Oliver Emmerich (1896–1978) of the *McComb Enterprise*; Hodding Carter, Jr. (1907–72) and Hodding Carter III at the Greenville *Delta Democrat-Times*; the young editors of the *Kudzu*, a radical underground tabloid published at Jackson in the early 1970s; and Bill Minor, a well-known Mississippi journalist who became editor of the weekly *Capital Reporter* in 1976.[12]

Mississippi's extreme right continued its press work during the decade. Such white organs as the Citizens' Council published the *Citizen* at Jackson, and the *Woman Constitutionalist*, the official tabloid of Women for Constitutional Government, appeared at Summit.[13]

Because blacks still did not produce a daily newspaper in Mississippi during the seventies, they had to buy local white-controlled papers to get news. Most of the white journals, such as the *Clarion-Ledger*, remained conservative and even pro-segregationist. To eliminate the negative treatment of blacks by most of the white press, black Mississippians used protests and threatened boycotts. Such techniques had a small amount of success, for by the end of the decade a higher degree of professionalism appeared in the major white papers. Blacks did not succeed, however, in gaining a major foothold as reporters or editors on the staffs of white newspapers.[14]

Two of the sixteen black papers published during the 1970s typify the black press—the *Jackson Advocate* and the Meridian *Memo Digest*, both of which published throughout the decade. For the *Advocate*, Percy Greene remained publisher and editor until his death in 1977. An enigmatic personality, Greene did not radically alter his views during the last years of his life. Indeed, his statement of the philosophy and principles of Booker T. Washington continued to appear each week at the top of the editorial page of the *Advocate*.[15]

The *Advocate* continued to decline during the early and middle seventies. It became a reprint sheet, totally dependent on the wire services, especially the *National Publishers Association*, and other newspapers, such as the *New York Times*, the *Charlottesville-Albemarle* (Virginia) *Tribune*, the *Yazoo City* (Mississippi) *Herald*, the *Charlotte* (North Carolina) *Post*, the *Chicago Defender*, and the *Christian Science Monitor*, for articles, news, and even editorials. In addition to these sources, the paper also reprinted heavily from the Congressional Black Caucus Release, Mississippi State University, Jackson State University, and other organizations.

In 1970, the paper appeared as an eight-page weekly tabloid on Thursdays or Saturdays. Single issues cost twenty cents, and a one-year subscription cost for $6.00 or $3.50 for six months. Greene claimed that the paper had "80,000 weekly readers" during the early 1970s, but this figure was exaggerated, because the *Advocate* had rapidly declined during the 1960s. A 1973 study estimated that the *Advocate's* circulation stood at 12,000; but this total remained too high, because basically it gave away copies during this period.[16] As for content, the *Advocate* did not focus on local news, and made little effort to conduct investigative reporting. Part of the problem lay in the fact that since the 1960s, the paper had only two employees, editor Greene and his wife, Frances, who worked as society editor.[17] In general, the editorial policy remained a mixture of black conservatism and black economic nationalism.

An old supporter of the status quo in Mississippi, Greene found little encouragement in the political quests of Charles Evers, perhaps the major black political figure in Mississippi during the early 1970s. When in 1971 the idea of an Evers run for governor of Mississippi emerged, Greene viewed the campaign as "an exercise in futility."[18] This criticism extended nationally to include the Black Panthers and other black radicals.[19] From an international perspective, Greene supported Israel and African independence (especially if the new nations embraced the West). In a striking omission, the *Advocate* failed to print editorial comments on the Nigerian civil war of 1970; instead, Greene reprinted articles from other papers, particularly the *New York Times*.[20]

Jimmy Carter's 1976 "ethnic purity" statement (which implied that discrimination against any ethnic group was wrong, yet groups had the right to retain the best of their traditions, as represented by ethnic neighborhoods) offered Greene an opportunity to express his old views on black separatism. In general, he agreed with Carter's "stand for the right of people of different ethnic or racial groups that make-up the population of the United States to establish and maintain their own separate neighborhoods." Greene still viewed integration as a dead-end position for black Americans. He still blamed the "titular Negro leaders" for "putting the word 'integration' into the political dialogue and debate to take the place of the phrase 'equality under the law' upon the mind of the Negroes of the nation." In Greene's viewpoint, Carter's statement constituted a reminder that blacks needed "their own neighborhoods to the point that they can no longer be looked upon as slum dwellers."[21]

The decline of the *Advocate* during the 1970s becomes apparent in the issue of January 29, 1977, three months before Greene's death. The entire issue contained reprints from news agencies, except for an obituary column and several society items. The paper also included a series of advertisements on pages four, five, six, eight, and ten.[22]

The *Advocate* survived financially on the services of Greene and on money from white advertisers who had supported the paper through the 1950s and 1960s. In 1970, this list included Seale-Lily Ice Cream, Tupelo Concrete Products Company, Friendly Finance Company, and the U.S. Air Force.[23] Such advertisements helped to pay for the printing costs of the paper.

On April 16, 1977, Percy Greene died in Jackson of a heart attack.[24] Many black Mississippians could not yet forgive him for his negative policies toward the civil rights movement, but the *Atlanta Daily World* editorialized that "After the U.S. Supreme Court decision on public school segregation, some Northern journalists misrepresented Editor Greene's position. However, we knew Editor Greene as a courageous young man before and after he started his paper. We believe Jackson is better by his having lived and published his paper there."[25]

After Greene's death, his wife, Frances Reed Greene, the *Advocate's*

Frances Reed Greene (1902–88)
played an active role as society
editor of the *Jackson Advocate*
from the 1940s to 1977. On the
death of her husband, Percy
Greene, she became its editor in
1977–78. Courtesy Dr. Lorraine
Greene Parker.

society editor, took over as acting editor and publisher until July 1, 1978,
securing the assistance of Charles Tisdale, a veteran black editor and
business manager. Under Frances Greene, the paper did not improve,
continuing as a reprint and advertisement sheet, particularly during the
remainder of 1977.[26] A small improvement occurred in early 1978, however, when Tisdale and Deborah LeSure, a news editor, began to play
an active role in the paper's affairs. Although the editorial page continued
to rely heavily on other sources, Tisdale and LeSure brought a welcome
change to the paper with fresh editorials and other news items.

In general, the paper did not break with the official policies of the
Greene family, which remained conservative after Percy Greene's death.
The theme of black pride and nationalism remained. The *Advocate* suggested that by 1978, blacks had developed a tendency "to misunderstand
the need for the maintenance of institutions which are solely black. It is

only by this method that we can set examples and develop images which black youngsters can emulate. . . . Pride in the accomplishments of a people is the sine qua non of the development of that people. If blacks learn this lesson, practiced so well by other ethnic groups, they will succeed as a race."[27] The paper also criticized the Democratic party, because "They have managed to control the majority of the black 'leadership vote' and in so doing have consistently raped the black community of any leadership." The only way for blacks to break out of this situation, the paper suggested, was for them to "split their votes between the Democratic and Republican Parties."[28]

The *Advocate* also worried about the problems produced by organized crime's role in American labor unions; about homosexual rights (fearing for children); and about United States policy toward Africa. On this issue, the *Advocate* wanted to see "a clearly developed, comprehensive U.S. policy" developed for the continent, as "enunciated by U.N. Ambassador Andrew Young that fulfills long-term U.S. and African needs."[29]

Frances Greene's declining interest in the day-to-day affairs of the *Advocate* offered an opportunity for Tisdale to assume the role of publisher in July 1978. Tisdale ushered in a new era, expanding the staff and broadening the scope and direction of the *Advocate*, as evidenced by the paper's new motto: "Individuals of goodwill must concern themselves with and act to curb repression, and to defend human rights. The ordinary individual can make a difference."[30] This represented a departure from the *Advocate*'s historical policy. A new editor, Colia Liddell LaFayette, an activist, poet, actress, teacher, and historian, turned the *Advocate* into a paper of record, information, insight, and inquiry.

Under Tisdale and LaFayette's leadership, the *Advocate*'s price increased to twenty-five cents for a single issue and ten dollars for a yearly subscription. The number of pages in an average issue of the paper increased from eight to ten or more pages. By September 1978, the staff consisted of four individuals: Tisdale as publisher, LaFayette as executive editor, Gemuh Akuchu, associate editor, and LeSure, news director.[31]

Such development began to make a difference in the paper's outlook, tone, and contents. Readers could see the changes in each weekly issue. LaFayette's improvements included the use of the work of local artists and scholars; wider news coverage from local to international, and an emphasis on items of particular interest to the readers, for example black prisoners, women's interests, black culture, black political interests, and

Africa; higher quality and variety of pictures; coverage of Native-American affairs; book reviews; improved society page and items of interest to youth; the development of the interview format and an emphasis on local history and culture; and a strong editorial page. These achievements brought praise from blacks throughout the nation. From northern Mississippi, the Reverend Donald Jenkins wrote that the paper was "moving well . . . in Tupelo." From New Orleans, noted black writer Tom Dent wrote: "I think the paper moves in the direction black people should, and I like the emphasis on history, photography and stories which are not duplicates of the white dailies."[32]

Between July 1978 and December 1979, the *Advocate* developed the strongest editorial page among Mississippi's black newspapers. The paper took special interest in the political condition of blacks in Mississippi and the rest of the nation and in the social and economic plight of the black masses. The paper remained critical of the political efforts of Charles Evers, mayor of Fayette; of communism's role in world affairs; of black leadership's failure to address fully all of the options open to black people in America; of discrimination and racism; of the oppression of women, supporting the Equal Rights Amendment; and of black economic serfdom in the United States, stressing the need for continued affirmative action and equal employment opportunities and for black economic institutions.[33] Much of this emphasis followed the historical focus of the paper, especially on such topics as the significance of vocational education, the need for new black leadership, the quality of and need for black colleges and schools, and the need for a strong program of self-determination and self-development (meaning black institutions rather than integration) for American blacks. The *Advocate* now expressed this old philosophy as "Our wisest course lies in the direction of proficiency in the trades. A search for quality education, and an inner growth which is not concerned with integration, per se, but with the quality of self-development within the confines of traditionally black institutions."[34] Black nationalism remained alive and well at the *Advocate*. Traces of programs and philosophies from Booker T. Washington to Malcolm X permeated the paper's editorial positions during the late 1970s. LaFayette left the *Advocate* in October 1978, to resume other interests; after her departure, Gemuh Akuchu, a native of Cameroon, West Africa, served as managing editor of the paper until May 1979, when he returned to his homeland.[35] During Akuchu's editorship, the price of the paper remained twenty-five cents for a single issue; however, the rate for a one-year subscription increased to fifteen dollars to raise much-needed funds. The staff increased to five members,[36] and further improvements included a special section devoted to business, consumer, labor, and management affairs. The earlier themes of black political, economic, and social plights continued during this period. The *Advocate* became deeply disturbed in early 1979 when a fourteen-year-old black boy, Robert Earl May, received a sentence of forty-eight years, without the possibility of parole, in Parchman State Penitentiary, for stealing.[37] To the *Advocate*, this case represented the depths of black injustice in Mississippi.[38]

During the summer of 1979, Charlotte Graham became acting general manager of the *Advocate*, with a staff of four others and Tisdale as publisher. Later in the year, however, LeSure became general editor.[39] Political issues dominated the pages of the *Advocate* from June to December 1979, followed by social and economic concerns. The paper took special interest in three issues: threats by Mississippi whites to the continued existence of public black colleges in the state; protests against the all-white Mississippi Health Care Commission; and the Iranian Revolution and its aftermath (which the paper noted because of Iran's strategic importance in the Middle East and the country's nearness to and impact on Africa) and Iranian student demonstrations at Jackson State University.[40] In general, the paper's tone continued to reflect a dedication to the black perspective or to black self-determination in Mississippi and elsewhere.[41]

The major black newspaper in eastern Mississippi during the 1970s was the Meridian *Memo Digest*, published and edited by Robert E. Williams. A native of Meridian, Williams received his education in the public schools of that city. He began his career as a professional photographer in 1946, when he opened a studio in Meridian. He also developed an interest in printing, and in 1952 he opened a job printing shop, followed by a religious bookstore in 1960, and a weekly newspaper in January 1961. He currently owns and operates Williams Studio, Williams Printing Company, and Williams Book Department, in addition to the *Memo Digest*.[42]

A ten- to twenty-page weekly tabloid published on Tuesdays, during the seventies the *Digest* claimed a circulation of 5,000, of which 4,000 represented paid subscriptions. A single issue of the *Digest* cost ten cents for most of the decade, increased to fifteen cents by 1979. A one-year subscription to the paper cost $5.20 for Mississippi and Alabama residents and seven dollars for all other locales. The paper's major distribution points included Lauderdale County (site of Meridian), the surround-

Brotherhood, Columbus, August 30, 1976. A bimonthly organ active in the late 1970s, this newspaper served the four northern Mississippi counties of Lowndes, Oktibbeha, Clay, and Monroe. It cost $3.00 a year or fifteen cents a copy. Courtesy *Brotherhood*. *Weekly Communicator*, Jackson, August 12, 1977. This general community newspaper published by James H. Meredith (who in 1962 was the first known black student to enter the University of Mississippi) and edited by Louis Armstrong was active from 1975 to the early 1980s. Courtesy *Weekly Communicator*.

ing counties in eastern Mississippi, and western Alabama. A staff of four, editor Williams and three black women, Mary Jones (advertising manager), Verna Gordon (production manager), and Janice Johnson (composer), ran the *Digest* during the late 1970s.[43]

A strong subscription and advertisement base enabled the *Digest* to appear weekly throughout the decade. An average issue of the paper carried twenty-four advertisements in 1979.[44] In addition to these sources of revenue, the paper could always depend on the income from printing jobs. Its advertisement base resembled that of other black newspapers in Mississippi. The list of advertisers for the paper included such black businesses as Cole's Record and Wig Shop; Sister Williams, spiritual adviser; *Players Magazine*; and other local concerns, such as groceries, cleaners, and so forth. White advertisers included Buck Gleen Pontiac-GM, Goodyear, Lerner Jewelers, and Merchants and Farmers Bank.[45]

As the only paper published in eastern Mississippi, the *Digest* had the field almost to itself—only the *Jackson Advocate* also reached the area; but because it was located in Hinds County, eighty-seven miles west of Meridian, it could not offer the local coverage that the *Digest* provided. Thus, the *Digest* securely held its base of operations at Meridian, a city of 47,000 people in 1972.[46] The *Meridian Star*, a white daily, also did not create any difficulties for editor Williams, as both papers benefited from a large advertisement pool in Lauderdale and the surrounding counties.[47]

The *Digest* placed special focus on the following items: pictures, local news events, cartoons, sports, a women's page, black personalities, especially those in show business, and a Bible column. The paper also covered news items in nearby areas such as Philadelphia, DeKalb, and Enterprise. The editorial page did not constitute one of its major features, except for syndicated columns from national agencies such as the National Black News Service; however, editorials written by the staff frequently appeared.

Between 1970 and 1979, the *Digest* remained deeply committed to the campaign to have Martin Luther King, Jr.'s birthday declared a national holiday. A day in King's honor would help to heal the nation, the *Digest* editorialized, and would indicate the nation's "commitment to the ideals for which he labored." The holiday would also honor the black minority "that has been oppressed, discriminated against and suffered for many centuries."[48]

The *Digest* remained politically moderate, but it had no problem in publishing the opinions of conservative staff writers. It also supported the Democratic party. In early 1970, D. Talmedge Webster, a Meridian black, expressed his extremely arch-conservative viewpoint in the paper: "I don't think now that civil rights is a paramount issue. Nor do I think desegregation is to save the greatness of this country. It is the duty of every loyal American to help eliminate disorder, communist, racial or political conditions and bring this country to peaceful, loyal and progressive society where it deserves to stand."[49] Such political sentiments carried over from the conservative themes of the 1960s, from such organs as the New Albany *Community Citizen*. They did not adequately reflect the black condition in America.

The *Digest* placed a high priority on better economic conditions for blacks and also for better housing and educational opportunities. The paper viewed racism as a continuing problem, especially for black children, because "In this day of surging black consciousness, black parents face a greater responsibility than ever before to help their children learn to live happily in a society that is still basically racist."[50]

The *Digest*'s style as a primarily local news and reprint organ continued from 1970 to the end of the decade, when few changes had occurred in the makeup, coverage, and direction of the paper. In fact, by 1979 the editorial page had become largely a digest of reprints and the opinions of individuals, such as then U.S. Ambassador to the United Nations Donald F. McHenry, on world affairs.[51]

Seven other substantial black Mississippi commercial newspapers existed: the *Natchez News Leader* and the *Bluff City Post*, both in Natchez; the Greenville *Mississippi News*; the Columbus *Brotherhood*; the Moss Point *Pas-Point Journal*; and the *Metropolitan Observer* and the *Mississippi Enterprise*, both of Jackson. These papers shared the following characteristics: all were weeklies published in areas with sizable black populations; all were established (except for the *Enterprise*) in the 1970s to meet the critical need for information by local blacks; all were extremely hard pressed for advertisement dollars, forcing them to cease publication after only one to four years; volunteers and very small, poorly paid staffs (usually consisting of the publisher/editor and one other individual) performed all of the work for the papers; and all had small circulations, generally between one thousand and two thousand copies weekly. Like the *Jackson Advocate* and the Meridian *Memo Digest*, they rate mention because of their attempts to develop black newspapers under severe circumstances.[52]

Five other black commercial papers also published during the seventies in Mississippi; however, this segment remained weak because they focused on yellow journalism, sensationalism, and exploitation of black readers. This group included the New Albany *Community Citizen*, the *Pascagoula–Moss Point 50/50*, the *Tutwiler Whirlwind*, and two Jackson sheets, the *Weekly Communicator* and the *Highlighter*. They collectively represented the worst side of black publishing in Mississippi. The major problems associated with them lay in the following areas: most were simply given away; advertisements consumed most of the papers; very little hard news or editorials appeared; these papers generally focused on crime, family disturbances, and "society" items of a sensational nature, especially in such organs as the *Weekly Communicator* and the *Highlighter*; and fillers, such as pictures, often dominated an average page of these papers.[53] None of these papers continued publication after 1979.

Three community organs also must be discussed. First, the monthly Mound Bayou *Voice*, established in 1968 by Johnny Magee and later edited by Milburn J. Crowe, with the help of between three and five other people. It ranged from four to twelve pages in length, and cost ten cents. Second, the Jackson *Drummer*, a bimonthly created in 1971 by the Drummer Associates and edited by Steve Wilson. The *Drummer's* five-person staff produced a twelve-page journal priced at twenty cents per issue. Finally, in 1978 Henry Kirksey established the Jackson *Mississippi Mirror*, which he published monthly with the help of only one other person. The *Mirror* ran from four to twenty-eight pages and cost one dollar per copy.[54] As community organs, the above papers concerned themselves particularly with the political, economic, and social conditions in their local areas and in other parts of Mississippi. They offered additional commentary on the pressing situation for most blacks in Mississippi during the seventies, adding their voices to strengthen the work of the major black newspapers of the state, such as the *Jackson Advocate*.

Mississippi had five monthly black magazines during the 1970s, all published at Jackson: *Close-Up Magazine*, established by W. Clayton Neely in 1965 and active until 1971; *Outlook Magazine*, created in 1974 by James Meredith (of Ole Miss fame); *Reaction Magazine*, produced by R. T. Sanders, Rufus Rawls, and Theodore Bozeman, Jr., in 1976; *Street Talk*, established in 1978 by Jerry Sutton; and *Sunbelt: Black Life in Mississippi*, created in 1979 by Thomas H. Espy.[55] Only *Sunbelt* and *Street Talk* continued publication after 1979.

Only three of these magazines practiced serious journalism, *Sunbelt* (the clear leader), *Close-Up*, and *Reaction*. *Street Talk* and *Outlook* were

The Drummer, Jackson, June 15, 1971. Mertis Rubin and Milburn J. Crowe served as editors of this general interest journal in the early 1970s. A yearly subscription to the paper cost $10.00 and single issues sold for twenty cents. Courtesy *The Drummer*. *The Voice*, Mound Bayou, May 27, 1970. This weekly, active in the all-black township of Mound Bayou from 1968 into the early 1970s, was edited by Johnny Magee in 1970 and by Milburn Crowe in 1971. It was "Dedicated to the Total Freedom and Independence of the African American people in this country." Courtesy *The Voice*.

sensational journals, placing a major emphasis on black engagements, marriage and divorce records, police reports, pictures, and personal statements from Hinds County residents. Both journals emphasized black activities and the personal problems of individual blacks in the county. A single twenty-page issue of *Outlook* sold for sixty cents; a one-year subscription for six dollars. *Street Talk*, with thirty pages in each issue, had a higher price, seventy-five cents per copy and eight dollars for a one-year subscription. Although both journals accepted advertisements, an average issue contained as few as three.[56] A staff of three worked at *Street Talk*, editor Sutton, photojournalist Jai Barnes, and cartoonist Harold Gater. Meredith represented the driving force behind *Outlook*. Both magazines had a small circulation and were generally distributed in Jackson, Hinds County, and central Mississippi.

Close-Up, *Reaction*, and *Sunbelt* magazines practiced better journalism. Active in the 1960s, *Close-Up Magazine* featured articles and essays on black life, with a focus on Mississippi. *Reaction Magazine*, with fifty pages in its maiden issue in 1976, contained essays on economic, political, and social topics of interest to black Mississippians, poetry, human interest short pieces, art, and news. A staff of four served the journal; however, *Reaction* published only this single issue.[57]

In late 1979, *Sunbelt* appeared. It immediately became the leading black magazine and, next to the *Jackson Advocate*, perhaps the second most important black publication in Mississippi. The journal's success lay in its soundness from the first issue in October 1979 onward. The well-designed fifty-page periodical included essays on black life in Mississippi, an interview with B. B. King, and feature articles on family history, health, music, business, home life, travel, book reviews, creative fiction, art and culture, and other items. Single issues cost $1.25, and a year's subscription sold for twelve dollars. A staff of fifteen worked at *Sunbelt*, including the publisher, Espy; an editor, Patricia C. Murrain (and later, Lynette J. Shelton); two associate editors, Art James and Rose R. Bozeman; an art director; two staff writers; a circulation manager; a technical engineer; and five photographers.[58] Not all of the staff members worked full time for the magazine, but staff commitment to the journal resulted in an excellent product. Martha Ceaser Dismuke of Columbus, in a letter to the editor of *Sunbelt*, believed that the magazine met an urgent need, offering information and insight to blacks who had "long needed a magazine that explores black life in Mississippi for us who live here as well as for the Mississippians who live elsewhere in the world."[59] Such senti-

Sunbelt magazine, Jackson, October 1979. *Sunbelt*, a monthly publication, was active in Jackson in 1979 and 1980. Under the leadership of Thomas H. Espy, publisher, and Patricia Churchill-Murrain, editor, it placed special emphasis on covering black cultural, social, economic, and political developments in Mississippi and the South. Courtesy Thomas H. Espy, Jackson, Mississippi. The *Bluff City Post*, Natchez, November 2, 1979. Edited by William H. Terrell, this paper was created in 1978 as a "forum for the presentation and discussion of issues, ideas and opinions" of black Mississippians in one of the state's oldest cities. Courtesy *Bluff City Post*.

ments appear to represent the views of many individuals on the significance of the new publication.[60]

Another facet of the black press in Mississippi consisted of journals published by black organizations. Mississippi boasted more than fifty such organs, mostly newsletters, during the 1970s, two of which merit special recognition:[61] first, the *New African*, the official publication of the Republic of New Africa (RNA), a black nationalist movement, seeking a black homeland in the Southern United States; second, *Forty Acres and a Mule*, the organ of the Emergency Land Fund (Mississippi branch). This organization strove to preserve black land ownership in the South and to aid black farmers.

The RNA's *New African* began in Detroit, the home of the movement, in 1969. It later transferred to Jackson, where the organization initiated a plan to acquire land as the first stage in the development of a black nation in North America.[62] The *New African* worked to promote the RNA and thus to seek "an African nation in the Western Hemisphere struggling for complete Independence." In addition, the organ pressed for "reparations from the U.S.A. for Black people living here, as repayment for . . . illegal kidnapping and transportation, slavery, cultural genocide, physical and educational deprivation, and post-slavery exploitation and oppression, all with complicity of U.S. law."[63] Under the leadership of President Imari A. Obadele I (Milton R. Henry), the *New African* published an eight- to twenty-four-page tabloid. It appeared sporadically, and cost twenty-five cents an issue; a one-year subscription was advertised at six dollars for twenty-four issues.[64] Because of the radical nature of its work, the state of Mississippi, the Jackson Police Department, and the FBI closely watched and harassed the RNA and the *New African*. An August 18, 1971, raid on two RNA houses in Jackson led to a shootout in which "a Jackson policeman was killed and a second policeman and an FBI agent wounded."[65] The eleven RNA members present were "beaten, paraded half-dressed through city streets in chains, tear gassed, and charged with murder, assault, and waging war against the state of Mississippi. The latter charge was based on a pre–Civil War statute. Eventually certain charges were dropped and some RNA citizens were released after serving long jail terms." Three of the eleven, however, received life sentences, and one received two concurrent ten-year prison terms.[66] The state and federal efforts created a period of uncertainty for the RNA; however, the *New African* continued to appear in the mid-1970s and afterward. Its circulation always remained small, but

Mississippi News, Greenville, March 13, 1976. Active between 1974 and 1976, this commercial weekly newspaper focused its coverage on black life with a special emphasis on the Delta region of northwestern Mississippi. An eight-page paper published on Saturday, it sold for $7.50 a year or ten cents an issue. David Johnson served as its publisher and Katie M. Johnson as editor. Courtesy *Mississippi News*. *Republic of New Africa Newsletter*, Jackson, March 1975. This publication served as the official organ of a political group that sought to create a new African nation for black Americans out of five Deep South states (Louisiana, Mississippi, Alabama, Georgia, and South Carolina) in the 1970s. Courtesy *RNA Newsletter*.

it reached activists, intellectuals, and the general public in Mississippi and in major American cities such as Detroit.

In 1978, *Emergency Land Fund Digest* became *Forty Acres and a Mule*. Jessie Morris, a civil rights veteran, and Regina Banks, a young black woman, served as the journal's editors. The organ was

> edited primarily for minority landowners. It covers problems of land ownership and land loss, examples of alternative crops and farm produce. It also covers current research and experimental developments in agricultural technology, technological innovations appropriate to the energy needs of small farmers, resources, services, and programs available from governmental and private organizations. In addition, it discusses issues on legislative developments and stances taken by elected officials as to proposed legislation that might have an effect on our readership.

Forty Acres and a Mule carried regular features in each issue: "(1) a story on a successful black farmer; (2) a question-answer column; (3) a sketch of an organization operating in the rural South whose primary purpose is improving the economic condition of black people; (4) a profile of a small rural town with a majority black population and government."[67]

Some issues of the journal were distributed free to poor people; a single issue sold for twenty-five cents in 1978 and thirty-five cents in 1979. In 1978, a one-year subscription cost two dollars, raised to four dollars in 1979. Generally a monthly, the organ usually contained between eight and sixteen pages.[68] The Emergency Land Fund and *Forty Acres and a Mule* filled an urgent need in Mississippi and elsewhere: in the five-year period between 1969 and 1974, U.S. blacks lost over 2.5 million acres of land, 499,541 of them in Mississippi.[69] The organ's success lay in its attempt to reach the poor and to use creative approaches to describe, analyze, and interpret the problems that faced black farmers and landowners during the 1970s, "providing a source of information for many of [its] readers."[70]

Five historically black colleges and universities in Mississippi constituted active press centers during the seventies: Alcorn State University, Jackson State University, Mississippi Valley State University, Rust College, and Tougaloo College.[71] During this period, activities at black colleges maintained their historical focus on student newspapers and other publications, yearbooks, alumni news bulletins, and general newsletters

Mississippi Mirror, Jackson, December 1978. Henry Kirksey edited the *Mississippi Mirror* in 1978 to focus black attention on major political, economic, and social issues in Mississippi. A twenty-eight-page tabloid priced at $1.00 an issue, it appeared only irregularly in the late 1970s. Courtesy Henry Kirksey, Jackson, Mississippi. The *Alcorn Herald*, Lorman, March 31, 1977. This official student newspaper at Alcorn State University has been active at the school since the 1930s. Alcorn, a historically black public institution, was created in 1871, the first black land-grant college in the United States. Courtesy *Alcorn Herald*.

on the schools' work. Alcorn State, the oldest predominantly black publicly supported university in the state, at Lorman, published four key institutional publications during the 1970s: the *Alcorn Herald*, a student newspaper active since the 1930s; the *Alcornite*, a school yearbook, which had published for more than thirty years by 1970; the *Alcorn Alumni Magazine*, active since 1952; and the *Weekly Bulletin*, a newsletter on university affairs. Student organizations, academic departments, the office of public information, the athletic department, the department of student affairs, and fraternities and sororities published more than two dozen other newsletters, bulletins, and pamphlets at Alcorn. Alcorn also had an underground student press that came to life whenever a problem demanded student expression outside of the *Alcorn Herald*. The *Alcorn Herald* and the *Alumni Magazine* had a wide circulation among Alcorn's students, alumni, and friends.[72]

The oldest private black college in Mississippi, Rust College, established in 1866 at Holly Springs, produced five key publications during the decade: the Rust College *Sentinel*, mailed quarterly to alumni, friends, and donors; the *Alumni Newsletter*, mailed eight times a year to alumni; *Campus News Briefs*, mailed weekly to faculty, staff, and students; the *Rustorian* student newspaper, published monthly; and the *Bearcat*, a yearbook published since 1927.[73]

The largest predominantly black institution in Mississippi, Jackson State University, had the largest volume of press materials among black institutions in the state. Among other factors, the school had the largest faculty, budget, and student population. Its most important press publications included the *Blue and White Flash*, a weekly student newspaper active since 1940; the *Jacksonian*, a yearbook active since 1925; the *Scope*, a weekly campus news bulletin; the *JSU Alumni Magazine*; and the *Jackson State University Review*, an academic journal published by the JSU Faculty Research and Publication Committee.[74]

At Itta Bena, Mississippi Valley State University published four press journals of note: the *Valley Voice*, a student newspaper; the *Review*, a literary magazine; the *Delvian*, a student yearbook; and a campus news bulletin.[75] The second-oldest black college in Mississippi, Tougaloo College, a private institution, boasted a number of quality publications. Tougaloo's strength as a publishing center reflected its historical commitment to academic excellence and social change. Its publications included *The Harambee*, a monthly student newspaper; *Eagle Queen*, an

Blue and White Flash, Jackson, September 29, 1979. The *Blue and White Flash* serves as the official student newspaper at Jackson State University, the largest historically black university in Mississippi, established in 1877. Courtesy *Blue and White Flash*. *The Harambee*, Tougaloo, October 1978. *The Harambee* has served since 1969 as the official student newspaper at Tougaloo College, the second oldest historically black college in Mississippi, created in 1869 by the American Missionary Association. Courtesy *The Harambee*.

TABLE 5-3.   Circulation Figures of Black College Student Newspapers, 1973

Institution	Paper	No. pages	Circulation
Alcorn State U.	*Alcorn Herald* (m)	4	4,100
Mary Holmes Jr. College	*The Growl* (m)	4	10,000
Jackson State U.	*Blue & White Flash* (w)	4	8,000+
Miss. Ind. Col.	*Miss. Ind. Col. News* (m)	4	500
Miss. Valley State U.	*Valley Voice* (m)	4	2,000
Rust College	*Rustorian* (m)	4	900
Tougaloo College	*Harambee* (m)	4	1,000+
Utica Jr. Col.	*Black People Speak* (formerly *The Bulldog Growl*) (m)	4	2,000

Note: w = weekly; m = monthly.

annual yearbook; *Tougaloo News*, an alumni bulletin; *Pound: The Literary Magazine*; and a campus news bulletin.[76]

Six historically black junior colleges also served as black press centers in Mississippi during the seventies. Utica Junior College had *Black People Speak* (formerly *The Bulldog Growl*), a student newspaper, and the *Uticanite*, an annual yearbook, and Holmes Junior College published the *Growl*, a student newspaper, *Reflections*, a college magazine, and *Horizons*, a college yearbook. Coahoma Junior College, Natchez Junior College, and Piney Woods School also published student newspapers and yearbooks.[77]

During the seventies, black educational journals in Mississippi generally printed college and university news, student concerns and problems, national and state news, syndicated columns, book reviews, literature, special poetry, film reviews, sports, cartoons, and pictures. Because black administrators closely monitored most black student publications, few of the journals developed as radical organs. They generally confined their editorial positions to school concerns and perhaps local or state events. They reached primarily students, staff members, and alumni.[78]

Black students who attended historically white universities in Mississippi during this period also produced black-oriented organs. At Mississippi State University, in Starkville, black students established the *Afro-Times Newsletter* in 1971. At the University of Mississippi, in Oxford, where approximately three hundred blacks studied during the early seventies, the *Spectator* served as the black student newspaper.[79]

The major educational organ of blacks in Mississippi, the *Mississippi Educational Journal*, the official publication of the Mississippi Teachers Association, published until 1976, when the association combined with the historically white Mississippi Education Association to form a new group, the Mississippi Association of Educators.[80]

The black religious press did not grow during the 1970s. In fact, the religious press had been declining since the height of the civil rights movement in Mississippi during the 1960s. Few modern black editors have been ministers, in comparison to earlier periods when black Baptist and Methodist preachers dominated the press. In addition to the pressure created by the civil rights movement's call for a less conservative, more progressive black press, factors discouraging black ministers from pursuing press careers appear to have included the lack of money created by modern-day black newspaper publishing, greater interests in other activities, and the decline in the black public's interest in religious newspapers. Nevertheless, a half dozen or so black religious organs published in Mississippi during the seventies. In addition, numerous black churches, especially the Baptist and Methodist denominations, have produced their own newsletters and other press materials. Black religious journals of the decade include the Jackson *Reconciler*, a monthly organ of the Voice of Calvary Ministries edited by John Perkins; the Mound Bayou *Light*, edited by Zee Anderson Barron; the Jackson *Metropolitan Baptist Ministers Fellowship*; and the Bay Saint Louis *Divine Word Messenger* (formerly *Saint Augustine's Messenger*), a Catholic periodical.[81]

Blacks controlled three radio stations in Mississippi during the 1970s: Hattiesburg's WORV-AM, Circuit Broadcasting Company, Vernon Floyd, owner and executive manager; Greenville's WBAD-FM, William D. Jackson, owner and executive manager; and Meridian's WTNK, East-West Communication Corporation, Charles Young and Len Miller, owner and executive managers.[82] Whites controlled fifteen black-oriented stations during the same period.

The small number of black-owned radio stations limited the options available to blacks with an interest in this medium. Perhaps the fact that most people viewed radio largely as a means of obtaining entertainment and music rather than hard news and analysis constituted the largest obstacle to the development of radio as an effective black communication tool.[83] In addition, black news did not make money, and, except for WJSU, a nonprofit educational radio station of Jackson State University, blacks in Mississippi did not control any other radio medium.[84] Such attitudes remained widespread despite the addition of new press agencies, such as the National Black Network, that offered fresh approaches to black news.[85]

During the 1970s, black presence on Mississippi television resembled that on radio. By 1976, blacks represented 24 percent of Mississippi's 463 television employees.[86] Blacks worked primarily on local television newscasts and in off-camera positions. Unlike radio, where blacks controlled three stations, blacks still did not fully control a single television station in the state.[87]

With television almost totally in the hands of whites, blacks could never count on receiving a black interpretation of the news, even with black employees. As elsewhere, Mississippi's television stations aimed for the vast white middle class, relegating black considerations to a thirty-minute program called "Sunday Morning Hour" or a segment on a weekly documentary program, at most. Blacks also disliked the available entertainment television programming, which limited and distorted the black experience, especially through the use of disparaging comedies and other network shows.[88]

During the 1970s black Mississippians gained a foothold on WLBT, channel three in Jackson. In June 1971, the Federal Communications Commission (FCC) finally ruled on a petition filed against the station (owned by Lamar Life Insurance Company) in the early 1960s by the United Church of Christ's communication office. The FCC approved a nonprofit group, Communications Improvement, Inc. (later Civic Communications), as the temporary manager of the station, until the appointment of a new permanent licensee. Five petitioners contended for the license, which was finally awarded to Civic Communications, a group of black investors including Aaron Henry and other black business leaders from throughout the United States. A new manager, William Dilday, Jr., a black, came to the station in 1972 from Boston, where he had served as personnel director for radio station WHDH. Educated at the Boston University School of Business, Dilday became the first black to hold such a position in the United States.[89] A 1975 study rated his tenure as "serious and hard line. He has an open-policy public affairs department and a creed which in effect states that his news team will report any and all news, without regard for Southern 'etiquette' and 'sacred cows'. He expects competency from the entire staff which is composed of 28 blacks and 52 whites."[90]

Under Dilday's leadership, the station maintained its record as the

Women in Media, a group of black Mississippi women, formed in 1978 to foster women in the print and broadcasting industries and to promote media education. *Left to right, rear:* Joyce Hughes, Regina Harris, Josephine Hobbs, Deborah Burk, Deloris Ballard; *front,* Paula Pittman, Doris Saunders, Marcia Clinkscales. Courtesy *Jackson Advocate.*

leading television station (in terms of viewership) in Mississippi, and it also received several awards during the seventies, including a Peabody Award for its work on Mississippi. Although the station added black reporters on and off camera, increased the amount of black material that reached the airwaves, and became more balanced in its general treatment of all groups, the station, unlike black newspapers, still did not reflect all black viewpoints. Channel three's motto remained "Let's keep a good thing going."[91] This problem continued until 1978, when blacks put together a package giving them 51 percent control at the station.[92]

Black newspapers clearly continued to serve as the major form of black-controlled communications in Mississippi during the 1970s. Blacks' weak position in ownership and lack of influence on the content of radio and television made black newspapers even more important in fulfilling the black quest for information, news, and analysis based on a black viewpoint. Nor was the black newspaper's central role in securing and interpreting black news vastly affected by the employment of a small number of blacks on the staffs of white dailies during this period.[93] Although white dailies, such as the *Clarion-Ledger*, increased the percentage of black news they covered during the decade, such news remained outside of the papers' primary focus. Perhaps their greatest area of competition with the black press lay in the fact that the white papers appeared seven days a week, with up-to-the-minute news, whereas black Mississippians did not produce a single daily paper during the decade. Radio and television also used the immediacy issue to attract black listeners to their programs: In reality, all of the major white media attempted to gain the black audience. For the black press, however, this issue constituted one of life or death.[94]

Throughout the 1970s, Mississippi's black press faced severe economic difficulties, so much so that by 1979, only eight black newspapers and three magazines remained active.[95] Black businesses (and many white ones too) continued to support the black press; however, the black economic base was concentrated in Jackson and in approximately ten other Mississippi cities, but its advertisement strength had declined as a result of desegregation during the 1970s. Most white advertising dollars went to the white papers and to radio and television; what was left over went to the black press.

Small inexperienced staffs, who often did not have college degrees or training in journalism programs, also plagued the black press. Technological innovations in publishing and use of computers in publishing also represented shortcomings for black journalists—largely as a result of the high cost of the machines.

By 1979, blacks in Mississippi looked back on a decade of desegregation efforts that had changed the state to a degree. The public schools were open to all children without regard to race, and public accommodations, such as hotels, restaurants, libraries, and movie theaters, were desegregated. Most blacks could vote, and blacks served at all levels of state government. The black middle class grew during the decade. Lingering shadows of segregation still prevailed in the state, however. The withdrawal of many whites from the system and the creation of private white academies throughout Mississippi damaged the public school system. Black principals, teachers, coaches, and students suffered varied forms of discrimination, including the loss of status and jobs, demotions, and diminishing educational options. Unemployment and underemployment remained high, so that many blacks could not take advantage of the desegregation of public accommodations. Blacks remained underrepresented, and many (especially those who lived on Delta farms) feared voting, because of the possibility of economic reprisals. Throughout the state, blacks suffered disproportionately in terms of housing, health care, number of state jobs held, positions in police departments, and other areas. Blacks also continued to suffer from the racism of many white Mississippians, especially in rural areas or small towns.[96]

In this environment, the black press in Mississippi struggled to stay alive and to continue to bring black communities the black point of view on local, state, national, and international issues. Weakened by the economic strains of the 1970s, which affected the black press throughout the United States, Mississippi's publishers, editors, reporters, and other press personnel kept the black printed tradition alive in weekly newspapers, magazines, and other media.[97] The appearance of a younger generation of black radio and television journalists, who worked under the limitations of white newscasts, helped in this task. These individuals began to present the news to the public from black newscasters on the state's airwaves. It represented a beginning.

CHAPTER 6

Change and Continuity

1980–1985

The 1980s opened with the election of Ronald Reagan as president and the expansion of a conservative outlook in the United States. It represented a period of mixed progress for American blacks, particularly in Mississippi, where Afro-Americans faced an economic system in which most blacks endured high rates of unemployment and underemployment, poverty, hunger, and an inadequate social-service system. In January 1982, the unemployment rate for all Mississippians stood at 10.3 percent, increasing to 14.7 percent in February 1983 and declining to 10.7 percent in 1985. One-fourth of all Mississippians and 62 percent of the state's black families lived below the poverty line during the early 1980s. Mississippi remained at the bottom on a number of national economic indicators, including the dubious distinction as the state with the lowest per capita income, measured at $7,256 in 1981, versus a national average of $10,517. The state also depended heavily on funds from the United States government. In fact, among the states, Mississippi received the highest amount of federal monies—$6.56 billion in 1982.[1]

The eighties represented a period of black political assertiveness in Mississippi. Between 1980 and 1983, the total number of registered black voters in the state increased from 350,000 to 410,000, while the number of registered whites decreased from 1,152,000 to 1,140,383. During the early 1980s Mississippians elected more than 439 blacks to political positions, including 20 black mayors, more than 140 city councillors, and 20 members of the state legislature. In 1984, Mississippi held the distinction

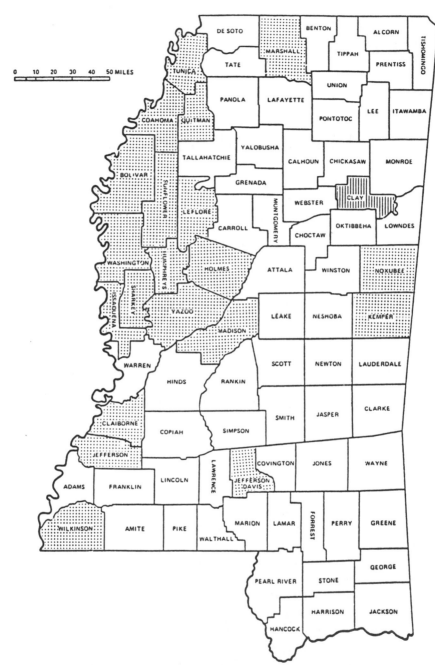

Mississippi's Black Majority Counties, 1980. Dots = black majority. Stripes = 49.9 percent blacks, no clear racial majority.

of having the largest number of black elected officials in the United States. Such achievements, however, did not reflect the total percentage of the black population of Mississippi—887,206, or 35.2 percent of the total in 1980. In the legislature, for example, blacks held only 11 percent of the seats.[2]

A mixed state of social affairs also existed in Mississippi during the 1980s. Although de jure segregation no longer existed, aspects of customary segregation and discrimination continued to operate, as evidenced by the negative beliefs some whites still held about blacks, such as their inferiority to whites. Furthermore, many whites continued to view blacks primarily as a source of cheap labor for white economic interests. In spite of such attitudes, blacks and whites could observe the changes that had taken place in the state since the 1960s—the disappearance of rigid segregation laws and practices in education and public accommodations, black voting, black elected officials—but all could also see the degree to which many aspects of life had not changed. The greatest black disappointments came in the areas of housing, education, and employment, where discrimination and the lingering effects of segregation still influenced events and public policy in the 1980s.

As blacks surveyed the Mississippi landscape during this era, they found that segregation remained a way of life for most churches, public education remained beleaguered because of white private schools (and the average number of years of education for a black Mississippian stood at 6.7 in 1983), discrimination existed in housing (with Mississippi leading the United States in substandard and poor housing), and black employment in business and government continues low as a consequence of their poverty. Those few middle-class blacks who have jobs, like poor blacks, face the problem of subtle racism. In addition to these problems, a large number of blacks remain in Mississippi's prisons.[3] Thus, the economic, political, and social conditions of black Mississippians continue to indicate that further progress remains necessary.

The black press has joined the search for solutions to Mississippi's problems. Yet the black press in Mississippi has also continued to decline in the 1980s. Of the twelve black commercial papers of the 1970s, only four survived into the eighties: the *Jackson Advocate*, the *Mississippi Enterprise*, the *Memo Digest*, and the *Bluff City Post*. In addition to these papers, a new journal, the Port Gibson *Claiborne*, founded by Regina Devoual published from 1980 to 1981. In 1983, Eddie Taylor and Joyce Jones created the *Hub City Community News* in Hattiesburg.[4] Three of the five commercial magazines of the 1970s continued publication into the 1980s: *Outlook Magazine, Street Talk,* and *Sunbelt.* A new journal, *TOF Weekly Magazine,* appeared in 1980.

Except for church and organizational religious newsletters, the black religious press remained weak in the 1980s. The *Reconciler,* published by Jackson's Voice of Calvary Ministries, continued during this period, as did the many historically black educational journals of the predominantly black colleges and universities. Outside of the newsletters of major fraternal organizations such as the Elks and the Masons and social groups such as Alpha Phi Alpha, Omega Psi Phi, Alpha Kappa Alpha, Delta Sigma Theta, and Kappa Alpha Psi, the black fraternal press also remained weak, especially in comparison to its major role during the early twentieth century.

The greatest growth in Mississippi's black press in the 1980s occurred in the area of the organizational press—the organs of the black social, political, and economic groups. More than fifty such publications appeared regularly during this period, including *Forty Acres and a Mule,* the *Political Action League Newsletter, Monitor* (of the Mississippi Cultural Arts Coalition), and the Black Arts Music Society's *Keynotes.* Groups such as the state NAACP, the Jackson Urban League, the United League of Mississippi, Mississippi Action for Community Education, Co-Blossom (formerly Council of Black Leaders of State Organizations of Mississippi), the Oxford Committee for the Promotion of Black Art, the Mississippi Legislative Black Caucus, the Southern Black Cultural Alliance, and the Mississippi Coalition of Black Human Service Workers all have issued newsletters.[5] This increase in black organizational journals indicates the additional effort to promote advancement of blacks and other groups in the state.

In general, the economic pressures of publishing—the lack of adequate advertisers—increased in the 1980s, a factor contributing to the decreasing number of black commercial newspapers and magazines. The press also continues to suffer from high staff turnover, small offices, a lack of modern equipment, and inadequate distribution outlets.[6] In television and radio, the conditions of the 1970s prevailed during the 1980s; however, blacks continued to play a major role in the operation of Jackson's WLBT (channel three).

Minor changes occurred in the white press of Mississippi in the 1980s. First, although in 1980 the number of white daily newspapers remained the same as in the 1970s (23), the number of weeklies declined from 119 papers to 91. By 1984, the number of white dailies had declined by one, but the weekly press had increased to a total of 107. White Mississippians also produced 30 magazines and journals in 1981 and 31 in 1984.[7]

In most cases, Mississippi's white press continued its 1970s conservative outlook and attitude toward political, economic, and social issues. Changes did occur at some papers with the death of veteran editors, such as George McLean (1905–83) at the *Tupelo Journal*, and Leonard Lowrey (1920–82) at the *Hattiesburg American*.[8] By 1984 Mississippi also lacked moderate papers, such as the weekly *Capital Reporter*, published at Jackson from 1956 to 1981.[9] The transfer of ownership perhaps represents the greatest change among white Mississippi papers during the eighties. First, in 1980, the Carter family of Greenville sold the *Delta Democrat-Times* to Freedom Newspapers, Inc., a thirty-newspaper chain with its home base at Santa Ana, California. By 1983, many local citizens believed that the paper had become extremely conservative and less public service–oriented in comparison to its history of moderate positions on public issues.[10] Second, in 1982 the Gannett chain, based at Rochester, New York, purchased the *Clarion-Ledger*, the *Jackson Daily News*, the *Hattiesburg American*, and six weekly papers in Mississippi.[11] Gannett bought the three daily newspapers from the Hederman family of Jackson, which had a major influence on Mississippi journalism for more than fifty years.[12] Under new management, the *Clarion-Ledger* and the *Jackson Daily News*, which have the largest circulations in Mississippi, became more moderate in their coverage, interpretation, and assessment of both black and white Mississippians. After decades of antiblack and negative reporting, the new mood set by the state's largest papers brought a welcome change in white publishing.[13] Although a small number of blacks continued to work on papers such as the *Clarion-Ledger* and the *Jackson Daily News*, most white newspapers employed few blacks. For example, as the 1980s opened, the *Jackson Daily News* had a staff of forty journalists, only three of them minorities.[14]

Between 1980 and 1984, the major political issues found on the pages of the black press in Mississippi included the political trial of a murder charge of former Tchula Mayor Eddie Carthan; the 1980 and 1984 presidential elections, the role of Jesse Jackson, problems created by Ronald Reagan's administration, and the political status of Afro-Americans; the NAACP's success in overturning a 1974 decision by the Hinds County Chancery Court that directed the organization and ninety-one Port Gibson blacks to pay 1.2 million dollars to twelve local whites for damages they claimed resulted from a boycott of their businesses beginning in 1966; events in Africa, especially hunger and white minority control of Namibia and South Africa; the creation of a national holiday to honor the work and life of the Reverend Dr. Martin Luther King, Jr.; the conservative domination of the U.S. Supreme Court; the Middle Eastern events, such as the Iranian Revolution and the murder of Egyptian President Anwar Sadat; the plight of Haitian refugees in the United States; the attempt to elect a black congressman from Mississippi (Mike Espy, a Democrat from Yazoo City, became the first black congressman from the state in 1986); and the campaigns of Leslie McLemore and Robert Clark.

The black press of Mississippi addressed five economic areas in particular during the 1980s: black unemployment; the loss of black land-holdings; the poor state of black businesses; black poverty; and the Reagan administration's cuts in public-service programs and the resulting plight of blacks and other groups.

The black press's major social interests during this period included black education and the survival of black colleges; the role of black journalists at historically white newspapers and in other media (e.g., Janet Cooke and Milton Coleman, especially his disclosure in 1984 that Rev. Jesse Jackson had described Jews as "hymies"; race relations, racism, and discrimination and the related problems of extremist white organizations, such as the Ku Klux Klan and the White Citizens' Councils, and police brutality against blacks (e.g., the 1980 Jackson case of Gregory Lowe and especially the case of Robert Earl "Bubba" May of Brookhaven); the number of blacks, especially males, who were in jail and on death row in Mississippi; the work of civil rights organizations in Mississippi, such as the NAACP and the United League, and conflicts among black organizations over the direction of the freedom movement in the state; the murders of black children in Atlanta and the problem of random violence against blacks in the South; and the status of black culture in the United States.[15]

The editors of the state's five black commercial papers of the 1980s represented a highly educated group. All of the editors completed high school, and six of the eight held college degrees.[16] Black women worked on the staffs of all black newspapers in the 1980s, and Regina Devoual at the *Claiborne*, Deborah LeSure and Colia LaFayette at the *Advocate*, and Lucille Miller at the *Mississippi Enterprise* had particular influence at their respective newspapers, where black women served as editors.[17]

Black men, however, still dominated the ranks as publishers, including Charles Tisdale at the *Advocate*, Willie Miller at the *Enterprise*, Robert E. Williams at the *Memo Digest*, and Theodore C. Johnson at the *Bluff City Post*.

A summary of the four major black newspapers of this period (the *Advocate*, the *Enterprise*, the *Digest*, and the *Post*) in table 6-1 shows that papers ranged from eight to twenty-four pages in length, varied in size and published once weekly by a staff ranging from 4 to 11 individuals; a single issue was generally priced at 25 cents; and all had a moderate circulation rate, between 2,000 and 8,000 issues weekly.

The *Jackson Advocate* clearly emerges as the leading black paper in terms of circulation, number of staff members, total pages printed, and the range of advertisements. The *Advocate* also provided the best amount, quality, and interpretation of news, not only for events in Mississippi, but also for those elsewhere in the world. Consequently, the *Advocate* became the only statewide black newspaper in Mississippi.

Although papers such as the *Enterprise*, the *Digest*, and the *Post* continued to publish, their major achievement during the eighties lay in their continued publication. But they often fell short of appearing as outstanding weekly newspapers. In general, their problems, historic in nature, included poor coverage of state, national, and international news; inadequate investigative reporting on local and state affairs; and very weak editorial pages. Despite such problems, these papers contributed to the black citizens of Natchez, Meridian, and Jackson by offering black press voices, however inadequate, to these communities.

TABLE 6-1.   Major Black Mississippi Commercial Papers of the 1980s

Paper (location) (date of est.)	Estimated cost	No. pages	Size	No. staff in 1983	No. ads	Range of circulation
Advocate (Jackson) (1940)	35¢ $20.00	22–24	Standard	11	65 (10/18/84)	8,000
Mississippi Enterprise (Jackson) (1933)	25¢ $15.00	8	Standard	8	27 (12/18/82)	5,000
Bluff City Post (Natchez) (1978)	25¢ $7.00	8–12	Standard	7	39 (2/25/83)	2,000
Memo Digest (Meridian) (1966)	15¢ $4.20	20	Tabloid	4	35 (4/9/80)	3,150

Note: all are weekly papers.

Mississippi Enterprise, Jackson, December 18, 1982. This commercial newspaper was active in Jackson from 1933 to the late 1980s. Willie J. Miller was its publisher for more than fifty years. Courtesy *Mississippi Enterprise*. *Jackson Advocate*, September 1, 1983. The *Advocate* is the oldest black newspaper in continuous operation in Mississippi. Led by Charles Tisdale as publisher since 1978, it is the best-known black newspaper produced in Mississippi. Courtesy *Jackson Advocate*.

The *Mississippi Enterprise* constituted the oldest black paper in the state, dating from 1933, when it was called the *Mississippi Weekly*. From 1980 to 1985 the paper remained eight pages long, filling those pages largely with reprint materials from news agencies, religious items, and advertisements. Its editorial page, like that of most black weeklies, depended heavily on materials by national black columnists, such as Vernon E. Jordan, Jr., and John E. Lewis, both of the Urban League, and Manning Marable.

The *Enterprise* had its own editorial voice in William Harvey, associate publisher–executive editor. Harvey's weekly "Roaming" column touched on a variety of Afro-American concerns. Harvey supported black political, economic, and social rights in the United States. Among the issues of special interest to him was the need in 1981 for an extension of the 1965 Voting Rights Act. This act helped to safeguard the franchise of minority groups, such as blacks, Hispanics and American Indians.[18] American economic problems represented another area of interest, especially the high black unemployment rates in the 1980s.[19] Harvey lso addressed social issues such as mental health, drug and alcohol abuse, and general problems created by poverty in the column, as well as third world issues, such as events in India.[20] Such concerns, however, did not receive in depth treatment from week to week, a traditional problem for the *Enterprise* and most other black Mississippi weeklies. The other major commercial papers of this period— the Meridian *Memo Digest* and the Natchez *Bluff City Post*—resembled the *Enterprise*.

The *Digest*, a tabloid, continued in the 1980s as a community-oriented organ. It focused on sports and entertainment, local and state news, and other items of interest to the black public, often reprinting articles from press agencies.[21] The *Digest* also emphasized advertisements. The editorial page depended on national black columnists for points of view on the pressing issues of the day. In the 1980s, the *Digest* did not improve as a serious newspaper.

At Natchez, the *Bluff City Post* also served as a community paper, bringing local blacks news and items of concern in southwestern Mississippi. Natchez had a total population of 22,209 in 1980, 52 percent black. It had always constituted one of the major black press centers of Mississippi except for the 1950s and 1960s, when the migration of blacks from Natchez and the general difficulty of publishing a paper led to the decline of the black press.

Issues of special concern to the *Bluff City Post* in the early 1980s included support for a 1981 campaign to keep Charity Hospital in Natchez open; the murders of black children in Atlanta; support for the NAACP; the need for black political participation and voting; foreign affairs and the negative leadership characteristics of Ronald Reagan and Menachem Begin of Israel; and the rich legacy of Afro-American history, as observed during Black History Month, celebrated every February.[22]

Stronger editorially than the *Digest* or the *Mississippi Enterprise*, the *Bluff City Post* remained true to its community base, an important function for small weekly newspapers. The paper's seven staff members—Theodore C. Johnson, William H. Terrell, Josie G. Anderson, Mildred Fletcher, C.W. Taylor, James Gibson, and Marvin Muhammed—maintained close community ties through activity in political, economic, and social organizations, such as black churches and the Adams County NAACP. The paper has provided a deeper interpretation of the black experience than, for example, the *Natchez Democrat*, a white daily.[23]

The *Jackson Advocate*, the second-oldest black newspaper in continuous publication in Mississippi, remained the most significant black journal in the state during the 1980s. The paper's chief importance lay in its widespread distribution and in the overall quality of the journal.[24] The *Advocate's* professional staff—including four contributing editors, Jerry W. Ward, Jr., Tom Dent, Acklyn Lynch, and Ivory Phillips—also enhanced the paper's position.[25] In addition, the *Advocate* successfully obtained work from outstanding black intellectuals, scholars, critics, artists, and writers free of charge. This list includes such figures as Vincent Harding, Imari Obadele, L.C. Dorsey, Virgia Brocks-Shedd, and Barbara Watkins.

The publisher of the *Advocate* since 1978, Charles Tisdale, remained in place, although the Greene family (now based in Atlanta) still maintained an interest in the paper. The primary editors of the *Advocate* from 1980 to 1985 included Deborah LeSure (1979–80), Rose R. Bozeman (1981), Raymond K. Yancey (1981–82), and Alice Thomas (1985–).[26] Yet despite these individuals' importance to the *Advocate*, Tisdale dominated the struggle to keep the paper alive during the eighties. His efforts included extending the distribution base outside of Jackson and Hinds County, increasing the range of advertisements, and securing a wide range of individuals to write commentaries and creative poetry and articles. One cannot overestimate Tisdale's role as the driving force behind the paper. While other black newspapers disappeared, he has kept the *Advocate* alive. Perhaps only the *Memo Digest*, the state's third-oldest black newspaper has rivaled the *Advocate*'s strength. As noted earlier, however, the *Digest*'s location in Meridian and Lauderdale County gave it a special hold on the interests of blacks in that region, even though the *Advocate* remained the stronger paper. The weakness of the other black papers of this period—the *Bluff City Post*, the *Claiborne*, and the *Enterprise*—prevented them from becoming serious challengers to the *Advocate* in its campaign to remain the preeminent black newspaper in Mississippi.

A review of the *Advocate* for the years 1980–85 indicates why it dominated so. Simply stated, the *Advocate* remained the best-produced black newspaper in the state. The editorial page represented one factor in this success. It included in-house commentaries by contributing editors such as Ivory Phillips and pieces by syndicated national columnists, such as Manning Marable, Louis Farrakhan, Charles E. Belle, M. Carl Holman, Alfreda L. Madison, Robert L. White, Tony Brown, Nathaniel Wright, Jr., John E. Jacob, and Ethel Payne. Other elements contributing to the *Advocate*'s strength included coverage of black state news; creative works on black history, culture, art and motion pictures, and poetry and book reviews; attention to the concerns of black women; sports and entertainment pages; a focus on local history; and concern for international affairs, especially relating to blacks and Third World interests.[27]

Compared to the other black newspapers, the *Advocate* published the most outstanding editorial page, especially in terms of its coverage of major political, economic, and social questions. Yet even the *Advocate* often did not publish an "official" unsigned editorial reflecting the paper's position on matters of public interest. Thus, as late as the 1980s, the leading black newspaper in Mississippi demonstrated continued fear of taking a position on certain issues. In the eight issues of the *Advocate* published in March and April 1981, only two unsigned editorials appeared. For January through October 1984, a similar pattern held; during those ten months, only six official editorials appeared.[28] Although the *Advocate* did not fear white Mississippians as much as earlier black newspapers did, its frequent avoidance of an editorial stand indicates a very real concern about alienating the public. To deal with this problem, the *Advocate* published the work of black writers from other areas of the United States, enabling the *Advocate* to offer a variety of opinions on a wide range of topics.

During this period the *Advocate*'s major concerns reflected a black perspective on American political, economic, and social issues. This concern often expressed itself in the traditional forms of American liberalism, but at other points a strong emphasis on black nationalism has been of paramount interest to the paper. The *Advocate* focused during the 1980s on demanding total equality—and self-determination—for blacks to develop the independent institutions of the black community to their fullest while participating in the larger American society. All other concerns stem from these interests.

For the six years between 1980 and 1985, five political themes dominated the pages of the *Advocate*. The first of these involved a series of attacks on the paper both by whites and by blacks, particularly from 1981 to 1983. The *Advocate* viewed its black critics as failing to support an independent black press in Mississippi. A segment of the paper's own staff also challenged the *Advocate* in December 1980, when a group including editor Deborah LeSure attempted unsuccessfully to create a new black newspaper.[29] The *Advocate*, as it had under editor Percy Greene, survived its first major crisis of the 1980s, but other challenges followed in rapid succession.

In late 1981 and early 1982, a series of shootings occurred in the paper's office at 115 Hamilton Street in Jackson. A former Ku Klux Klansman, Larry Walker, was convicted on September 30, 1982, for the January 1982 incident.[30] Also in 1982, police arrested Gail Hall, an *Advocate* photojournalist, while she worked on a story about evictions at Sunset Plaza Apartments in Jackson. The paper viewed the arrest as an example of the harassment of the black press by whites. The *Advocate* also saw the *Clarion-Ledger* and the *Jackson Daily News* as hostile to the black press and black people for their negative treatment of some black issues.[31] Finally, in 1983, the *Advocate* received a number of items in the mail allegedly from the Ku Klux Klan, including cards, letters, and photographs. To make matters worse, the *Advocate* felt that many "Black leaders [were] silent about [the] Klan attacks."[32]

Second, the *Advocate* supported the development of an American black agenda that would successfully address black economic, political, and social freedom, overcome the obstacles of the black bourgeoisie, promote healing and unity among all black groups, especially the black underclass, and lead to a period of heightened and effective black leadership. The keys to the success of this black agenda included such black leaders as State Senator Henry Kirksey of Jackson; Ben Chavis of the Wilmington Ten; Imari Obadele of the RNA; Skip Robinson of the United League of Mississippi; Robert Walker, former field secretary of the Mississippi NAACP; Eddie Carthan, former mayor of Tchula; State Representative Robert Clark of Holmes County; Rev. Jesse Jackson, 1984 Democratic presidential candidate; Jobie Martin of Jackson; Harold Washington, mayor of Chicago.[33] On the other side of the equation stood those black leaders that the *Advocate* viewed with suspicion: Charles Evers, former field secretary of the Mississippi NAACP and former mayor of Fayette; Dr. Robert W. Harrison of Yazoo City, chairman of the Mississippi College Board; State Representative Horace Buckley of Jackson; William Dilday, former general manager of television station WLBT in Jackson; and Charles Bannerman, director of Mississippi Action for Community Education at Greenville. In general, the *Advocate* disagreed with these black leaders on various aspects of their political or economic outlooks.

Third, the *Advocate* criticized white political leadership on the national, state, and local levels, but especially in Mississippi. On the national scene, the paper disagreed with the policies of the Reagan administration and the New Right, and it alleged that racism colored the work of the white media and of white Southern historians.[34] At the state level, the *Advocate* criticized the administration of Governor William Winter (1980–83). Although blacks had strongly supported Winter's election, the *Advocate* believed that once in office, he had turned a "cold shoulder to Black concerns."[35] The *Advocate* also expressed concern about the Ku Klux Klan and about white attitudes towards redistricting. Locally, the paper lamented the political situation of blacks in Jackson. Although blacks amounted to more than 40 percent of the city's population in 1980, they did not have a representative on the three-member city commissioner. The paper also criticized the leadership of Mayor Dale Danks.[36]

Fourth, the *Advocate* addressed the problem of nuclear power development in the United States and the related issue of atomic warfare. The *Advocate* opposed the development or use of such weapons, and supported very strong safeguards on nuclear power development.

Finally, the fifth area of special political interest to the *Advocate* involved development and events in Africa, particularly South Africa, and hunger throughout the continent, as well as related issues of importance to the Third World.[37] The *Advocate* espoused a pro–Pan African and –Third World editorial policy on these matters, with an emphasis on politically and economically strong black, brown, and yellow states.

In the 1980s, the *Advocate* stressed the need for black economic freedom in America for Afro-American people to fully enjoy their political and social rights. In the *Advocate*'s perspective and that of the black press in general, black political, economic, and social equality maintain close connections—one cannot be fully gained and protected without the other two.

A mixture of support for black economic self-determination and for distribution of the wealth of the United States to the poor and the black underclass filled the pages of the *Advocate* during this period. The paper often suggested that black leaders had a special role to play in helping blacks to understand the capitalist system. From this base of knowledge the black middle class and the black poor needed to forge a common agenda. Out of such unity, black economic progress would occur. Although the federal and state governments had a role to play, the *Advocate* expected much more from the national policymakers in Congress because they set the central policy goals for the entire nation. The *Advocate* called for strong federal action to deal with the black economic crisis—unemployment, underemployment, and poverty. The paper vigorously supported all efforts to enhance black economic opportunity through affirmative action programs, and it criticized the Carter and Reagan administrations for what the paper perceived as a lessening of federal interest in black economic equality in the late 1970s and 1980s. On the local level, the *Advocate* emphasized the unequality of high utility bills for the poor and economically pressed families of Mississippi. It was, the paper noted on several occasions, "a matter of life or death."[38]

Four broad social concerns dominated the pages of the *Advocate* during the 1980s: black education in Mississippi; the crisis caused by the related problems of crime, police brutality, and the criminal justice system; the celebration of black history and culture in the United States; and the need for blacks to strengthen black institutions such as the family, the church, and the black press.

The *Advocate* viewed progress in black education as the cornerstone of the Afro-American struggle for total equality in the United States. The more than one hundred black colleges—five senior-level ones in Mississippi—have constituted the base of black educational strength since the 1860s. The paper believed that the black colleges deserved to survive because of their tremendous contributions to American life and because of their history of quality opportunity for all people. The *Advocate* spoke out against the possibility that black colleges, such as Alcorn State University or Jackson State University, might be annexed to Mississippi's historically white universities in the state, such as the University of Mississippi, Mississippi State University, or the University of Southern Mississippi. When predominantly black Utica Junior College became incorporated into the Hinds Junior College system, the *Advocate* viewed the decision as an attempt by white Mississippi to weaken the school while adding the additional burden of direct white control.[39] The paper also opposed the Reagan administration's educational policies; the decreased status of many black educators in Mississippi; the lack of morality among some teachers; the exploitation of black athletes by whites; and the lack of black control of education at all levels in the state.[40]

On the issues of crime, police brutality, and the mistreatment of blacks by the criminal justice system, the *Advocate* adamantly denounced such ills, whether black-on-black crime or the abuse of blacks by police during an arrest or by prison guards in places such as the infamous Parchman Prison.[41] In fact, the *Advocate* viewed the overrepresentation of blacks in Mississippi's prisons as another indicator of the oppressive nature of the criminal justice system. The paper also saw the unsolved murders of black Mississippians in the 1980s as evidence of a period of modern-day lynching.[42]

The *Advocate* also worked to celebrate black history and culture in the United States. The paper saw itself as aiding the cause, first set forth by Carter G. Woodson in the 1930s, of setting aside a special time to reflect on the meaning of the culture, life, and historical experiences of black people. During each February, the *Advocate* devoted a special issue of as much as thirty-six pages to an extensive examination of issues in Afro-American history. These special issues contained commentaries on the black economic, social, and political condition in the United States and abroad, editorials and stories on black history, pictures of Afro-American leaders, poetry and excerpts from the works of black writers, book reviews, and regular features.[43]

As an interest related to black history, the *Advocate* focused on the legacy of black heroes, such as Martin Luther King, Jr., Marcus Garvey, Ida B. Wells-Barnett, and Malcolm X. The treatment of such historical figures throughout the year served to advance the paper's black perspective and to carry the theme of Black History Month beyond February.[44] This theme also appeared in the paper's strong support for Afro-American studies from the elementary grades to the university level. The *Advocate* also criticized American white culture whenever the paper perceived it as having a negative impact on black people. The paper believed that blacks suffered from the negative interpretation of their lives by American television and movies such as "The Jeffersons" and "Beulah Land," from the control of the music industry by whites, and from the general stereotyping of blacks by some segments of the white American mass media.[45] During the 1980s the *Advocate* expressed a commitment to black poets by publishing their poetry. From 1981 to 1984, the poets published in the *Advocate* included Dudley Randall, L.C. Dorsey, Imamu Amiri Baraka, Virgia Brocks-Shedd, Julius Thompson, Barbara Watkins, Charles R. Braxton, C.K. Chiplin, Jerry W. Ward, John M. Wesley, and Dorothy Sims Winston.[46] In this way, the *Advocate* has helped to promote black history and culture, as well as aided the development and visibility of black writers, particularly those from Mississippi.

The *Advocate* has also concentrated on the need for stronger black institutions, especially families, churches, schools, housing, and black newspapers. Without effective, independent black institutions, the *Advocate* feared the future for blacks in America.[47]

In essence, in the 1980s the *Advocate* remained a local paper, yet one with broader interests. Although committed to black economic and social equality, an examination of the organ for 1980–85—a time of considerable black political activity—shows that political concerns dominate. One can easily understand the *Advocate*'s special emphasis on black efforts in this area. Blacks have found greater roadblocks to economic progress than they have in voting and running for political office. Since the 1960s American blacks have focused on gaining political power, using that clout to pressure for black economic equality. This theme runs through the *Advocate* and other black newspapers in Mississippi for this period.

Throughout the 1980s the *Advocate*'s position as the leader among black newspapers in Mississippi remained strong. As in the 1970s, the paper secured better professional staff, took full advantage of its Jackson location, and gained active support from blacks in Mississippi and in other states.[48] These advantages and others have carried the paper through a number of financial troubles.

In general, the economics of publishing have remained a problem for all black newspapers in the state. In 1984, the *Advocate* developed a campaign to inform black readers of those white businesses (where blacks shopped) that did not advertise with the paper. The program had some success, inducing a number of white establishments to advertise in the *Advocate*.[49] During this period, the other three commercial papers (the *Memo Digest*, the *Mississippi Enterprise*, and the *Bluff City Post*) continued to receive advertising from both black and white businesses in Meridian, Jackson, and Natchez, respectively. Like the *Advocate*, however, funds always remained in short supply, and the financial conditions prevented the papers from expanding from weekly to daily newspapers. This situation persisted throughout the eighties, in spite of Mississippi's large black population and the sizable black middle class with funds to purchase and support a daily newspaper.[50]

Two major black commercial magazines remained active in Mississippi during the early 1980s: *Sunbelt: Black Life in Mississippi* (later entitled *Sunbelt: Black Life in the South*) and *Street Talk*.[51] Both journals published at Jackson and had similar make-ups, staffs, and general focuses as in the 1970s. A total of four black magazines published in Mississippi during the 1980s, down from an all-time high of five during the 1970s. This marked the first time since World War II that the number declined from the previous decade.

The brainchild of publisher Thomas H. Espy, *Sunbelt* remained the most significant black magazine published in Mississippi during the early 1980s. A staff of fifteen plus free-lance writers enabled the journal to develop rapidly as a major organ not only of black Mississippi, but of the South and the nation as a whole. In design and range of articles, *Sunbelt* had little real competition in the South, except for a publication like *Sepia*, of Fort Worth, Texas, which had begun publishing in 1955. It approached the national stature of *Ebony*, and compared favorably to such organs as *Encore, American and World Wide News, Essence Magazine,* and *Black Family*.

In 1980, an average issue of *Sunbelt* contained forty-eight pages and had a circulation of 25,000, both numbers comparable to other national black publications.[52] *Sunbelt* also had a good range of advertisers who, although mostly from Jackson, represented many of the state's blue-chip advertisers. Table 6.2 demonstrates the problems a black publication faces in finding and keeping advertisers. Although *Sunbelt* secured about half of its advertising from black businesses in January and February 1980, this was not the case in June and August, when whites contributed 68 percent of the ads.[53]

The social essays in *Sunbelt* during this era included interviews with state and regional figures and subjects such as the following: health care, with an examination of the conditions of black doctors, the rewards of breastfeeding, pregnancy after age forty, and problems associated with

TABLE 6-2.   Advertisements in *Sunbelt* for Six Months during 1980

No. of ads	Date	No. and % black		No. and % white	
15	Jan.	8	53	7	47
15	Feb.	8	53	7	47
23	Mar.	9	39	14	61
34	June	11	32	23	68
25	July	7	28	18	72
28	Aug.	9	25	19	75

stress; religion, with articles on African and Afro-American religion; education, with an emphasis on the need for and history of black colleges and universities and pieces on everyday matters such as "What Parents Should Know about Beginning Band Programs"; topics of particular interest to blacks, such as Jackson's WLBT-TV 3, family histories, children and the elderly, and the U.S. Census's undercounting of blacks; travel, black sports personalities, home care, fashion, and marriage and relationships; and black culture, including music, poetry, and fiction by Mississippi writers like Aurolyn C. Jacobs, Katana Lazet Hall, Ralph Thurman, and J.C. Wilson. *Sunbelt* also printed reviews of such books as *Just above My Head,* by James Baldwin, *Mississippi: The View from Tougaloo,* by Clarice T. Campbell and Oscar A. Rogers, Jr., *Cotton Candy on a Rainy Day,* by Nikki Giovanni, and *Black Society,* by Geraldyn Mayor and Doris E. Saunders.

Sunbelt's political articles remained moderate in tone and centered on the following themes: black leadership in Mississippi, with works on figures of the 1980s and of the Reconstruction era of the 1860s and 1870s; modern national black leaders and problems they have faced; the black political situation in the United States; and the role of the federal government in Afro-American life.

The economic essays in *Sunbelt* during this period focused on general individual concerns, such as coming to grips with difficulties like inflation and taxes, starting small businesses, and job interviewing and career outlooks; black success stories in Mississippi; and how to benefit from the government programs such as those run by the Small Business Administration during the 1980s.

In many respects, *Sunbelt's* foci closely correlated with the interests and goals of black newspapers in Mississippi during the 1970s and early

1980s: black social and cultural history and affairs and black political and economic growth. As a magazine, *Sunbelt* developed these themes in short, effective essays, and thus positioned itself to reach a large audience through advertising campaigns and distribution to individuals, churches, barbershops, and other black institutions.

From January through April 1980, *Sunbelt* published four issues with the subheading of *Black Life in Mississippi*. In May 1980, the title of the magazine became *Sunbelt: Black Life in the South* to expand the journal's audience and advertisement base. An examination of *Sunbelt* for the first three months of this period reveals that fifty-six major articles appeared, of which thirty-seven had a cultural focus, nine had a political orientation, and ten concentrated on economic matters.[54] A breakdown of this data indicates that a high percentage of the articles concerned black Mississippians: seventeen of the thirty-seven social articles (45 percent), five (55 percent) of the political articles, and three (30 percent) of the economic items. Emphasis on black Mississippi served to attract black readers and advertisers from both black and white businesses.

After *Sunbelt* expanded its focus to include all of the South, its coverage of other states in the region increased. From June through August 1980, forty-six major articles appeared in the magazine, thirty-seven of them on social and cultural topics, three of a political nature, and six with an economic orientation. An assessment of this data reveals that of the thirty-seven social articles, eight (22 percent) had black Mississippians as subjects; of the political articles, none centered on black Mississippi; and of the economic works, one (17 percent) chiefly related to the state.[55] Eighteen articles (39 percent of the total) concerned other Southern states. Thus, a clear pattern emerges—*Sunbelt* changes from a publication concentrating on one state to one with a regional orientation and a wider scope.

Social and cultural issues continued to dominate the pages of *Sunbelt*. The magazine's coverage expanded from the areas listed earlier to include profiles of black personalities like John Perkins of Mississippi's Voice of Calvary, author Margaret Walker Alexander, educators Benjamin Mays and Jane Ellen McAllister, and Monica Kaufman, a television journalist from Atlanta; articles on the media and food; and creative works by poets such as Patrisha Frazier and fiction by Toni Cade Bambara.

Sunbelt published few articles during this period on political matters—one on mayor Richard Arrington of Birmingham, Alabama, one criticizing black assimilation in the United States and abroad, and a general article on "What is a Good Lawyer?"[56] Of the assimilation article, however, the editors felt compelled to state for the first time that the views of the article did "not necessarily reflect the views of the management and staff."

On economic issues, Sunbelt concentrated on black farming and the loss of black land in the South, successful Southern black business leaders, and business opportunities for blacks, with review articles on Sam Baker, a black administrator at the Small Business Administration, and the economic possibilities of gasohol.

Thus, Sunbelt's movement from a Mississippi-centered publication to a regional organ represented a change only of degree, rather than of focus. Although significant, the change did not save Sunbelt from the ravages of the economics of publishing a black magazine in the South. In the history of black publishing in Mississippi, many publications have begun with grand ideas, only to see them quickly die. Sunbelt erred in expanding too rapidly from a state to a regional publication. Although black public interest in Sunbelt undoubtedly existed, the South is a huge region, and each state's black population had its own loyalties to locally produced publications.

Sunbelt's end came in late 1980. For eleven months it had served as a new voice, a little Ebony, bringing creative articles reflecting on the black experience in Mississippi and the rest of the South. It leaves this legacy for others to follow.[57]

Street Talk, a controversial, thirty-six-page monthly magazine, also published during the early 1980s. A staff consisting of Jerry Sutton, editor, Jai Barnes, photojournalist, and Harold Gater, cartoonist, compiled the publication, targeted at readers in Jackson, Hinds, and Madison counties and priced at seventy-five cents an issue or eight dollars for a one-year subscription. Although the magazine's exact circulation is not known, it most likely remained very small, perhaps 500 to 1,000 copies per issue.[58]

Unlike Sunbelt, Street Talk did not appeal to the black middle class. Instead, its contents suggest that it viewed lower-income blacks as its market. An examination of the magazine for five months in 1980 reveals that Street Talk did not attempt to meet high journalistic standards in its coverage. Instead, the magazine published local citizens' legal troubles. In fact, each issue of Street Talk cautioned, "Warning: the information in Street Talk may be considered controversial, or personal. The material is selected without regard to race, creed, sex or ethnic background. It is not the intent of the editor or staff to slander, ridicule or demean anyone personally. All information is open to the public."

In each issue, *Street Talk* printed a list of the names and addresses of individuals in Hinds and Madison counties who had legal difficulties. The list of legal actions printed generally included divorces; child support cases; bankruptcies; and police reports on individuals charged with shoplifting, prostitution, buying or selling drugs, assault, burglary, larceny, carrying concealed weapons, drunk driving, and other crimes. Such information filled more than 50 percent of an average issue. Publishing such lists of people's sorrows did not represent the best traditions of black journalism.

Street Talk's other features included a monthly top-twenty chart of contemporary disco and black gospel music; pictures of black models; cartoons; items on black education; articles on black religious concerns; and pieces discussing police brutality against blacks and other aspects of the criminal justice system in Mississippi.[59]

Street Talk did not comment on the political issues of the day. The organ expressed its regrets about the financial setbacks suffered by a group of black businessmen when the Fidelity Bank of Mississippi closed in 1980,[60] but the magazine said little else about economic matters. It was, in essence, a haphazardly constructed sensationalist journal.

Advertising provides an indicator of *Street Talk*'s weak position among Mississippi's black publications. The five issues published between February and December 1980 contained a total of only twenty-seven ads, divided almost evenly between black and white businesses. Over the same period, *Sunbelt* averaged more than twenty-three advertisements per issue. Such a small range of advertising could not keep a monthly publication alive. Few black or white businesses contributed to *Street Talk*'s financial base. Those black business concerns that did advertise included the magazine itself, which did not pay for the publicity, the Emergency Land Fund, whose ads also probably ran at no charge, musical shows, Jon Ya's Health and Beauty Salon, the Masonic Temple, Talk of the Town Recording Studio, and Trucks Unlimited Club. White advertisements came from such businesses as Stop-N-Go, Jitney Jungle, Howard's Brandiscount, the city of Jackson, and Big Star food stores.[61] Such ads for food stores, music shows, clubs, and personal appearance services attracted lower-income individuals.

By 1984, all the black magazines in the state had ceased to publish. In-

Soul Force! Oxford, February 1984. *Soul Force!* is an organ of the Oxford Development Association, created in 1984 to promote programs to improve the lives of black children. A monthly, this twenty-eight-page organ cost $8.00 a year in the 1980s. Courtesy *Soul Force! Monitor*, Jackson, September 1982. Nayo (Barbara Malcolm Watkins) was the first editor of *Monitor*, an organ of the Mississippi Cultural Arts Coalition, an organization created in 1982 to promote the work and interests of black community arts groups and artists in Mississippi. Courtesy *Monitor*.

terest in magazines remained because of the large number of talented blacks living in the state, and the need for a journal of political, social, economic, and cultural expression remained tremendous. The economic crisis of publishing persisted, however, and no journal successfully overcame it.

In the absence of an effective magazine the black organizational publications helped somewhat to deal with this crisis, but none of these organs had the statewide influence or distribution that *Sunbelt* possessed. The Emergency Land Fund's journal, *Forty Acres and a Mule*, also active in the mid-1970s, represents a prime example of an organizational publication in Mississippi. In 1980 Jessie Morris and Regina Banks remained as editor and associate editor, respectively, with seven additional staff members.[62] During the early 1980s, the paper continued to address the issues of black landownership and farming. Financial obligations became severe for this organ as well, however, and it ceased publication in 1981.[63]

Two cultural organs of this period provided high-quality and wide ranging information to black Mississippians. *Monitor*, the official publication of the Mississippi Cultural Arts Coalition, a group of black cultural bodies statewide, began to publish during the summer of 1982 at Jackson.[64] A monthly four-page newsletter edited by Barbara Watkins, *Monitor* chiefly strove to link black arts groups and artists. It also published articles on the state of the black arts; book reviews; conference reports; news on cultural events, workshops, grants, and proposal writing; deadlines for publication possibilities; creative poetry and fiction; and short essays on cultural and social affairs.[65] No other organization in Mississippi distributed successfully a newsletter that promoted black culture.

Keynotes, the official organ of the Black Arts Music Society, approached *Monitor*'s success. The society's president, John Reese, established *Keynotes* in 1982 to foster a commitment for "the production/preservation and promulgation of African-American classical music—jazz."[66] *Keynotes* printed reviews of performances by jazz artists in Mississippi, highlights of musical activities in Jackson and elsewhere in Mississippi, commentary on black culture, creative works, such as poetry, and items of special interest about jazz artists from throughout the South.[67] *Keynotes*'s special significance lay in its status as the only black publication in Mississippi devoted to jazz.

Monitor and *Keynotes* published for a time in the 1980s because of assistance from local sponsors and government agencies. *Monitor* received support from the National Endowment for the Arts and City Arts Program of the city of Jackson and from sponsors such as First National Bank of Jackson, South Central Bell, and Miller High Life.[68] *Keynotes* received support from Nu-South Typesetting and from patrons such as Mississippi Valley Gas Company, Apollo Hair Designs, Mississippi Power and Light Company, Coors Central Mississippi outlets, South Central Bell, Dr. D.E. Magee, IBM, Mississippi Family Health Center, Paige's Upholstery, Westside Printers, and Collins Funeral Home. It has also received public funds from the Jackson Arts Alliance, City Arts Program, and the National Endowment for the Arts.[69] Such a variety of aid sources helped to keep the newsletters alive. Their size, circulation, and distribution remained small, however, largely as a result of the financial restraints of publishing for black cultural organizations. Nevertheless, *Keynotes* and *Monitor* served as important voices of the black arts community in Mississippi, more so because no statewide black magazine remained active. Together, they helped to fill a critical void.

The black religious and fraternal press in Mississippi remained weak in the 1980s, despite the very strong position of both the church and the fraternal orders. Newsletters constitute a common form of communication among Baptist and Methodist congregations, the primary denominations of blacks in Mississippi. The Mississippi Baptist Convention Board and the Mississippi Conference (Methodist) also produce other press materials. In Jackson, the *Reconciler*, the official organ of the Voice of Calvary Ministries, also remained active.[70] A number of major black fraternal organizations in Mississippi published journals, including the Prince Hall Grand Masters; the Elks; the Federation of Masons of the World; the Federation of Eastern Stars; and state chapters of national black social fraternities and sororities like Alpha Phi Alpha, Phi Beta Sigma, Kappa Alpha Psi, Omega Psi Phi, Alpha Kappa Alpha, Delta Sigma Theta, Zeta Phi Beta, and Iota Phi Lambda. The membership of these groups included some of the most influential black people in Mississippi; as a result, the social fraternity world played an important part (despite its small numbers relative to the general black leadership in Mississippi) in determining black concerns.[71] Generally small and inexpensive to produce, the newsletters of black churches and fraternal organizations stayed alive by keeping their focus on the membership of each group and by controlling costs. The expenses often involved only the cost of a typewriter and of reproduction, plus postage.

Historically black public and private educational institutions—from

Rust College Sentinel, Holly Springs, March 1981. The *Sentinel* was created in 1946 to serve as a general-interest magazine of Rust College in northern Mississippi, the first historically black institution established in the state, in 1866, by the Methodist Episcopal Church. Courtesy *Rust College Sentinel*. *Delvian Gazette*, Itta Bena, May 1981. Active at Mississippi Valley State University since 1980, the *Delvian Gazette* serves the institution as a newsletter of campus events and interests. Courtesy *Delvian Gazette*.

grade schools to colleges and universities—produced well over 100 publications during the 1980s, including student newspapers, yearbooks, news bulletins, alumni affairs magazines, and research publications. As in earlier years, Jackson State University, Alcorn State University, Mississippi Valley State University, Tougaloo College, and Rust College produced the bulk of this material. The publications of these institutions and of historically black junior colleges reached tens of thousands of Mississippians each year,[72] serving as significant voices on blacks' varied educational and social interests.

By 1985, the black press in Mississippi remained in a crisis position in terms of the number and range of active commercial black newspapers and magazines produced. Only four black newspapers and no magazines operated at this point. Without the organizational and educational publications, the different avenues of the black cultural and social experience in Mississippi would have had little expression. The loss of a number of commercial newspapers and magazines forced those that survived to shoulder a greater burden of the journalistic promotion and defense of black interests. In Jackson, Natchez, and Meridian, the surviving black newspapers—the *Jackson Advocate*, the *Mississippi Enterprise*, the *Bluff City Post*, and the *Memo Digest*—at least found themselves in areas of high black population. In addition, blacks in these cities had high educational levels and had demonstrated interest in cultural matters. Such cities constituted good bases for the future of the black press; however, the economics of publishing did not change, a factor inhibiting survival for these journals.

The great hope for black print journalism lies in the historical pattern of individual black commitment to publishing and of community efforts to develop small- to moderate-size papers within localized circulations ranging between 10,000 and 25,000. These papers also must develop advertising connections to all segments of society. Black Mississippians also must do more to promote the development of a strong statewide newspaper. The *Jackson Advocate* has assumed part of this role, but central Mississippi still remains the heart of its operations. Black Mississippians need a newspaper that reaches into all corners of the state and that reflects in its news, analysis, and interpretation the citizens' lives, hopes, and aspirations. Black people in Mississippi have the resources and know-how to achieve such goals in print media; however, greater problems appear to lie ahead in radio and television, where black control remained insufficient in the 1980s.

Blacks in Mississippi increased their control of radio stations in the state from three (WORV-AM, Hattiesburg, WBAD-FM, Greenville, and WTNK, Meridian) in the 1970s to five in the 1980s. The two new stations, both located in Jackson, began broadcasting in 1984. John Pembroke received a license to operate WOAD, and the J.C. Maxwell Broadcasting Group, Inc., created WMPR.[73] Thus, of the twenty black-oriented radio stations in Mississippi during the 1980s, 75 percent remained under white control.

Most black-oriented stations remained predominantly focused on music—news and commentaries took a back seat to music, sports, and commercials. Most stations continued to devote less than ten minutes during an average broadcast hour to news; the news portion generally amounted to only five minutes—12 percent of an average hour of programming. Unfortunately, many blacks depend too heavily on radio news for the information and analysis they receive about state, national, and international events.[74]

Jackson dominated black radio in Mississippi during the 1980s, when six black-oriented radio stations operated in the city. Whites controlled WOKJ-AM, WJMI-FM, and WKXI-AM, all "soul" music stations. Blacks controlled WOAD-AM, a gospel station, WJSU, an educational station operated by Jackson State University's Department of Mass Communication, and WMPR, a National Public Radio station adjacent to Tougaloo College. Both of the latter stations offer a diversified selection of music, cultural, news, and public-affairs programs.[75]

Some black Mississippians in the 1980s expressed concern about white control of black-oriented stations, with protest centering on white control of WOKJ and WJMI, two of the most popular black-oriented stations in Jackson. Owned by Tri-Cities Broadcasting Company, operated by E.O. Roden and Associates, and managed by Zane Roden, a white man, WOKJ and WJMI received criticism from black club owners, the *Jackson Advocate*, and former black employees of WJMI. Although both stations attracted both black and white listeners as a result of their soul music programming, black critics charged that the stations claimed to represent the black community, although ownership remained in white hands.

In 1981, the United Black Club Owners of Jackson organized a series of demonstrations and boycott against WOKJ and WJMI. The club owners accused the white-owned stations of having damaged black businessmen by supporting "a series of Friday-night dances at Club Zanyo, a large club owned by a white businessman from Monroe, La. The two radio stations have heavily promoted the dances in exchange for a share of the proceeds." The black club owners believed that they suffered the loss of black business thereafter. "But Zane Roden, station manager at WJMI-WOKJ, saw nothing unusual about the deal, which he said is similar to ones the stations have had with other clubs." Activist James Meredith, a club owner and member of the United Black Club Owners, noted another major black concern: "Ninety-nine percent of the blacks I talk to think they [the stations] are black-owned."[76] After a month of protests, WOKJ and WJMI refused to back down from their deal with Club Zanyo, and the picketing of the stations came to an end, largely as a result of the additional time and money lost by the black club owners. Black anger at the stations' white owners did not end, however, as a 1982 editorial by the *Jackson Advocate* reflected. Zane Roden, manager of WOKJ and WJMI, did not respond to a request by a local Eddie Carthan March Committee for support in publicizing a rally in the mayor's defense on October 16, 1982. The *Advocate* editorialized:

> The negative silence which the Committee received from the station was thunderous in its implications for Black people. WOKJ and WJMI have milked millions of dollars from the Black community by misrepresenting themselves as Black stations. The only things Black at the station are a few underpaid employees and Roden's whip, if he uses one now. Eddie Carthan's case was a cause celebre all over the world. To this writer's personal knowledge, no news person from WOKJ-WJMI covered any phase of the trial. This reflects, of course, the racist attitude of this "Black" radio station. . . . A steady diet of boogie, bodies, booze and just plain pornographic filth permeates the minds of Black youth, partially, but not fully because of these stations, WOKJ and WJMI. If Roden can censor efforts for Black progress, he can also censor the filth emanating from his stations.[77]

A third controversy emerged in 1983 when WJMI fired disc jockeys David Stafford and Ray St. Vincent. The two men alleged that their dismissal resulted from a protest letter sent to the management about the station's programming goals and priorities. The letter suggested that WJMI develop programming beyond the field of music because "people in Jackson are missing out on a lot of newsworthy programs."[78]

Despite black protests such as those described above, WOKJ and

WJMI continued to operate with mostly blacks on the air while top management remained primarily in white control.[79] WJMI's popularity has, however, been overtaken by WKXI. Critics, such as Ray St. Vincent, believed that, although white-owned, WKXI built a position of supremacy by getting involved in the community and by offering a variety of programming to its listeners.[80]

Jackson's first black-owned radio station, WOAD, went on the air in February 1984 with a range of forty-five miles, and 1,000 watts of power during the day and 250 watts during the night. Pembroke created the station as "the only station in Jackson to offer a forum for continuous black gospel music." In contrast to WOKJ, which "plays gospel music from 10 a.m. until 3 p.m. Monday through Saturday . . . WOAD plays it from 5 a.m. until midnight each day." Pembroke viewed as the major difference between black-owned and black-programmed stations "that the Black community will demand more from me."[81] In an article on Earl Anderson, vice president of WOAD, the *Advocate* noted in September 1984 that in addition to gospel music, the station offered its public "a variety of community sponsored programs geared toward providing meaningful information to its listeners." Such efforts made WOAD the number four station in the market area of Jackson and central Mississippi.[82]

WJSU-FM, a noncommercial radio station, remained very active in the Jackson area as an educational outlet for students at Jackson State University. *Monitor* noted that WJSU became successful because the station "provides educational, information and cultural programming for the metropolitan Jackson area each day from 6 a.m. till 12 midnight. In addition to daily musical programs of jazz, blues and reggae, WJSU offers gospel on Sunday mornings, a special hour of blues on Saturday evenings, and a variety of public affairs programs."[83] The station was noted in the 1980s, as in the 1970s, for its contributions to black American jazz. WJSU also received a series of state and national awards for its achievements as an educational station, including the small-market Corporation for Public Broadcasting development award for outstanding achievement in public awareness, June 1982; the 1982 Station of the Year Award from Black College Radio, a division of Collegiate Broadcasting Group, Inc.; the Mississippi Broadcasting Association's 1980 and 1982 Public Service Award for a minidocumentary series on black history entitled "Family Tree" and the association's best in the state award for an educational radio station for mini magazine (a format of short public affairs programs) and "Community People" (special events).[84]

In the early 1980s, however, WJSU had a few problems with the university. One issue of major importance concerned how much power and independence the university administration under President John A. Peoples would allow the station's manager, Professor Omega Wilson, and its chair, Dr. Marcia Clinkscales of the Department of Mass Communications, in the day-to-day operation of the station. An answer came in 1981, when the administration decided to transfer WJSU to the Office of University Relations. This policy decision met a negative reaction, and eventually both Professor Wilson and Dr. Clinkscales left the university.[85] In spite of these setbacks, the station continued to play a significant role in developing radio in the Jackson area.

Finally, WMPR-FM began a period of test broadcasting of National Public Radio programming on April 12, 1984, and regular daily transmission on November 16, 1984.[86] WMPR's creators—"Maxwell Broadcasting, Inc., a minority controlled, nonprofit and tax exempt community organization—took five years to complete the task of constructing the first full-service public radio station in Jackson and central Mississippi."[87] Along the way WABG-TV-6 in Greenwood "filed a motion to stop WMPR's construction and a petition to substantially reduce its power with the FCC." Located more than one hundred miles from WMPR, WABG claimed that WMPR's "100 KW signal will cause interference in its secondary coverage area." WABG did not succeed, and WMPR successfully offered a "diversified program format of multi-cultural and cross-cultural material, including: programs from National Public Radio; concert music and drama; expressions of culture from Mississippi's Black and White communities; art, culture and thoughts from all parts of the world; news and public affairs programs affording community self-expression on a wide range of issues."[88] Under the leadership of station manager Omega Wilson, Aurelia N. Young, president of the Maxwell Group, and the twenty-four local citizens on the Maxwell Board, WMPR demonstrated a commitment to excellence in broadcasting. Its 100-kilowatt signal extends over an 80-mile radius and reaches an estimated 1.25 million people in Mississippi and parts of Arkansas and Louisiana.[89] The station's significance lies in its promise to "primarily serve the programming interest of Mississippi's 40-plus percent Black population" and "the handicapped and rural" citizens of the state.[90]

In spite of the contributions of Mississippi's five black-owned radio stations and of its fifteen white-controlled ones, black journalism has not flourished on the airwaves. Contemporary black music dominates black radio stations in the state. News, analysis, and commentary take a distant fifth place at most stations, behind music, advertisements, gospel programs, and sports. Blacks in and around Jackson have benefited from the educational programs and additional newscasts of WJSU and WMPR; however, their signals do not reach most black Mississippians, even in central Mississippi. With three-fourths of all black radio stations in Mississippi under white control, radical change in the nature of their operations does not seem imminent. Nor does it seem likely that many new black radio stations will come into existence in the near future. Yet radio will play an increasingly important role as more and more blacks turn to it as a source for a quick summary of the day's news.

Black control of television in Mississippi follows a similar pattern. Mississippians express high interest in television programs and news. A recent study conducted by the A.C. Nielsen Company indicates that the total time Americans spend watching television has increased from an average of four and a half hours daily in the early 1950s to seven hours and two minutes each day in 1983.[91] Television has particular attraction for Mississippi blacks because it is inexpensive and remains the major source of culture and entertainment in most rural and small-town communities. As in the rest of the United States, whites dominate programs and commercials except for a few predominantly black shows.[92] The television industry in Mississippi remained under white management in the 1980s. As a result, only seven areas of Mississippi had stations, more than one-third of them in central Mississippi. In 1981, ten commercial network stations and eight Mississippi Educational Television Network affiliates broadcast in the state. By 1985, the state added five additional stations, for a total of fifteen. Four network stations operate in Jackson, three in Meridian, and one each in Hattiesburg-Laurel, Biloxi, Greenwood, Natchez, Columbus, Tupelo, Bruce, and West Point. Geographically, central Mississippi (Jackson and Meridian) contains nearly 50 percent of the state's television stations, although Meridian may also be considered part of east Mississippi. North Mississippi contains two, WTVW-TV at Tupelo and WOBN at Bruce, and depends on Memphis, Tennessee, for much of its programming needs. Besides Meridian's three stations, east Mississippi also has WCBI-TV, at Columbus. In south Mississippi, WDAM-TV lies halfway between Hattiesburg and Laurel, and southwestern Mississippi has WNTL at Natchez. WABG-TV, at Greenwood, serves the Delta region. Finally, the Gulf Coast region has one television station, WLOX-TV at Biloxi. The state's eight educational stations are located in Biloxi, Boonesville, Bude, Greenwood, Jackson, Meridian, Oxford (the University of Mississippi), and Starkville (Mississippi State University).[93]

Out of Mississippi's fifteen commercial and eight educational stations, blacks had a controlling interest in two commercial stations, WLBT-TV in Jackson and WLBM-TV in Meridian. In the early 1980s TV-3, 51 percent black-owned, controlled WLBT.[94] Blacks also held administrative and on-the-air positions at other television stations, particularly in Jackson. For example, Larry Nicks worked as an account executive and Paula Pittman served as a reporter, anchor, and production staff member at WAPT-TV, and Ruth Campbell held the position of executive producer for public affairs at WMAA (PBS), after 1974.[95] Yet programming and news broadcast policies remained generally set by whites rather than blacks. In addition, the total number of blacks employed at Mississippi television stations remained small in the 1980s.[96]

At WLBT, where blacks played a major role in the management and on the air, a number of changes and problems occurred after 1980. In the early 1980s, WLBT, under the management of William Dilday and a board of directors headed by activist Aaron Henry, remained the number one commercial station in Mississippi. *Black Enterprise* magazine recognized its financial success in 1980, listing the station among the top 100 black businesses in the United States.[97] Not all elements of the black community agreed with the programming policies of the station or of its general manager, Dilday. The *Jackson Advocate* declared in a critical editorial in 1981 that "Those in control of WLBT have retreated to a much more conservative stance on Black-white issues." Two years later, the *Advocate* alleged that Dilday held negative attitudes toward the *Advocate* and toward certain parts of the local black community (e.g., the Farish Street area).[98] Despite such coverage by the *Advocate*, WLBT maintained its ranking as the leading television station in the state. Another major event for WLBT took place in early 1983, when TV-3 sold the station to Civic Communications Corporation. Prior to the sale, both black and white TV-3 board members had tried to sell the station to a white firm. Prominent board members, such as Aaron Henry, expressed opposition to the sale. Under Civic Communications, blacks maintained a 52.6 percent controlling interest in WLBT, divided among three men: Henry (26 percent), Charles Young (24 percent), and Frank E. Melton, vice president of Buford Television, of Tyler, Texas (2.4 percent). White interest in the new company included Robert C. Travis, Owen Cooper, Interfirst Venture Corporation, Eric Newman, and Buford Television.[99]

A series of disputes over WLBT's operating policies immediately emerged between Melton, the new chief executive officer, and Dilday. In quick succession, Melton fired Dilday; Tom Walsh, a white who served as sales manager, resigned and also received notice that he, too, was fired; and Walter Sadler, news director, was fired.[100] In response to these events, the Community Coalition for Better Broadcasting, a group of Jackson and Hinds County political and labor leaders called for a boycott of WLBT's six and ten p.m. news broadcasts.[101] Ill feelings also developed between the station's new management and the International Brotherhood of Electrical Workers, who charged that WLBT's management with antiunion bias. Local blacks accused the company of decreasing minority involvement in the station. Melton denied all of the charges against the station.[102] The boycott leaders attacked Melton, Henry, and Young.[103] A special movement developed against Henry, a veteran civil rights leader and chairman of WLBT's board. Coalition leader Bennie Thompson and others accused Henry of serving as "a 'front' for the Texas owners" of the station. In May 1984, at the Mississippi state Democratic Convention, Thompson and other political leaders expelled Henry from his eight-year-old position as a Democratic National Committee member and awarded the seat to Thompson. It represented a blow to Henry, who still served as a state representative in Mississippi and had served since the early 1960s as the president of the Mississippi NAACP.[104] Despite personal damage to Henry, Melton suggested that the boycott against WLBT had little effect. In late May 1984, he noted that "the station's advertising revenues were higher than ever and he had received only one letter—'and it supported us'."[105]

The battle of nerves continued through the summer, when Civic Communications Corporation fired eleven workers at WLBT and eight at WLBM in Meridian, another of its properties. Five of the WLBT workers belonged to unions.[106] By September 1984, tempers had calmed a bit, and Sadler had become managing editor of news at WJTV, channel twelve, Jackson.[107]

The conflicts over management policies at WLBT and white dominance of news programs at other Mississippi television stations clearly demonstrate why black newspapers and newsletters will remain the major forms of communication among the Afro-American people in

Mississippi. In comparison to television and radio, the print media are inexpensive, and a variety of black groups, individuals, and interests can effectively use newsletters, magazines, and newspapers to reach significant numbers of people. Cable television may one day offer black Mississippians another option for gaining control over a segment of the television industry; however, current financial conditions make this an unrealistic goal in the near future.[108] Nevertheless, low-power television stations, such as WOBN at Bruce, may offer an opportunity for financially secure urban blacks to create a small number of new stations. Yet the problem of raising at least $75,000 to operate such a station remains a burden for most blacks, and the Federal Communications Commission must first approve all applications.[109]

Black journalists in Mississippi speak positively about the future of the black press.[110] Not surprisingly, however, many blacks see newspapers as the most important vehicle for black-controlled communications in the state. On the historical importance of the black newspaper, they speak with two voices. Scholar and editor Jerry W. Ward of Tougaloo College expresses the majority view when he states that the "role of the Black press in Mississippi has been to serve as an instrument in the long struggle for freedom and literacy. Even when the press took positions that we would today consider *Uncle Tomish*, it kept the folk reading; it definitely served psychological needs to have something of our own. The press has served, too, as a historical record, documenting events that are certainly not to be found elsewhere. It gave us the alternative to mainstream views." Scholar and editor Ivory Phillips of Jackson State University best expressed the minority view that the Mississippi black newspaper "has kept a relatively low profile. Too often rather than forthrightly exposing white racism and championing Black power, it has remained relatively quiet and conservative. In some instances, it has actually been critical of progressive movements among Black Mississippians."[111] Thus, the black press in Mississippi had a dual history of support for black uplift and of reactionary views on the black condition in the United States. The special strength of Mississippi's black newspapers lies in the sense of consciousness they give black people and in "carrying out the important role of being the organ of protest for the Black community."[112] The black newspapers' central weakness comes from their "too many ties to the white power structure . . . advertisements" and from "white control and manipulation" of the black press. Others add that the lack of capital and of distribution outside of Mississippi also represents key failures. A minority view places a great deal of emphasis on "the lack of support from the Black community, especially certain key leaders."[113] One view holds that for the black press to succeed in Mississippi, it must "be political in its nature and militant in its stances with regard to Black needs, concerns and problems." A moderate view measures the press' success in giving "an account of the progress our [black] people have made and how they struggle to achieve these small goals." A third opinion suggests that the black newspaper "should concentrate on in depth coverage of events, opinions, criticism, and analysis from a black perspective."[114]

In the final analysis, Phillips suggests that the future of the black press in Mississippi lies in "the courage of its maturing generation." To insure the survival of black newspapers, magazines, and broadcast stations, they will have to "match their ability with courage and commitment." If they are able to do so "they can easily live up to the ideal set by Frederick Douglass, David Walker and other pioneers in Black journalism."[115] As in the past, journalists must begin with little and strive through hard work to create media forms that will "speak the truth to the people" on the black condition throughout the world.[116]

Conclusion

Begun during the 1860s, a time of great crisis, Mississippi's black press evolved during the Reconstruction era. In the nineteenth century it strove to develop the institution of the newspaper and to promote and defend black interests. By 1899, however, the press had reached a mixed position. For the most part, it remained religious, dominated by the philosophy of Booker T. Washington. This conservatism produced a press that in many ways did not—perhaps could not—address black problems.

After the turn of the century, the black press increased in total number until 1928 and then began to decline as a result of the effects of the Great Depression and harsh segregation and racism in Mississippi. The great tasks facing the black press during this period remained the same as in the previous century: to define black freedom, to help secure it with a solid foundation, and, finally, to protect black interests. This period also offers mixed contributions by the press to black life. Although some voices in the 1940s demanded black rights (Percy Greene at the *Jackson Advocate*, for example), the majority, as in the case of the *Mississippi Enterprise*, represented an obstacle rather than a force for action and service in the long black struggle for freedom.

Finally, during the decades of the civil rights movement and its aftermath, 1950–85, the black press in Mississippi reached its lowest ebb. After World War II, even the *Jackson Advocate* became an obsolete mouthpiece for the status quo. Many segments of the black press were devoid of reality and irresponsible. And yet, through the hardships of the era, a few papers (*Freedom's Journal* of McComb, the *Mississippi Free Press*, and more recently the *Mirror*, edited by Henry Kirksey of Jackson), like much of the national black press, stood with a bright sense of hope for progress. In the last decades of this period a certain amount of indifference set in, brought on by the cruel destruction of the civil rights movement and by the continuation of severe black economic and social problems in Mississippi. Yet the period yielded a few surprises, such as the healthy thrust that Colia L. LaFayette and Charles Tisdale gave to the *Jackson Advocate* in the 1970s and 1980s.

The black press in Mississippi has always faced severe economic conditions. Most of the black press now finds itself in a week-to-week struggle to stay afloat. Good sources and current, accurate information also remain problems. The white press of the state, for the most part, still follows a conservative approach on social, political, and economic matters of great interest to black people, and the white press, along with television and radio, serves as major competition for the black market, especially for general advertising.

A central theme that runs through the black experience from Africa, through slavery, to the present is that blacks will support those institutions that relate to their lives and interests. A need will always exist for a black press to define, promote, and secure black freedom and interests throughout the world.

Although the black newspaper has represented the major forum of journalistic activity among blacks in Mississippi, more recently a new emphasis has emerged on the use of radio and television as news outlets. Historically, however, blacks in the state have had little success in gaining access to the news media, as remained the case in 1985. Nevertheless, more than twenty radio stations in the state have black programming, but news, information, and cultural programs take a back seat to contemporary music. Blacks have gained a controlling interest in WLBT, a Jackson television station, but the programming has not changed.

The future of the black press in Mississippi is, therefore, inextricably tied to the general condition of black people in Mississippi, where in 1985 two of every five blacks lived in poverty. The rural concentration of blacks in the state also remains a problem for the distribution of black journals in Mississippi. Wider distribution must occur to reach blacks in rural areas and to increase circulation in towns and cities. To combat the lack of fulltime professional journalists on the staffs of the various papers, the problems of attracting and keeping such personnel must be solved. Then, too, the black press can never take for granted that their audience will buy the product. Intensive efforts must attract readers from all economic levels as consumers. Such efforts will battle the fact that "Blacks buy white newspapers at four times the rate that they purchase Black newspapers."[1] To guarantee its future, Mississippi's black press must secure advertising from all elements, and it must produce a product that speaks to the core of economic, political, and social conditions of black people in the United States and abroad, in particular by covering black news. The black press has to come to grips with the fact that it is the first line of black defense in the new world information order. To secure the future of black people and to define and promote black freedom and interests, an effective black press, including newspapers, magazines, newsletters, and radio and television outlets, remains necessary. This challenge has confronted the black press in Mississippi for the past 120 years. The need for the black press to promote information sharing among people at home and throughout the world will always continue.

Black Mississippi Newspapers

1865–1985

Aberdeen Advance
Advance (Durant)
Advance (Mound Bayou)
Advance Dispatch (Mound Bayou)
Advance Dispatch (Vicksburg)
Advocate (Durant)
Advocate (Winona)
Advocate Journal (Vicksburg)
African Methodist Advocate (Vicksburg)
Afro-American Studies Newsletter (University of Mississippi)
Afro-Times Newsletter (Mississippi State University)
Alcorn Alumni Magazine (Alcorn State University)
Alcorn Herald (Alcorn A&M College/Alcorn State University)
Alcornite (Alcorn A&M College/Alcorn State University)
Alumni Newsletter (Rust College)
American (Signal)
Appeal (Meridian)
Aristocrat (Aberdeen)
Avalanche (Beulah/Clarksdale)
Baptist Advocate (Port Gibson)
Baptist Echo (Mound Bayou)
Baptist Headlight (Biloxi)
Baptist Headlight (Carriere)

Baptist Herald (Vicksburg)
Baptist Journal (Greenville)
Baptist Messenger (Jackson)
Baptist Preachers' Union (Greenville)
Baptist Record (Jackson)
Baptist Reporter (Jackson)
Baptist Sentinel (Lexington)
Baptist Signal (Greenville)
Baptist Signal (Natchez)
Baptist Trumpet (Enterprise)
Baptist Women's Union (Greenville)
Baptist Women's Union (Mound Bayou)
Beacon Light (Greenwood/Hattiesburg)
Bearcat (Rust College)
The Bee (Greenville)
Benevolent Banner (Edwards)
Black Man (Vicksburg)
Black People Speak (Utica Junior College)
The Blade (Greenville)
The Blade (Meridian)
The Blade (West Point)
Blue and White Flash (Jackson State University)
Bluff City Post (Natchez)
The Brookhaven Leader
Brotherhood (Columbus)
Brotherhood (Natchez)
Bulldog Growl (Utica Junior College)
Bulletin (Greenville)
Calanthian Journal (Jackson/Edwards)
Campus Communicator (Jackson State University)
Campus News Briefs (Rust College)
The Center Light (Greenwood)
Central Mississippi Signal (Cary)
Central Mississippi Signal (Kosciusko)
Central Voice (Yazoo City)
Charleston Star
Chenier's Black Woman Magazine (Jackson)
Christian Informer (Edwards)
Christian Plea (Shaw)

Citizen (Canton)
Citizen (Rosedale)
Citizens' Appeal (Vicksburg)
City Bulletin (Natchez)
Claiborne (Port Gibson)
Close-Up Magazine (Jackson)
Colored Alliance Advocate (Vaiden)
Colored Citizen (Vicksburg)
Colored Citizen's Monthly (Jackson)
Colored Journal (Jackson)
Colored Journal of Mississippi (Lyon)
Colored Messenger (Canton)
Colored Messenger (Coffeeville)
Colored People's Messenger (Senatobia)
Colored Veteran (Greenwood/Jackson)
Community Citizen (New Albany)
Conservative (West Point)
Conservative Echo (Okolona)
Cotton Farmer (Scott)
Defender (Mound Bayou)
Delta Beacon (Vicksburg)
Delta Leader (Greenville)
Delta Lighthouse (Greenville)
Delta Messenger (Clarksdale)
Delta Ministry Newsletter (Greenville)
Delta Ministry Reports (Greenville)
Delta News (Greenville)
Delta Progress (Shelby)
Delvian Gazette (Mississippi Valley State University)
The Demonstrator (Mound Bayou)
District Gazette (McComb)
Divine Word Messenger (Bay Saint Louis)
The Douglass Report (Jackson)
The Drummer (Jackson)
Eagle Eye (Jackson)
Eagle Queen (Tougaloo College)
Eastern Banner (Enterprise)
Echo (also *Weekly Echo*) (Meridian)
Educator (Clarksdale)

Elevator (Booneville)
Enterprise (Oxford)
Faculty Resource Center Newsletter (Jackson State University)
Fair Play (Meridian)
Field Hand (Jackson)
Floreyville Star (Rosedale)
Forty Acres and a Mule (Jackson)
Freedom's Journal (McComb)
Freedom Village Progress Report (Greenville)
Free Press (Brandon)
Free State (Brandon)
Galaxy (Hattiesburg)
Gazette (Biloxi)
Golden Eagle (Vicksburg)
Golden Rule (Quitman)
Golden Rule (Vicksburg)
Gospel Messenger (Fort Adams)
The Gospel Plea (Edwards)
The Gospel Truth (Jackson State University)
Greenville Mississippian
Growl (Mary Holmes Junior College)
Guide (Natchez)
Gulfport Coast Vigilante (Scranton)
The Harambee (Tougaloo College)
Headlight (Greenville)
Headlight (Jackson)
Headlight (Meridian)
Herald (Greenville)
Herald (Hattiesburg)
Herald (Jackson)
Herald (Natchez)
Highlighter (Jackson)
Hinds County Freedom Democratic Party Newsletter (Jackson)
Horizons (Mary Holmes Junior College)
Hub City Community News (Hattiesburg)
Informer (Gulfport)
Insight (Jackson)
It's the Gospel (Jackson)
Jackson Advocate

Jacksonian (Jackson State University)
Jackson Rodet (Jackson State University)
Jackson State University Review
Jackson Tribune
Jackson Urban League Newsletter
Jacob's Watchman (Jackson)
Journal (Clarksdale)
Journal (Coffeeville)
Journal (Moss Point)
JSU Alumni Magazine (Jackson State University)
JSU Faculty News (Jackson State University)
JSU Focus (Jackson State University)
JSU Now (Jackson State University)
The JSU Researcher: A Journal of Interdisciplinary Studies (Jackson
      State University)
Keynotes (Jackson)
Lancet (Jackson)
Leader (Greenville)
Leader (Jackson)
Lever (Port Gibson)
Light (Jackson)
Light (Mound Bayou)
Light (Vicksburg)
Maroon and Gold Flash (Utica Junior College)
Marshall Herald (Holly Springs)
Memo Digest (Meridian)
Meridian Morning Sun
Messenger (Jackson)
Metropolitan Baptist Ministers Fellowship (Jackson)
Metropolitan Observer (Jackson)
Mid-South Informer (Walls)
Mississippiana (Greenville)
Mississippi Baptist (Canton)
Mississippi Baptist Herald (Senatobia)
Mississippi Brotherhood (Robinsonville)
Mississippi Educational Journal (Jackson)
Mississippi Enterprise (Jackson)
Mississippi Freedom Democratic Party Newsletter (Jackson)
Mississippi Free Press (Jackson)

Mississippi Letter (Okolona Industrial Institute)
Mississippi Mirror (Jackson)
Mississippi Monitor (Meridian)
Mississippi News (Greenville)
Mississippi Newsletter (Tougaloo College)
Mississippi Republican (Vicksburg)
Mississippi Snaps (Brandon)
Mississippi Teachers Association—NOW (Jackson)
Mississippi Weekly (Jackson)
Monitor (Jackson)
Morning Star (Columbus)
Mound Bayou Digest
Mound Bayou Weekly
Natchez News Leader
Natchez Reporter
National Defender (Clarksdale)
National News Digest (Mound Bayou)
National Standard Enterprise (Fayette)
National Star (Vicksburg)
Negro Herald (Magnolia)
Negro Leader (Greenville)
Negro Reminder (Houston)
Negro Star (Greenwood)
Negro Star (Rosedale)
Negro World (Cary)
New (Greenville)
New African (Jackson)
New Era (Hernando)
New Era (Indianola)
New Light (Columbus)
New Light (Edwards)
New Light (Lexington)
New Light (Stratton)
New Messenger (Marks)
News (Granada)
News-Dispatch (Mound Bayou)
News Journal (Laurel)
New South (Jackson)

New Visions: A Journal of Contemporary Literature (Jackson State
    University)
North Jackson Action (Jackson)
Observer (Macon)
Oddfellow (Holly Springs)
Opera/South Newsletter (Jackson)
Outlook Magazine (Jackson)
Pascagoula–Moss Point 50/50
Pas-Point Journal (Moss Point)
Pathfinder (Greenville)
People's Advisor (Jackson)
People's Defender (Jackson)
People's Elevator (Independence)
People's Journal (Jackson)
People's Pilot (Moss Point)
People's Relief (Brookhaven)
People's Relief (Jackson)
Pike County Tribune (McComb)
Pine Torch (Piney Woods School)
Political Action League Newsletter (Jackson)
Pound: The Literary Magazine (Tougaloo College)
Practical Pointer (Aberdeen)
Practical Pride (Aberdeen)
Preacher and Teacher (Kosciusko/West Point)
Preacher's Safeguard (West Point)
Prentissite (Prentiss Institute)
Progress (Laurel)
Progressing Together (Tupelo)
Progressive Torchlight (Greenwood)
Race Pride (Okolona)
Reaction Magazine (Jackson)
Reconciler (Jackson)
Reflections (Mary Holmes Junior College)
Reflector (Jackson)
Republican (Natchez)
Republican Times (Summit)
Review (Mississippi Valley State University)
Rising Sun (Toomsuba)

RNA Newsletter
Rural Plea (Prentiss)
Rust College Sentinel
Rustorian (Rust College)
Saint Augustine's Messenger (Bay Saint Louis)
Saturday Times (Hollandale)
Scope (Jackson State University)
Searchlight (Port Gibson)
Sentinel (Mound Bayou)
Sentinel (Rust College)
Sentinel-Signal (Lexington)
SLRA Advocate (Forest)
Social Science Speaks (Jackson State University)
Soldiers of Faith (Brandon)
Soul Force! (Oxford)
Southern Advocate (Holly Springs)
Southern Advocate (Mound Bayou)
Southern Afro-American (Tupelo)
Southern Black Cultural Alliance Newsletter (Jackson)
Southern Forum (Greenville)
Southern Popular Athletic Sports (Jackson)
Southern Progress (Holly Springs)
Southern Register (Jackson)
Southern Sun (Greenville)
Spectator (University of Mississippi)
The Spirit of Mississippi (Jackson)
Star (Columbia)
Star (Lambert)
Street Talk (Jackson)
Sun (Greenwood)
Sunbelt (Jackson)
Taborian Bulletin (Mound Bayou)
Taborian Leader (Greenville)
Taborian Star (Mound Bayou)
Teacher and Preacher (Meridian)
Times (Benoit)
Times (Hattiesburg)
TOF Weekly Magazine (Jackson/Canton)
Tougaloo Enterprise

Tougaloo News (Tougaloo College)
Tougaloo Quarterly
Truth (Jackson)
Tutwiler Whirlwind (Tutwiler)
Uticanite (Utica Junior College)
Valley Voice (Mississippi Valley State University)
Vanguard (Gunnison)
Vicksburg Tribune
Vindicator (Mound Bayou)
Voice (Mound Bayou)
Voice of the Black Youth (Mayersville)
Weekly (Mound Bayou)
Weekly Bulletin (Alcorn State University)
Weekly Communicator (Jackson)
Weekly Recorder (Jackson)
Weekly Recorder (Mound Bayou)
What's Happening (Mississippi Valley State University)
Wilkerson County Appeal (Woodville)
Woodman Sentinel (Holly Springs)
Woodmen Sentinel (Crystal Springs)
Workmen of the World (Oxford)
Zion Harp (Greenville)

APPENDIX B

White Mississippi Newspapers

Batesville Panolian
Biloxi-Gulfport Herald
Capital Reporter (Jackson)
The Citizen (Jackson)
Citizens' Council (Jackson)
Clarion (Jackson)
Clarion (Meridian)
Clarion and Standard (Jackson)
Clarion-Ledger (Jackson)
Clarion-Ledger/Jackson Daily News (Jackson)
Clarksdale Press-Register
Delta Democrat-Times (Greenville)
Enterprise-Journal (McComb)
Fayette Chronicle
Greenwood Commonwealth
Hattiesburg American
Hinds County Gazette
Inside World (Parchman)
Issue (Jackson)

Jackson Daily News
Kudzu (Jackson)
Lexington Advertiser
McComb Enterprise
Meridian Star
Mississippi Pilot (Jackson)
Natchez Democrat
Pascagoula Chronicle
Petal Paper
Pike County Summit Sun
Reporter (Jackson)
State Times (Jackson)
Tunica Times-Democrat
Tupelo Journal
Tylertown Times
Vicksburg Commercial
Vicksburg Post-Herald
Vicksburg Times
Woman Constitutionalist (Summit)

Other Publications

Afro-American (Baltimore)
Atlanta Daily World
Black Dispatch (Oklahoma City)
Chicago Defender
Commercial Appeal (Memphis)
Crisis (New York/Baltimore)
Free Speech (Memphis)
Los Angeles Times

Miami Herald
New York Age
New York Times
Pittsburgh Courier
Southwestern Advocate (New Orleans)
Times Picayune (New Orleans)

Mississippi Radio and Television Stations

WABG (Greenwood)
WAPT (Jackson)
WBAD (Greenville)
WCBI (Columbus)
WCLD (Cleveland)
WDAM (Hattiesburg/Laurel)
WDBD (Jackson)
WESY (Greenville)
WFLZ (Belzoni)
WHII (Bay Springs)
WHOC (Philadelphia)
WHTV (Meridian/Tupelo)
WIWV (Tupelo)
WJMI (Jackson)
WJPR (Greenville)
WJSU (Jackson)
WJTV (Jackson)
WJXN (Jackson)
WKXI (Jackson)
WLBM (Meridian)
WLBT (Jackson)
WLOX (Biloxi)
WMAA (Jackson)
WMAB (Mississippi State University, Starkville)

WMAE (Booneville)
WMAH (Biloxi)
WMAO (Greenwood)
WMAU (Bude)
WMAV (Oxford)
WMAW (Meridian)
WMPR (Jackson)
WNAT (Natchez)
WNSL (Hattiesburg/Laurel)
WNTL (Natchez)
WOAD (Jackson)
WOBN (Bruce)
WOKJ (Jackson)
WORV (Hattiesburg)
WQBC (Vicksburg)
WQIC (Meridian)
WROB (West Point)
WROX (Clarksdale)
WTNK (Meridian)
WTOK (Meridian)
WTVW (Tupelo)
WVIM (Vicksburg)
WYAX (Yazoo City)

NOTES

Chapter 1

1. John R. Skates, "Mississippi," in *The Encyclopedia of Southern History*, ed. David C. Roller and Robert W. Twyman, 835; William K. Scarborough, "Heartland of the Cotton Kingdom," in *A History of Mississippi*, ed. Richard Aubrey McLemore, 1:102. See also Charles Sydnor, *Slavery in Mississippi* (New York: D. Appleton-Century, 1933).

2. Edwin A. Miles, "The Mississippi Insurrection Scare of 1835," *Journal of Negro History* 42 (January 1957): 48–60; Harvey Wish, "Slave Insurrection Panic of 1856," *Journal of Southern History* 5 (May 1939): 218; Davidson Burns McKibben, "Negro Slave Insurrections in Mississippi, 1800–1865," *Journal of Negro History* 34 (January 1949): 73–90.

3. John Hope Franklin, *From Slavery to Freedom: A History of Negro Americans*, 145; *Clarion-Ledger/Jackson Daily News*, November 27, 1977; H.G. Gutman, *The Black Family in Slavery and Freedom, 1750–1925* (New York: Vintage, 1976), 201–16.

4. Charles S. Sydnor, "The Free Negro in Mississippi before the Civil War," *American Historical Review* 32 (July 1972): 779; Vernon Lane Wharton, *The Negro in Mississippi, 1865–1890*, 12; Leon Litwack, *Been in the Storm So Long: The Aftermath of Slavery*, 509.

5. See Lawrence W. Levine, *Black Culture and Black Consciousness: Afro-American Folk Thought from Slavery to Freedom* (New York: Oxford University Press, 1977); W.E.B. Du Bois, *The Souls of Black Folk*, 181–90; Vincent Harding, *There Is a River: The Black Struggle for Freedom in America*, 82–84; John White, "Veiled Testimony: Negro Spirituals and the Slave Experience," 251–63.

6. The white population of Mississippi numbered 353,899 in 1860. U.S. Bureau of the Census, *Census*, 1860. See also James M. McPherson, *The Negro's Civil War*, ix; Herbert Aptheker, "Notes on Slave Conspiracies in Confederate Mississippi," *History* 29 (January 1944): 75–79; Robert Fulton Holtzclaw, *Black Magnolias: A Brief History of the Afro-Mississippian, 1865–1980*; Ken Lawrence, "Mississippi's First Labor Union" (Tougaloo, Miss.: Freedom Information Service, 1974), 1–3.

7. *The Black Republican* (New Orleans), May 20, 1865.

8. Wharton, *The Negro in Mississippi*, 270–72; Alferdteen Harrison, *A History of the Most Worshipful Stringer Grand Lodge: Our Heritage Is Our Challenge*, 17, 25–42; John K. Bettersworth, "The Reawakening of Society and Cultural Life, 1865–1890," in McLemore, *A History of Mississippi* 1:626;

George Alexander Sewell and Margaret L. Dwight, *Mississippi Black History Makers*, 87–88.

9. Wharton, *The Negro in Mississippi*, 273, quoting the *Hinds County Gazette*, May 10, 1867. The first black bank in Mississippi was created at Vicksburg in 1865. See Arthur James, "A Historical Look at Black Business in Mississippi," 12; Arthur James, "Black Banking in Mississippi," in *Selected Proceedings of the Symposium on the State of the Black Economy in Mississippi*, ed. Leslie G. Range. See the *Arkansas Freeman*, October 5, 1869; Allen Woodrow Jones, "Alabama," and Alton Hornsby, Jr., "Georgia," in *The Black Press in the South, 1865–1979*, ed. Henry Lewis Suggs, 27, 120.

10. Boston *Daily Evening Transcript*, January 9, 1870.

11. Wharton, *The Negro in Mississippi*, 273; N.R. Clay, "40th Anniversary of Rust University," *Voice of the Negro* 3 (June 1906): 401–3, Clarice T. Campbell and Oscar Allan Rogers, Jr., *Mississippi: The View from Tougaloo*, 6.

12. *American Newspaper Directory*, 678; *The Methodist Advocate* (Atlanta), February 23, 1870; Wharton, *The Negro in Mississippi*, 272–73; Armistead Scott Pride, "A Register and History of Negro Newspapers in the United States: 1827–1950," 111; E.C. Foster, "A Reflection on Afro-Mississippi Political Reconstruction from a 1980 Perspective: A Tribute to Mississippi Black Legislators," *Jackson State University Researcher* 7 (Summer 1980): 51–52; William C. Harris, "James Lynch: Black Leader in Southern Reconstruction," *Historian* 34 (November 1971): 43; Patrick H. Thompson, *The History of Negro Baptists in Mississippi*, 78, 136, 170, 172–73.

13. Thompson, *History of Negro Baptists*, 172–73; John T. Morris, "The History and Development of Negro Journalism," *A.M.E. Church Review* 6 (July 1889): 390; Illinois Writers' Project, *Cavalcade of the American Negro* (Chicago: Diamond Jubilee Exposition, 1940), 80; Bess Beatty, "Black Newspapers: Neglected Sources for the 'New South'," *Negro History Bulletin* 43 (July–September 1980): 61.

14. *American Newspaper Directory*, 678; Emma Lou Thornbrough, "American Negro Newspapers, 1880–1914," 475; William C. Harris, *The Day of the Carpetbagger: Republican Reconstruction in Mississippi*, 230.

15. Cleopatra D. Thompson, *The History of the Mississippi Teachers Association*, 164–65; Melerson Guy Dunham, *Centennial History of Alcorn A.&M. College* (Hattiesburg: University and College Press of Mississippi, 1971), 3–7; Campbell and Rogers, *Mississippi*, 255; Lelia G. Rhodes, *Jackson State University: The First Hundred Years, 1877–1977*, 6–14; Bettersworth, "The Reawakening of Society and Cultural Life," 626–28; Wharton, *The Negro in Mississippi*, 250–55; Jesse Thomas Wallace, *A History of the Negroes of Mississippi from 1865 to 1890*, 134.

16. Wharton, *The Negro in Mississippi*, 272.

17. I. Garland Penn, *The Afro-American Press and Its Editors*, 108.

18. John Roy Lynch, *Reminiscences of an Active Life: The Autobiography of John Roy Lynch*, 259; Wharton, *The Negro in Mississippi*, 157–73; W.E.B.

Du Bois, *Black Reconstruction in America*, 442; Rayford W. Logan and Michael R. Winston, eds., *Dictionary of American Negro Biography*, 74; John R. Lynch, *The Facts of Reconstruction*, ed. William C. Harris (Indianapolis: Bobbs-Merrill Co., 1970); William C. Harris, "Blanche K. Bruce of Mississippi: Conservative Assimilationist," in *Southern Black Leaders of the Reconstruction Era*, ed. Howard N. Rabinowitz (Urbana: University of Illinois Press, 1982), 7; Julius E. Thompson, *Hiram R. Revels, 1827–1901: A Biography*, 57–60.

19. Penn, *The Afro-American Press and Its Editors*, 110; Wharton, *The Negro in Mississippi*, 273; William J. Simmons, *Men of Mark*, 930; Logan and Winston, *Dictionary of American Negro Biography*, 407; John Hope Franklin, "John Roy Lynch: Republican Stalwart from Mississippi," in *Southern Black Leaders of the Reconstruction Era*, ed. Rabinowitz, 39–58.

20. Wharton, *The Negro in Mississippi*, 282. Another scholar of the period lists forty white Republican papers during Reconstruction in Mississippi. See James W. Garner, *Reconstruction in Mississippi*, 326–27. For a general summary of the white press in Mississippi, see the following in McLemore, *A History of Mississippi*: James J. Pillar, "Religion and Cultural Life, 1817–1860," 1:417–19, and John K. Bettersworth, "The Home Front, 1861–1865," 1:537–39. See also Harris, *The Day of the Carpetbagger*, 31, 267, 414–17, 596–601.

21. Wharton, *The Negro in Mississippi*, 181–201; Garner, *Reconstruction in Mississippi*, 338–53, 372–414; Du Bois, *Black Reconstruction in America*, 448–50; Herbert Aptheker, *To Be Free: Studies in Negro History* (New York: International Publishers, 1948, 1968), 163–87.

22. Thompson, "Mississippi," in *The Black Press in the South*, ed. Suggs, 178. A copy of the June 26, 1880, issue of the Columbus *Tribune* is located at the Mississippi Department of Archives and History, Jackson.

23. N.W. Ayer and Sons, *American Newspaper Annual* (hereafter referred to as *Ayer's Directory*), 1880, 417; 1887, 207–9, 250; 1888, 265–67; 1889, 271–72, 274; *Tougaloo Enterprise*, May 1884, March 1885. See the Tougaloo College Archival Collection for a file of these and related press items for the 1880s and 1890s. See also Ida B. Wells, *Crusade for Justice*, ed. Alfreda M. Duster, 35–46; Thomas C. Holt, "The Lonely Warrior: Ida B. Wells-Barnett and the Struggle for Black Leadership," in *Black Leaders of the Twentieth Century*, ed. John Hope Franklin and August Meier, 39–61; Bert James Loewenberg and Ruth Bogin, eds., *Black Women in Nineteenth-Century American Life: Their Words, Their Thoughts, Their Feelings*, 252–62; Mildred I. Thompson, *Ida B. Wells-Barnett: An Exploratory Study of an American Black Woman, 1893–1930* (Brooklyn, N.Y.: Carlson Publishing, 1990). On the role of the national black press and the Colored Press Association, a grouping of black newspapers, see Lawrence D. Hogan, *A Black National News Service: The Associated Negro Press and Claude Barnett, 1919–1945*, 16–17.

24. Ayer and Sons, *American Newspaper Annual*, 1880, 1887, 1888, 1889.

25. Ibid., 1890, 377, 379–80, 382; 1893–94, 405–6, 408; 1896, 408; 1898, 424, 426–28, 431–32, 1095; 1899, 430–34, 436–37, 1117, 1120–21; Flora Ann Cald-

well McGhee, "Mississippi Black Newspapers: Their History, Content and Future," 18; *Tougaloo Quarterly*, September 1890; *Tougaloo News*, November 1890; Penn, *The Afro-American Press and its Editors*, 112–14.

26. James W. Loewen and Charles Sallis, eds., *Mississippi: Conflict and Change*, 161–63; August Meier, *Negro Thought in America, 1880–1915*, 38, 148, 224–25; Louis R. Harlan, *Booker T. Washington: The Wizard of Tuskegee, 1901–1915*, 220–63; Janet Sharp Herman, "Isaiah T. Montgomery's Balancing Act," in *Black Leaders of the Nineteenth Century*, ed. Leon Litwack and August Meier, 291–304.

27. Wharton, *The Negro in Mississippi*, 272–73; Roy F. Lee, *The Setting for Black Business Development: A Study in Sociology and Political Economy* (Ithaca, N.Y.: State School of Industrial and Labor Relations, 1973), 104; Albert L. DeMond, *Certain Aspects of the Economic Development of the American Negro, 1865–1900*, 106–8.

28. Wharton, *The Negro in Mississippi*, 273; Thompson, *The History of Negro Baptists in Mississippi*, 190.

29. Thompson, *History of Negro Baptists*, 198.

30. Wharton, *The Negro in Mississippi*, 82–83; Suggs, *The Black Press in the South*, 4–16, 423–29.

31. The following provide insight into the nature and extent of the oppression of this age: Meier, *Negro Thought in America*, 72–73, 108–10, 161–70; Ray Stannard Baker, *Following the Color Line* (1908; reprint, New York: Harper and Row Publishers, 1964), 97, 101–5, 175–76, 233; Franklin, *From Slavery to Freedom*, 272–76, 320–27, 348–71; C. Vann Woodward, *The Strange Career of Jim Crow*. Other minority populations in Mississippi during the later part of the nineteenth century included the Choctaw Indians, who numbered approximately 2,500 in 1903, and fifty-one Chinese inhabitants in 1880. These groups remained too small to support viable presses.

32. The major sources of data for this section include *Ayer's Directory*, and Monroe Work, *Negro Year Book*, 1912, 1918–19, 1947. The physical survival of black newspapers from 1900 to 1919 presents a major problem for students of Mississippi black press. The Library of Congress has one issue each of Brandon, *The Free State* (Brandon, Mississippi), January 20, 1900; the Vicksburg *Light*, January 18, 1900; and the Vicksburg *Golden Rule*, January 27, 1900. The character of each individual paper cannot be easily assessed from a single four-page issue. For this period see also Neil R. McMillen, "Black Journalism in Mississippi: The Jim Crow Years," *Journal of Mississippi History* 49 (May 1987): 125–38; I.W. Crawford, P.H. Thompson, and J.H. Ballou, eds., *Multum in Parvo*, 7–9; the *People's Relief*, a single copy of which (April 29, 1911) is also held by the Smith Robertson Museum, Jackson. Although published at Jackson, it served as the official organ of the Franklin and Copiah county branches of the Industrial Mutual Relief Association of America, which had as its motto, "Equal Rights to All, Special Favors to None." E.N. Bryant and E.H. Johnson served as editors.

33. *Ayer's Directory* 1900–1919.

34. Two fraternal papers published in each of these four cities: Holly Springs, Natchez, Edwards, and Jackson. The religious press was concentrated in Mound Bayou, with three papers, and in Jackson, with two. Finally, Holly Springs had the greatest concentration of educational journals for the period because of the two black colleges located there, followed by Jackson, which also had two black colleges during this period.

35. *Ayer's Directory*, 1900–1919; Thornbrough, "American Negro Newspapers, 1880–1914," 475–76. See also *The Leading Afro-Americans of Vicksburg, Mississippi, Their Enterprises, Churches, Schools, Lodges and Societies*, 1–80.

36. Thornbrough, "American Negro Newspapers," 472–73; P. Thomas Stanford, *The Tragedy of the Negro in America* (Boston: author's edition, 1898), 118; D.W. Woodward, *Negro Progress in a Mississippi Town: Being a Study of Conditions in Jackson, Mississippi*, 3–6.

37. More than 100 publishers, editors, and associate editors worked in Mississippi during this era. My data are based on a cross section of twenty-five papers. Sources surveyed for these data included standard biographical references, general histories of Mississippi and the South, and vertical files at Alcorn State University, Jackson State University, Utica Junior College, Tougaloo College, Millsaps College, the University of Mississippi, the University of Southern Mississippi, Mississippi State University, and the Department of Archives and History, Jackson, and *Ayer's Directory*, 1900–1919. Black women limited their press activities during this era primarily to church-related journals, educational papers, and black women's organizational publications.

38. Tony Martin, *Race First: The Ideological and Organizational Struggles of Marcus Garvey and the Universal Negro Improvement Association*, 364–65; Harlan, *Booker T. Washington*, 218–31; Pete Daniel, *The Shadow of Slavery: Peonage in the South, 1901–1969*, 21, 289–90; Neil R. McMillen, *Dark Journey: Black Mississippians in the Age of Jim Crow*, 172, 376.

39. William M. Strickland, "James Kimble Vardaman: Manipulation Through Myths in Mississippi," in *The Oratory of Southern Demagogues*, ed. Calvin M. Logue and Howard Dorgan, 66–82; William F. Holmes, *The White Chief: James Kimble Vardaman* (Baton Rouge: Louisiana State University Press, 1970); *Ayer's Directory*, 1907, 463. For a review of the other major Mississippi demagogue of the era, see Jerry A. Hendrix, "Theodore G. Bilbo: Evangelist of Racial Purity," in Logue and Dorgan, *The Oratory of Southern Demagogues*, 150–72.

40. David Gordon Nielson, *Black Ethos: Northern Urban Negro Life and Thought, 1890–1930*, 63; Frederick G. Detweiler, *The Negro Press in the United States*, 1, 21–22, 74; Leon Litwack, "The Ordeal of Black Freedom," in *The Southern Enigma: Essays on Race, Class, and Folk Culture*, ed. Walter J. Fraser, Jr. and Winfred B. Moore, Jr., 15. By 1925, Mississippi may have had as many as 93,040 Ku Klux Klan members. One black reaction to the violence of the era was the establishment in 1918 in Vicksburg of the first

NAACP chapter in Mississippi. See Lenwood G. Davis and Janet L. Sims-Wood, *The Ku Klux Klan: A Bibliography* (Westport, Conn.: Greenwood Press, 1984), 622–23; *Clarion-Ledger/Jackson Daily News*, February 12, 1984; Kenneth T. Jackson, *The Ku Klux Klan in the City, 1915–1930*, 237.

41. Schools also played an important role as a source of news and information for blacks during the age of segregation. See "The Negro Common School, Mississippi," *Crisis* 33 (December 1926): 90–102. See also V.P. Franklin, *Black Self-Determination: A Cultural History of the Faith of the Fathers* (Westport, Conn.: Lawrence Hill, 1984).

42. Woodward, *The Strange Career of Jim Crow*, 116; Daniel, *The Shadow of Slavery*, 149, 153–54; Loewen and Sallis, *Mississippi*, 202–18; Pete Daniel, *Deep'n as It Come: The 1927 Mississippi Flood* (New York: Oxford University Press, 1977); Nathan Irvin Huggins, *Harlem Renaissance* (New York: Oxford University Press, 1971). On the continued oppression of black newspaper agents and black journalists in Mississippi, see Roland E. Wolseley, *The Black Press, U.S.A.*, 53–54. Perhaps black Mississippians' greatest contribution to cultural history during the 1920s occurred in the area of music, especially the blues. See William Ferris, *Blues from the Delta: An Illustrated Documentary on the Music and Musicians of the Mississippi Delta* (Garden City, N.Y.: Anchor Press/Doubleday, 1978); Paul Oliver, *The Meaning of the Blues* (New York: Collier Brooks, 1960); Giles Oakley, *The Devil's Music: A History of the Blues* (New York: Harcourt Brace Jovanovich, 1976).

43. *Ayer's Directory*, 1920–29; Georgetta Merritt Campbell, "Extant Collections of Black Newspapers, 1880–1915, in the Libraries of the United States: The Need for a Scholarly Index," 132. Scattered copies of the *Rural Plea*, an educational organ of Prentiss Institute, edited by A.L. Johnson, the son of the institute's founder, J.E. Johnson, are available for 1928 and 1929 in A.L. Johnson's private collection at Prentiss. Jefferson Sainsbury, Letter to the author, April 16, 1992.

44. John B. Kirby, *Black Americans in the Roosevelt Era: Liberalism and Race* (Knoxville: University of Tennessee Press, 1980); Robert H. Brisbane, *The Black Vanguard: Origins of the Negro Social Revolution, 1900–1960*, 133–59; August Meier and Elliott Rudwick, *From Plantation to Ghetto*, 241–46; Peter M. Bergman and Mort N. Bergman, *The Chronological History of the Negro in America*, 447–86; Alferdteen Harrison, ed. *Black Exodus: The Great Migration from the American South*. It is difficult to evaluate the concerns of Mississippi's blacks during the 1930s about the position of the Communist party and its allies on black issues. On the Communist party and blacks, see Wilson Record, *The Negro and the Communist Party*; J. Oliver Emmerich, *Two Faces of Janus: The Saga of Deep South Change*, 66–71; Manning Marable, *Race, Reform and Rebellion: The Second Reconstruction in Black America, 1945–1982*, 8–11; James Silver, *Running Scared: Silver in Mississippi*, 18–30.

45. *Ayer's Directory*, 1930–39.

46. See Detweiler, *The Negro Press in the United States*, 101–26; Vishnu V. Oak, *The Negro Newspaper*; Wolseley, *The Black Press, U.S.A.*, 163–80.

47. Mound Bayou *Southern Advocate*, October 1, 1938. The *Southern Advocate* cost $1.50 per year and five cents per issue. The Department of Archives and History, Jackson, has on microfilm the *Southern Advocate* and the *Delta Leader* for 1938 and 1939 with scattered issues missing.

48. *Southern Advocate*, May 28, June 11, July 2, 16, 23, August 6, 13, 20, September 3, October 1, 8, November 26, December 10, 24, 1938; January 7, February 25, March 18, May 6, 13, July 22, 29, September 9, November 11, 18, December 9, 16, 1939. On the state level, the paper noted that the office had a copy of Mississippi Senator Bilbo's bill (introduced in the U.S. Senate on April 24, 1939) "to provide for sending good American Negroes back to Africa." For the good of the community, the paper stated that "anyone interested may see it" (April 29, 1939).

49. *Southern Advocate*, May 28, 1938, October 14, 1939.

50. Ibid., December 24, 1938.

51. *Delta Leader*, November 4, 1939.

52. Ibid., November 19, 1938, October 7, December 9, 19, 1939, November 4, 1949.

53. Ibid., November 19, 1938, October 7, 1939.

54. David L. Cohn, *Where I Was Born and Raised*, ix; George S. Schuyler, "Freedom of the Press in Mississippi," 302.

55. Rayford W. Logan, ed., *The Attitude of the Southern White Press toward Negro Suffrage*, 44–46. Other white papers of the period that followed the same line of reasoning included the *Meridian Star*, the *Vicksburg Post-Herald*, the *Fayette Chronicle*, and the *McComb Enterprise*.

56. Laurence C. Jones, *The Bottom Rail: Addresses and Papers on the Negro in the Low Lands in Mississippi and on Inter-Racial Relations in the South during Twenty-Five Years*, 62–63. For a recent study of Piney Woods School, see Alferdteen Harrison, *Piney Woods School: An Oral History*.

57. Schuyler, "Freedom of the Press in Mississippi," 302; Nickieann Fleener, " 'Breaking Down Buyer Resistance': Marketing the 1935 Pittsburgh *Courier* to Mississippi Blacks."

58. Ibid., 302–4; Leslie H. Fishel, Jr., "Blacks in the Roosevelt Era," in *A Reader in Afro-American History*, ed. Eric Foner, 504. For the early black press in Mississippi, see also McMillen, *Dark Journey*, 172–77. See also the *Mississippi Weekly*, February 12, 1938, held by the Smith Robertson Museum, Jackson.

Chapter 2

1. For a review of the political, economic, and social positions of blacks in Mississippi during the 1940s, see the following: Loewen and Sallis, *Mississippi*, 239, 243–45; John Ray Skates, Jr., "World War II and Its Effects, 1940–1948," in *A History of Mississippi*, ed. McLemore, 2:120–39; William F. Winter, "New Directions in Politics, 1948–1956," in *A History of Mississippi*, ed. McLemore, 2:140–44; Daniel, *The Shadow of Slavery*, 179; Woodward, *The Strange Career of Jim Crow*, 129–30; Meier and Rudwick, *From Plantation to Ghetto*, 246–49; Wolseley, *The Black Press, U.S.A.*, 55–57; Suggs, *The*

Black Press in the South, 433; Marable, *Race, Reform and Rebellion*, 12–41; "World War II and the Black Press," in *Perspectives of the Black Press: 1974*, ed. Henry C. LaBrie, 27–37; Richard Wright, "How Jim Crow Feels," *Negro Digest* 3 (January 1947): 44–53. Two events of 1947 particularly interested blacks. First, Senator Theodore G. Bilbo died of cancer of the mouth on August 21, 1947. Perhaps the greatest demagogue in modern Mississippi history, Bilbo firmly believed in the use of violence, physical and psychological, against blacks. The second event was a hurricane that destroyed property and took many lives when it hit the Mississippi Gulf Coast on September 19, 1947. Skates, "World War II and Its Effects, 1940–1948," 138; Loewen and Sallis, *Mississippi*, 239. For a general history of blacks and World War II, see Neil Wynn, *The Afro-American and the Second World War*.

2. *Jackson Daily News*, February 15, 1971. In 1940, blacks represented 49 percent of the population of Mississippi (ibid.). On black life in an east Mississippi city during World War II, see Cleveland Payne, *Laurel: A History of the Black Community, 1882–1962*.

3. *Ayer's Directory*, 1941, 1241; 1942, 1252; 1944, 1199; 1945, 1199; 1947, 1247; 1948, 1274; Oak, *The Negro Newspaper*, 159; *The Negro Handbook*, 1944, 266; Thompson, *The History of the Mississippi Teachers Association*, 164–65. On a major black Catholic publication of this period, *Saint Augustine's Messenger*, see Jessie Parkhurst Guzman, ed., *The Negro Year Book, 1941–1946*, 403.

4. Geneva Brown, Blalock White, and Eva Hunter Bishop, eds., *Mississippi's Black Women: A Pictorial History of Their Contributions to the State and Nation*, 1–102.

5. Percy Greene's devotion to the *Jackson Advocate* as a full-time journalist may help to explain why this paper has been one of the best black journals, in terms of its standards as a newspaper, in Mississippi. Next to the *Mississippi Enterprise*, the *Jackson Advocate* is also the second longest surviving black paper in Mississippi.

6. *Jackson Advocate*, June 4, 1949; *Ayer's Directory*, 1941–48; Oak, *The Negro Newspaper*, 159; Florence Murray, ed., *The Negro Handbook*, 266; Franklin, *From Slavery to Freedom*, 387–98; Mary Frances Berry and John W. Blassingame, *Long Memory: The Black Experience in America*, 165–66, 176–78. The circulation rates for four black journals in 1948 were as follows: *Saint Augustine's Messenger*, 7,900; *Delta Leader*, 7,622; *Jackson Advocate*, 3,000; and the *Central Voice*, 2,000 (*Ayer's Directory*, 1948, 1274).

7. Gunnar Myrdal, *An American Dilemma*, 924.

8. On a black underground paper, the *Eagle Eye*, published at Jackson during this period, see *Jackson Daily News*, September 6, 1946.

9. *Ayer's Directory*, 1928–48; *Negro Year Book*, 1948.

10. "Leads 400,000 Baptists," 24–26; Sharren Williams and Brenda Elizey, "The Jackson Advocate, 41 Years of Community Service," *Jackson Advocate*, August 2, 1979.

11. Sewell and Dwight, *Mississippi Black History Makers*, 270–73.

12. The exact editions surveyed were January 11, 18, February 1, 8, April 26,

May 10, 31, June 28, July 5, August 30, September 13, 1941. Often no editorials appeared in the *Southern Advocate.*

13. *Delta Leader*, January 11, September 13, 1941.

14. *Jackson Advocate*, August–December 1941.

15. *Mississippi Enterprise*, February–September 1941. See also *Jackson Advocate*, August 16, September 20, 1941.

16. *Jackson Advocate*, August 2, 1941; *Delta Leader*, November 4, 1939.

17. *Mississippi Enterprise*, January 1, 22, 1944, April 10, November 6, 1948; *Southern Advocate*, October 1, 1938.

18. Washington wrote: "In all things that are purely social we can be as separate as the fingers, but in all things that affect our mutual progress and development we can be as together as the hand": Booker T. Washington, "Speech at the Atlanta Exposition," in *The Negro Caravan*, ed. Sterling A. Brown, Arthur P. Davis, and Ulysses Lee, 675; *Jackson Advocate*, August 2, 1941.

19. For a recent discussion of the national black press during World War II, see Lee Finkle, *Forum for Protest: The Black Press during World War II* (Cranbury, N.J.: Associated University Press, 1975). I based my assessment of the black press in Mississippi during this period on a study of the *Jackson Advocate* for 1941–42 and 1947–49; the *Mississippi Enterprise* for 1942, 1944–45, and 1948–49; the *Delta Leader* for 1939–41; and the *Southern Advocate* for 1938–41.

20. Extensive documentation exists on this question. See *Jackson Advocate*, November 15, December 13, 1941, March 21, September 5, 1942; *Delta Leader*, May 18, June 29, July 6, August 3, 17, 31, 1940, January 4, February 1, September 27, December, 13, 20, 27, 1941; and *Mississippi Enterprise*, November 18, 1944, May 19, 1945, July 3, September 18, 1948.

21. *Southern Advocate*, January 25, June 14, 1941. Both of these cases were wire reports, not editorial statements on the war. The June item referred to the loss of thirty-three men in a submarine disaster off the coast of New Hampshire.

22. *Commercial Appeal*, March 6, 1949. See also *Southern Advocate*, February 8, 1949, on Greene's fifteen-point program for Mississippi; *Jackson Daily News*, November 23, 1948; Luther P. Jackson, "Race and Suffrage in the South since 1940," 3–4.

23. For *Jackson Advocate*, see September 5, October 3, 1942, November 1, 1947, May 1, October 30, November 6, 1948. The paper stands out again in news coverage as the only paper that offered reflections and opinions on issues of the 1940s, including hard news, editorials, and commentaries.

24. *Mississippi Enterprise*, July 3, September 18, 1948.

25. *Southern Advocate*, October 26, 1940. The *Delta Leader* only referred to politics and the suffrage issue (between 1939 and 1941) on December 9, 1939, when it praised the mayor of Greenville in his campaign for reelection in 1939. This support did not mention black voting but noted that the mayor had been "one of the most progressive mayors ever," and there the *Leader* left the matter.

26. *Delta Leader*, May 4, 1940, February 21, 1942, July 28, 1945; and *Jackson*

Advocate, January 10, 1948. The editors assumed that since they served as spokesmen and leaders in their communities, they, too, were in the "upper class" of their society.

27. *Mississippi Enterprise*, November 20, 1948; *Delta Leader*, November 22, 1941.
28. *Mississippi Enterprise*, November 20, 1949. The *Southern Advocate* demanded that blacks purchase all of their goods from black-owned stores in Mound Bayou (May 25, August 24, September 7, October 5, 26, 1940).
29. *Jackson Advocate*, August 16, 1941, September 4, 1948.
30. *Delta Leader*, November 15, December 20, 1941. On education, see *Jackson Advocate*, December 6, 1941. See *Mississippi Enterprise* on unions (February 10, 1945) and on education (April 9, 1949).
31. See *Delta Leader*, March 16, June 29, July 6, 20, November 23, 1940, February 15, March 1, 7, April 19, May 10, 17, October 25, November 22, December 20, 27, 1941; *Mississippi Enterprise*, February 21, 1942, September 16, 1944, April 11, May 12, June 9, 1945, January 8, 1949; *Southern Advocate*, January 7, 1939, February 1, 8, 1941; *Jackson Advocate*, April 5, 1947, February 13, 1948.
32. *Delta Leader*, December 9, 1939.
33. *Mississippi Enterprise*, December 18, 25, 1948. For criminal problems in the state see also *Southern Advocate*, April 20, 1940, April 19, July 4, 1941; *Delta Leader*, December 9, 1939, August 24, 1940, June 21, 1941; *Mississippi Enterprise*, October 24, 1942. On censorship of the black press during the war, see Patrick S. Washburn, *A Question of Sedition*, 154–55, 263.
34. *Delta Leader*, September 20, October 18, 25, November 15, 1941.
35. *Fayette Chronicle*, September 26, 1937.
36. See Walter Lord, *The Past that Would Not Die* (New York: Harper and Row Publishers, 1965); Pat Watters, *The South and the Nation* (New York: Pantheon Books, 1969); Logan, ed., *The Attitude of the Southern White Press toward Negro Suffrage*, 44–46; James Silver, *Mississippi: The Closed Society*; and Robert Hooker, "Race and the Mississippi Press."
37. Hodding Carter, Jr., editor of the *Delta Democrat-Times*, received the Pulitzer Prize in 1946 for his sensitive treatment of racial problems in a series of editorials. See *Jackson Daily News*, April 5, 1972. Ira Harkey, editor of the *Pascagoula Chronicle*, was forced to flee Mississippi because of his efforts to promote fair journalism in the state. See *Pittsburgh Courier*, August 1950.
38. Robert H. Kinzer and Edward Sagarin, *The Negro in American Business*, 116. In meeting costs at Jackson, Percy Greene received aid from the *Atlanta Daily World*, a black organ that during the 1940s printed the *Advocate* at its printing plant in Atlanta. See *Atlanta Daily World*, April 22, 1977.
39. *Southern Advocate*, October 12, 1940, September 13, 1941; *Taborian Star*, November 1941, December 1944; *Delta Leader*, June 22, 1940, January 4, 1941; *Mississippi Enterprise*, September 23, 1939, September 8, 1945; *Jackson Advocate*, August 2, 1941, December 5, 1942.
40. Interview with Bruce Payne, Jackson, Mississippi, March 20, 1981. On the history of white radio in Mississippi, see *Clarion-Ledger/Jackson Daily News*, February 8, 1981; West Point *Times Leader*, February 19, 1980; Bob

McRaney, Sr., *The History of Radio in Mississippi*. On national black radio in the United States, see Reginald Stuart, "Rise of Radio's 'Black Music' Source," *New York Times*, July 12, 1982; Bruce Payne, "Blacks in the Broadcasting Business," *Jackson Advocate*, March 5–11, 1981; Ellen Kay Bastron, "Black-Oriented Radio: Analysis of Broadcast Content and Policies: A Case Study," 1–2; John S. Lash, "The Negro and Radio", in *Issues and Trends in Afro-American Journalism*, ed. James S. Tinney and Justine J. Rector, 167–82.

41. Interview with Bruce Payne.
42. *Jackson Advocate*, January 22, 1949; *New York Times*, June 28, 1989.
43. *Jackson Advocate*, March 5, 1949.
44. Ibid. A good example of the early black choral groups on radio in Mississippi was the "Gospel Quartet announcers who gave information about religious activities on white stations" (ibid.).
45. W.E.B. Du Bois, "The American Negro Press," *Chicago Defender*, February 20, 27, 1943.
46. Ibid.
47. *Fortune*, May 1945, 235. For a sample of other opinions on the black press during the 1940s, see also Oak, *The Negro Newspaper*, 43–63, 84–87, 128–32; Doxey A. Wilkerson, "The Negro Press"; Roi Ottley, "The Negro Press Today," *Common Ground*, Spring 1943, 11–18; Marjorie McKenzie Lawson, "The Adult Education Aspects of the Negro Press," *Journal of Negro Education* 14 (1945): 431–35; Thomas Sancton, "The Negro Press," *New Republic*, April 26, 1943, 557–60; John H. Burma, "An Analysis of the Present Negro Press," *Social Forces* 26 (December 1947): 172–80; Roi Ottley, *"New World a-Coming": Inside Black America*, 269–88; John Pittman, "The Negro Press and America's Future," *Congress View*, June 1944, 1–2; V.V. Oak, "What about the Negro Press," *Saturday Review of Literature*, March 6, 1943, 4–5; Warren H. Brown, "A Negro Looks at the Negro Press," *Saturday Review of Literature*, December 19, 1942, 5–6; Wolseley, *The Black Press, U.S.A.*, 55–63, 116–17; Suggs, ed., *The Black Press in the South*, 44, 72–78, 167–68, 335–38; Richard Bardolph, *The Negro Vanguard*, 337–44.
48. *St. Louis Angus*, March 8, 1946.
49. Loewen and Sallis, *Mississippi*, 244.

Chapter 3

1. Haynes Johnson, *Dusk at the Mountain: The Negro, the Nation, and the Capital—A Report on Problems and Progress*, 42; *Jackson Daily News*, July 27, 1977; *1950 Census*.
2. Loewen and Sallis, *Mississippi*, 247.
3. Daniel Guerin, *Negroes on the March: A Frenchman's Report on the American Negro's Struggle*, 52.
4. Earl Black, *Southern Governors and Civil Rights: Racial Segregation as a Campaign Issue in the Second Reconstruction*, 41; Earl M. Lewis, "The Negro Voter in Mississippi," *Journal of Negro Education* 26 (1957): 335; *Jackson*

Daily News, July 27, 1977; Bergman and Bergman, *The Chronological History of the Negro in America*, 554; Steven F. Lawson, *Black Ballots: Voting Rights in the South, 1944–1969*, 146.

5. Robert Sherrill, *Gothic Politics in the Deep South: Stars of the New Confederacy*, 189; F. John Wade, "The Development of Mississippi's Economy since 1950," in *Sense of Place: Mississippi*, ed. Peggy W. Prenshaw and Jesse O. McKee, 180, 182; *Commercial Appeal*, January 29, 1962.

6. *Ayer's Directory*, 1950–59; *Jackson Daily News*, March 26, 1957; McGhee, "Mississippi Black Newspapers," 27.

7. Good accounts of this period, especially of the establishment of the White Citizens' Council and of the role of the Ku Klux Klan and other extremist groups, include Francis M. Wilhoit, *The Politics of Massive Resistance*; Stephen J. Whitfield, *A Death in the Delta: The Story of Emmett Till* (New York: Free Press, 1988); and Neil McMillen, *The Citizens' Council: Organized Resistance to the Second Reconstruction, 1954–64* (Urbana: University of Illinois Press, 1971).

8. *Mississippi Enterprise*, November 24, 1951. The decline of the black press in Mississippi occurred between 1910 and 1959, as follows: 1910–19, sixty-six papers; 1920–29, thirty-one; 1930–39, thirty-three; 1940–50, thirty-nine; 1950–59, twenty-six.

9. Loewen and Sallis, *Mississippi*, 246–58; Philip Abbott Luce, "Mack Parker," *Freedomways* 2 (Winter 1962): 95–96; Woodward, *The Strange Career of Jim Crow*, 132–68; Daniel, *The Shadow of Slavery*, 186–88; Thomas D. Clar, ed., *The South since Reconstruction* (Indianapolis: Bobbs-Merrill Co., 1973), 424–28, 449–53, 460–65; William M. Simpson, "Reflections on a Murder; The Emmett Till Case," in *Southern Miscellany: Essays in History in Honor of Glover Moore*, ed. Frank Allen Dennis (Jackson: University Press of Mississippi, 1981), 177–200; *Clarion-Ledger/Jackson Daily News*, December 16, 1979, May 9, 1982; Jack Mendelsohn, *The Martyrs* (New York: Harper and Row, 1966), 1–20; *Clarion-Ledger*, November 15, 1976, September 15, 1977; Wade, "The Development of Mississippi's Economy since 1950," 179–88; Brisbane, *The Black Vanguard*, 237–50; Robert H. Brisbane, *Black Activism: Racial Revolution in the United States*, 21–41; Meier and Rudwick, *From Plantation to Ghetto*, 255–57; Hodding Carter I, *The South Strikes Back* (Garden City, N.Y.: Doubleday, 1954); Silver, *Running Scared*, 67; Berry and Blassingame, *Long Memory*, 384–85; Franklin, *From Slavery to Freedom*, 454–62; Alton Hornsby, Jr., *The Black Almanac: From Involuntary Servitude (1619–1860) to the Age of Disillusionment (1964–1973)* (Woodbury, N.Y.: Barron's Educational Series, 1975), 78–88; Bergman and Bergman, *The Chronological History of the Negro in America*, 522–63; William F. Winter, "New Directions in Politics, 1948–1956," in *A History of Mississippi*, ed. McLemore, 2:144–53; Neil McMillen, "Development of Civil Rights, 1956–1970," in *A History of Mississippi*, ed. McLemore, 2:154–61.

10. *Ayer's Directory*, 1958, 1388. Black media interests in radio and television were also curtailed during the 1950s. For the most part, the patterns of the 1940s prevailed throughout the decade.

11. Silver, *Mississippi*, 69; *State Times*, February 26, 1959; Theodore J. Spahn, Janet M. Spahn, and Robert H. Miller, *From Radical Left to Extreme Right*, 1:332–82. On Jimmy Ward, editor of the *Jackson Daily News* during the late 1950s and one of the leading segregationist journalists in Mississippi, see Joe Atkins, "Jim Ward: Fiery editor's retirement ends an era," *Clarion-Ledger/ Jackson Daily News*, January 8, 1984. On a 1956 visit to Mississippi by twenty New England editors and publishers, invited to observe and experience "the truth about what segregation is, and why," see *Time*, October 22, 1956, 54. For the perspective of a leading white Mississippi writer of this period see William Faulkner, "Mississippi," *Holiday Magazine* (April 1954): 33–47. On the black press of the 1950s in general, see Lewis H. Henderson, "The Negro Press as a Social Instrument," *Journal of Negro Education* 20 (1951): 181–88; James A. Bayton and Ernestine Bell, "An Exploratory Study of the Role of the Negro Press," *Journal of Negro Education* 20 (1951): 8–15; J.J. Mullen, "Advertise to the Negro Market? A Case Study," *Journalism Quarterly*, 32 (Summer 1955): 353–56; Armistead Scott Pride, "Negro Newspapers: Yesterday, Today and Tomorrow." See also Gayle G. Yates, *Mississippi Mind*, 65–67.

12. On the white Mississippi moderate press, see the following: Ira B. Harkey, Jr., *The Smell of Burning Crosses: An Autobiography of a Mississippi Newspaperman*; *Pittsburgh Courier*, August 1950; Howard Rusk Long, ed., *Main Street Militants: An Anthology from Grassroots Editors*, 7–8, 119–24; William Peters, *The Southern Temper*, 31, 128–29; Guerin, *Negroes on the March*, 82; *Meridian Star*, December 28, 1958; Albert Vorspan, "The Iconoclast of Petal, Mississippi"; P.D. East, *The Magnolia Jungle: The Life, Times and Education of a Southern Editor*; Silver, *Mississippi*, 38–39, 44, 47, 143; Frank E. Smith, *Congressman from Mississippi*, 41, 266–69. Some white papers during this period devoted a page to the various activities of Afro-Americans in Mississippi. For example, the *Natchez Democrat*, March 7, 1954, published a page edited by J.R. Buck, a black man, who was president of Natchez Junior College.

13. For the 1950s, only the *Jackson Advocate*, the *Mississippi Enterprise*, and the Mound Bayou *Sentinel* (1952–54) are available on microfilm. They are located at the Mississippi Department of Archives and History, Jackson. On the activities of Rev. H.H. Humes, editor of the Greenville *Delta Leader*, see Andrew Michael Mainis, *Southern Civil Religions in Conflict: Black and White Baptists and Civil Rights, 1947–1957* (Athens: University of Georgia Press, 1987), 60–63; Julius E. Thompson, *The Black Press in Mississippi, 1865–1985: A Directory*, 115.

14. This assessment is based on a review of the *Jackson Advocate* for the period 1941–59. (I have already noted that Greene's position had been strong in the late 1940s and early 1950s, especially after the conservative-segregationist *Jackson Daily News* made a series of attacks on him and the *Advocate*.) See "Jackson Daily News Fails to Print Full Story" and "The Jackson Daily News Is at Us Again," *Jackson Advocate*, December 30, 1950.

15. In 1958, Greene claimed that the *Advocate* paid $5,000 to produce a special

issue of the paper devoted to reprinting Booker T. Washington's 1895 "Atlanta Compromise" speech. See *Clarion-Ledger/Jackson Daily News*, November 30, 1958; *Jackson Advocate*, July 1, August 5, 26, 1950. Greene criticized white South African leadership, but South Africa was thousands of miles away from the United States. See *Jackson Advocate*, September 30, 1950. He reserved his highest praise for the work of Dr. Ralph Bunche, winner of the 1950 Nobel Peace Prize, for his role in bringing peace to the Middle East. See *Jackson Advocate*, October 7, 1950. On Africa and the black press during the 1950s see Armistead S. Pride, "Emergent Africa and the Negro Press," *The Nation*, November 7, 1953, 369–70.

16. *Jackson Advocate*, May 22, 29, July 3, 24, August 28, September 4, 11, October 23, 1954.

17. In 1954, Percy Greene offered a seven-point plan and program, "For Interracial Harmony and Good Will in the State." See *Jackson Advocate*, September 4, 1954. The *Clarion-Ledger* (May 18, 1955) referred to Greene's educational efforts as "Voluntary Segregation Urged by Negro Editor."

18. *Jackson Advocate*, October 3, 1959. See also May 24, 1958. The paper noted that in Jackson "There has been a steady evolution for the better towards Negro citizens on the local buses." Thus, the *Advocate* saw no need for black protest there. Greene also supported FBI Director J. Edgar Hoover's charge of a Communist connection among some American black organizations (*Jackson Advocate*, January 5, 1957, May 24, 1958).

19. *Jackson Advocate*, May 27, 1957.

20. Ibid., September 21, October 12, 1957.

21. Ibid., May 25, October 21, 1957.

22. Ibid., February 16, 1957. The paramount goal consisted of the promotion of good race relations in Mississippi and the importance of black racial pride, achievement, and uplift. See *Jackson Advocate*, "More Uncle Toms Greatest Need of the Southern Negro," January 19, 1957; October 10, 1959; "Friendly Relations," November 21, 1959; and "Abolish Negro History Week?," March 8, 1958. See also "Negroes Vote in Mississippi," *Ebony*, November 1951, 15–18, 21–22.

23. *Jackson Advocate*, February 16, 1957.

24. Ibid., September 10, 1955. See also July 22, 25, September 10, October 1, 1950. For the Willie McGee case, see *Jackson Advocate*, July 22, 25, 1950; *Clarion-Ledger*, December 16, 1979. See *Jackson Advocate*, May 18, 1957, on G.W. Lee; June 14, 1959, on Gus Coates; and May 2, 9, 16, 1959, on the death of Mack Charles Parker. See also Howard Smead, *Blood Justice: The Lynching of Mack Charles Parker*.

25. *Jackson Advocate*, July 27, 1957.

26. Pride, *Negro Newspapers*, 112.

27. *Mississippi Enterprise*, June 3, 1950, January 29, 1954; *Ayer's Directory*, 1950, 1339, 1955, 1368.

28. *Mississippi Enterprise*, March 22, 1958.

29. Ibid., September 16, 1950.

30. Ibid., January 20, 1951.

31. Ibid., January 29, April 10, 17, 1954. The paper even allowed a good word to be said about the state NAACP in its support of the Progressive Voters' League, supporting both organizations because of their work on behalf of black freedom.
32. Ibid., June 3, 10, 1950, April 3, 1954.
33. Ibid., August 26, 1950; Robert Sherrill, *Gothic Politics in the Deep South*, 192.
34. *Mississippi Enterprise*, October 13, 1951.
35. Ibid., November 15, 1958. Despite several centuries of forced labor and slavery in America, the *Enterprise* could only offer this advice to students completing their educations: "Remember that when you take a job, you are supposed to work, not that you will know much about this word, but no kidding, it will be a fine thing for you to learn about it and learn real soon" (June 3, 1950).
36. Ibid., February 22, 1958. See also November 24, 1951, April 16, 1954, October 26, 1957.
37. On the role and influence of the State Sovereignty Commission, see Silver, *Mississippi*, 8.
38. *Eagle Eye*, October 9, 1954.
39. Ibid. On High's career, see the *Jackson Advocate*, April 28, 1988.
40. *Eagle Eye*, March 12, 19, October 22, 1955.
41. On the *Eagle Eye*'s point of view on the *Brown* decision, education, and "Uncle Toms," see March 12, 1955, June 9, 1956. On American labor, see March 19, 1955. On religion and segregation, see October 22, 1955. On race relations, see October 9, 1954. On the Mississippi Constitution of 1890, see February 19, 1955. On white supremacy and sexual relations between the races, see October 22, 1955, May 26, 1956.
42. The Mound Bayou *Sentinel*, September 13, 1952. The circulation of the *Sentinel* probably ranged between 500 and 1,000 copies each week, perhaps higher, during this period.
43. Ibid.
44. Ibid., October 11, 1952.
45. Ibid., January 17, 1953. See also May 9, 23, 1953.
46. Ibid., January 17, February 21, 1953. For the heavy local focus of the *Sentinel*, see "Our Volunteer Fire Unit," November 22, 1952; "Our Christmas Parade Drive," January 3, 1953; "You Can Help Clean Up Our Town," January 31, 1953; "Trees along Highway," February 21, 1953; "The Taborian Building," March 28, 1953; "Mound Bayou Moves Forward," July 18, 1953; "Our Christmas Fund," December 5, 1953; Loewen and Sallis, *Mississippi*, 344.
47. Mound Bayou *Sentinel*, August 8, 1953.
48. Ibid., September 13, 1952, February 27, 1954; *Jackson Advocate*, September 26, 1959.
49. Silver, *Mississippi*, 8; Erle Johnston, *Mississippi's Defiant Years: 1953–1973*, 48–52, 56–57.
50. Silver, *Mississippi*, 8; McMillen, "Development of Civil Rights," 159–60, 167. The black papers that received the backing of the Sovereignty Commission included the *Jackson Advocate* and the New Albany *Community Citizen*.

51. Interview with Bruce Payne.
52. *Jackson Advocate*, March 5, 1981.
53. Ibid.; interview with Bruce Payne.
54. *Jackson Daily News*, January 11, August 17, October 16, 1953, December 20, 1958; *Clarion-Ledger*, September 28, October 22, 1952. In December 1952 WJTV became the first station to go on the air in Mississippi. On blacks and American television during the 1950s, see J. Fred MacDonald, *Blacks and White T.V.: Afro-Americans in Television since 1948*, 1–74. During the 1950s Charles Evers, a political leader of the 1960s and 1970s, may have served as the first black disc jockey in the state, at WHOC, in Philadelphia, Mississippi. See Walter Rugaber, "We Can't Cuss White People Anymore. It's In Our Hands Now," *New York Times*, August 4, 1968; *Jackson Advocate*, August 8, 1953.

Chapter 4

1. On the general history of the civil rights movement and the 1960s see Loewen and Sallis, *Mississippi*, 249–85; Franklin, *From Slavery to Freedom*, 463–88; Meier and Rudwick, *From Plantation to Ghetto*, 251–98; Daniel, *The Shadow of Slavery*, 188–92; Woodward, *The Strange Career of Jim Crow*, 167–215. On the 1960s and Mississippi, see John R. Salter, Jr., *Jackson, Mississippi: An American Chronicle of Struggle and Schism*; Silver, *Mississippi*; McMillen, "Development of Civil Rights," 159–75; Myrlie Evers, "Why I Left Mississippi," *Ebony*, March 1965, 25–30. On black separatism/nationalism and the Black Power movement during this period, see Raymond L. Hall, *Black Separatism in the United States*; Stokeley Carmichael and Charles V. Hamilton, *Black Power: The Politics of Liberation in America* (New York: Vintage Books, 1967).
2. *Report of the National Advisory Commission on Civil Disorders*, 1.
3. *Jackson Daily News*, February 15, 1971, July 27, 1977; *Ayer's Directory*, 1978, 490; Harry Holloway, *The Politics of the Southern Negro* (New York: Random House, 1969), 34; Carlton R. Sollie, Wolfgang Frese, and Frederick D. Jones, *Changes in Quality of Life in Mississippi: 1960–1970* (Mississippi Agricultural and Forestry Experiment Station, Bulletin 824, March 1975), 3.
4. McMillen, "Development of Civil Rights," 167; Wilhoit, *The Politics of Massive Resistance*, 89; Robert Hooker, "Race and the Mississippi Press," 56; *Ebony*, November 1980, 110–12; Carl M. Brauer, *John F. Kennedy and the Second Reconstruction* (New York: Columbia University Press, 1977), 180–204.
5. This assessment is based on a review of the following papers for the 1960s: in Jackson, the *Jackson Advocate*, the *Mississippi Enterprise*, and the *Mississippi Free Press*; in Greenville, the *Delta Leader*; in Bay Saint Louis, *Saint Augustine's Messenger*; in Meridian, the *Memo Digest*; in Mound Bayou, the *Voice* and the *Taborian Bulletin*; in New Albany, the *Community Citizen*. See also Irving J. Sloan, ed., *The Blacks in America, 1492–1977: A Chronology and Fact Book*, 42–62; the *Clarion-Ledger/Jackson Daily News*, January

4, 1970; Bergman and Bergman, *The Chronological History of the Negro in America*, 536–616; Hornsby, *The Black Almanac*, 88–116; John Hope Franklin and Isidore Starr, eds., *The Negro in 20th Century America: A Reader on the Struggle for Civil Rights* (New York: Vintage Books, 1967); "The Ebony Years: Significant Dates," 110–12; Brauer, *John F. Kennedy and the Second Reconstruction*, 180–204; Frank R. Parker, *Black Votes Count: Political Empowerment in Mississippi after 1965* (Chapel Hill: University of North Carolina Press, 1990), 31–32.

6. A recent study notes that during the height of the movement the *Jackson Advocate* was "enthusiastically approved by the Sovereignty Commission." See McMillen, "Development of Civil Rights," 167. See also Wilhoit, *The Politics of Massive Resistance*, 89; Hooker, "Race and the Mississippi Press," 56; *Ayer's Directory,* 1960, 1969; Henry LaBrie, *The Black Newspaper in America: A Guide*, 47–48, 78; Frank B. Sawyer and Ruth Castor, eds., *U.S. Negro World, 1966: Directory of U.S. Negro Newspapers, Magazines and Periodicals*, 31; *Black List: The Concise Reference Guide to Publications and Broadcasting Media of Black America, Africa and the Caribbean*, 17.

7. Interview with Dilla E. Irwin, Vicksburg, April 16, 1981; Ollye Brown Shirley, questionnaire, April 5, 1980, Jackson; Vicksburg *Citizens' Appeal*, July 5, 1965; *Who's Who among Black Americans, 1977–78*, I, 491; *The Ebony Handbook, 1966*, 385; *Jackson Advocate*, November 8, 1967; *Mississippi Freedom Democratic Party Newsletter*, December 20, 1965; Levye Chapple, Jr., *History of Blacks in Greenville, Mississippi, 1868–1975*.

8. Silver, *Mississippi*, 289–96;7 Spahn, Spahn, and Miller, *From Radical Left to Extreme Right*, 1:283–84, 2:820–22; *Natchez Democrat*, September 30, 1968; *Clarion-Ledger/Jackson Daily News*, January 8, 1984; Watters, *The South and the Nation*, 185; *Time* Magazine, March 4, 1966.

9. Watters, *The South and the Nation*, 271.

10. Ibid., 276; Silver, *Mississippi*, 297; Noel E. Polk and James R. Scafidel, eds., *An Anthology of Mississippi Writers* (Jackson: University Press of Mississippi, 1979), 272–73, 528–29; *The Afro-American*, October 13, 1962; Emma G. Sterne, *They Took Their Stand* (New York: Crowell-Collier Press, 1968), 15–16; C.J. Wilson, "Voices from Mississippi," 62–71. See also Oliver Emmerich, "The Democratic Idea and the Southern Journalist," *Mississippi Quarterly* 18 (Fall 1965): 321–33; Charles Nutter, "A Crusading Editor Gets Results," *Reader's Digest*, January 1951, 134–37; Joseph Luther White, "Facing a Hostile Public: A Mississippi Editor's Dilemma"; Robert Canzoneri, "*I Do So Politely*": *A Voice from the South* (Boston: Houghton Mifflin Co., 1965); Willie Morris, ed., *The South Today: 100 Years after Appomattox* (New York: Harper and Row, 1965); Cohn, *Where I Was Born and Raised*. Hazel Brannon Smith received national recognition for her work in Mississippi in 1964, when she received the Pulitzer Prize for her antisegregation editorials in the *Lexington Advertiser*. In 1968, Charles Evers viewed the Greenville *Delta Democrat-Times* as the only progressive white newspaper in Mississippi. See Jack Lyle, ed., *The Black American and the Press*, 68–70; Emmerich, *Two Faces of Janus*, 116–18.

11. Spahn, Spahn, and Miller, *From Radical Left to Extreme Right*, 1:102.

12. Hazel Brannon Smith represented a special target for the Citizens' Councils and the State Sovereignty Commission for her progressive journalism standards. She charged in 1962 that opponents established a rival newspaper in her home county, the *Holmes County Herald*, to force her out of business. Furthermore, she faced public harassment and attacks from mailing campaigns against her by the Citizens' Council. See *Clarion-Ledger/Jackson Daily News*, January 6, 1962. See also *New York Times*, November 12, 1961; Hodding Carter, *First Person Plural* (Garden City, N.Y.: Doubleday Co., 1963), 217–25. See *Kudzu*, October 23, 1968, 5. The circulation figures for *Kudzu* averaged between 3,000 and 5,000 in the 1960s. The paper published once or twice a month (every two or three weeks). In 1965, the total circulation of Jackson's three papers, the *Clarion-Ledger* (morning), the *Jackson Daily News* (afternoon), and the *Clarion-Ledger/Jackson Daily News* (Sunday), stood at 164,500. The *Meridian Star* (evening and Sunday) had a circulation of 50,068 and the *Biloxi-Gulfport Herald* (evening) 7,798. Spahn, Spahn, and Miller, *From Radical Left to Extreme Right*, 1:102; *Benn's Guide to Newspapers and Periodicals of the World: Newspaper Press Directory, 1966*, 920.
13. *Natchez Democrat*, February 16, 1965.
14. New Albany *Community Citizen*, June 8, 1961.
15. Ibid.
16. Ibid., June 8, 1961, February 28, 1963.
17. *Ayer's Directory*, 1960, 1398; 1964, 1389; 1966, 1418; 1967, 1423; 1969, 1436. In spite of its segregationist support, the decline of the *Community Citizen's* circulation probably resulted from the successes of the civil rights movement and from the rising degree of black consciousness during the decade.
18. This assessment is based on a review of the *Community Citizen* for 1961–68.
19. *Clarion-Ledger/Jackson Daily News*, February 21, 1982.
20. *Community Citizen*, May 14, 1964. The *Citizen* also frequently attacked the federal government and national leaders such as President John F. Kennedy. On important individuals and organizations see issues of May 28, 1964, on democracy; July 25, August 22, 1963, on Martin Luther King, Jr.; February 28, April 25, 1963, on the NAACP; January 25, 1962, on John F. Kennedy; and November 22, 1962, on James Meredith.
21. Ibid., May 14, 1964.
22. Ibid., October 7, 1965. See also June 8, 1961, May 28, 1964.
23. Ibid., June 8, 1961, January 25, 1962, March 28, 1963.
24. Ibid., February 28, 1963.
25. Ibid., April 11, 1963.
26. Ibid., October 12, 1961.
27. Ibid., November 22, 1962.
28. Ibid., March 28, August 22, 1963, May 14, 1964.
29. Salter, *Jackson, Mississippi*, 113. See also Johnston, *Mississippi's Defiant Years*, 231–32; Benjamin F. Clark, "The Editorial Reaction of Selected Southern Black Newspapers to the Civil Rights Movement, 1954–1968."
30. Salter, *Jackson, Mississippi*, 113; *Clarion-Ledger/Jackson Daily News*, Feb-

ruary 21, 1982. See also Ashaki M. Binta, "Mississippi Spies," *Southern Exposure*, 9 (Fall 1981): 82–86; *Jackson Daily News*, November 27, 1960.

31. *Jackson Daily News*, May 7, November 27, 1960, January 23, 1965; *Ayer's Directory*, 1960, 1398; 1968, 1429.

32. *Jackson Advocate*, December 7, 1963, May 29, 1965, January 6, April 13, 1968.

33. For the *Jackson Advocate*'s "pro" positions during the 1960s, see May 7, 21, 23, 28, June 9, July 2, 23, October 8, 29, 1960; on the National Urban League, June 25, 1960; on voting, May 31, 1961, August 14, 1965; on economic development, July 15, 1961; on James Meredith, June 30, November 3, 1962; on the election of local blacks to office, December 3, 1966; on education, June 15, 1968; on race relations, January 6, 1968; and on freedom of the press, April 20, 1968. (The *Advocate* also noted that the black press had a special role to play in winning the Third World for the West. See "The Negro Newspaper and the Winning of Africa," February 6, 1960).

34. *Jackson Advocate*, February 6, March 5, 1960, June 15, 1968. For the *Advocate*'s negative positions, see the following issues: on the sit-in movement, April 1, 1961; on Freedom Rides, June 3, July 22, 1961; on Medgar Evers's death, June 15, 1963; on the March on Washington, August 24, 1963; on the death of John F. Kennedy, November 30, 1963; on the Freedom Summer, July 18, 1964; on the Council of Federated Organizations, March 6, 1965; on the Selma March, March 13, 1965; on the Freedom Democratic Party, August 7, September 25, 1965; on riots, August 21, 1965; on demonstrations in Chicago, July 31, 1965; on black elected officials, December 3, 1966; on the Civil Rights Act of 1966, August 20, 1966; on Martin Luther King, Jr., June 3, 1961, September 22, 1962, March 5, 1966, April 20, 1968; on Black Power, July 9, September 10, 1966; on Meredith's 1966 march, June 18, July 2, 1966: and on Charles Evers, April 20, 1968. Three significant works on the 1960s are Ann Moody, *Coming of Age in Mississippi*; Myrlie Evers, *For Us the Living* (Garden City, N.Y.: Doubleday and Company, 1967); Joyce Ladner, "What 'Black Power' Means to Negroes in Mississippi," *Trans-action* 5 (November 1967): 7–15.

35. Debra Ann Watson expressed the healing process that *Freedom Journal* viewed as necessary for a transformation of American society: "We, as citizens, should fight for: 1. Freedom, 2. Peace, 3. Kindness, 4. Better Schools, 5. Better Jobs, 6. A Better State, 7. A Better World." This was the counsel that *Freedom Journal* exerted in its pages as a foundation for the building of a new social order. See *Freedom Journal*, August 3, 1964. On the freedom schools see Mary Aickin Rothschild, *A Case of Black and White: Northern Volunteers and the Southern Freedom Summers, 1964–1965*, 93–121. The author is indebted to Professor Dorothy Smith of Dillard University, New Orleans, for a copy of *Freedom Journal*.

36. Charles L. Butt, ed., *Mississippi Free Press*.

37. Salter, *Jackson, Mississippi*, 29–31; *Commercial Appeal*, January 6, 1962, May 5, 1964. The civil rights movement produced a number of letters, leaflets, and pamphlets that also constitute part of the American black press.

We cannot escape their importance then (and now) as organs of information for the black community. One such publication was the *North Jackson Action*, an organ of the North Jackson NAACP Youth Council, headed at the time by Colia Liddell LaFayette. See Salter, *Jackson, Mississippi*, 58.

38. *Mississippi Free Press*, December 22, 1962; Charles L. Butt, *Philosophy of the Mississippi Free Press*, 2; *Negro Newspapers in the United States, 1966* (Jefferson City, Mo.: Lincoln University Department of Journalism, October 1966), 7.

39. Interview with Henry Kirksey, Jackson, March 15, 1981; *Jackson Advocate*, July 4, 1985. Subscriptions cost one dollar a year for Mississippians and four dollars for orders from outside the state. *Mississippi Free Press*, October 12, 1963.

40. Rothschild, *A Case of Black and White*, 23–24. See also Leslie Burl McLemore, "The Mississippi Freedom Democratic Party: A Case Study of Grass-Roots Politics" (Ph.D. diss., University of Massachusetts, 1971).

41. Rothschild, *A Case of Black and White*, 23–24; Louis L. Knowles and Kenneth Prewitt, eds., *Institutional Racism in America*, 88–91; Robert Brisbane, *Black Activism*, 73–104.

42. *Mississippi Freedom Democratic Party Newsletter*, December 20, 1965, September 23, 1967, March 12, November 5, 1968.

43. Dilla E. Irwin, questionnaire, Vicksburg, June 7, 1981; Vicksburg *Citizens' Appeal*, August 22, 1964. David Riley, a white civil rights movement worker, and other movement activists helped blacks create the *Appeal*. Interview with Dilla E. Irwin. On the role of Dr. Aaron Shirley (Ollye Brown Shirley's husband) at the *Citizens' Appeal* office during and after this period, see the *Washington Post*, August 30, 1971, A–3; *Sepia*, August 1975, 43–47; and the *Jackson Advocate*, September 20, 1984.

44. *Citizens' Appeal*, November 1, 1965; Ollye Brown Shirley, questionnaire. The *Appeal* was printed at New Orleans by a black printer and sent to Vicksburg by bus. Interview with Dilla E. Irwin.

45. *Citizens' Appeal*, November 1, 1965.

46. Ibid.; interview with Dilla E. Irwin.

47. Interview with Dilla E. Irwin. See also *Who's Who in the South and Southwest, 1978–1979* (Chicago: Marquis Who's Who, 1978), 666 (on Ollye Brown Shirley); Ralph McGill, *Southern Encounters: Southerners of Note in Ralph McGill's South*, ed. Calvin M. Logue (Macon, Ga.: Mercer University Press, 1983) (on Ralph McGill).

48. *Citizens' Appeal*, July 5, 1965.

49. Interview with Dilla E. Irwin.

50. *Jackson Advocate*, March 6, 1965; *Community Citizen*, June 8, 1961; *Citizens' Appeal*, October 12, 1963, August 22, 1964; *Rand McNally Standard Reference Map and Guide of Mississippi* (San Francisco: Rand McNally, 1972), 14; *Clarion-Ledger*, August 20, 1970; *Mississippi Free Press*, October 12, 1963. The sizes of the ads varied during this era.

51. Interview with Dilla E. Irwin.

52. U.S. Department of Justice, *Directory of Organizations Serving Minority Communications*, 46; *Black List*, 44; *Delta Democrat-Times*, August 11, 1974;

Fred Ferretti, "The White Captivity of Black Radio," in *Our Troubled Press: Ten Years of the Columbia Journalism Review*, ed. Alfred Balk and James Boylan (Boston: Little, Brown and Co., 1971), 87.

53. Ellen Kay Bastron, "Black Oriented Radio: Analysis of Broadcast Content and Policies, A Case Study," 55; *Jackson Advocate*, March 5, 1981; interview with Bruce Payne. See also Stuart H. Surlin, "Black-Oriented Radio: Programming to a Perceived Audience," *Journal of Broadcasting* 16 (Summer 1972): 289–98; Stuart H. Surlin, "Ascertainment of Community Needs by Black-Oriented Radio Stations," *Journal of Broadcasting* 16 (Fall 1972): 421–29.

54. William B. Monroe, Jr., "Television: The Chosen Instrument of the Revolution," in *Race and the News Media*, ed. Paul L. Fisher and Ralph L. Lowenstein (New York: Frederick A. Praeger Publishers, 1967), 85; Florence Halpern, *Survival: Black/White* (New York: Pergamon Press, 1973), 70, 167–69.

55. Fred W. Friendly, *The Good Guys, the Bad Guys and the First Amendment: Free Speech vs. Fairness in Broadcasting*, 90–95; Ford Rowan, *Broadcast Fairness Doctrine; Practice, Prospects: A Reappraisal of the Fairness Doctrine and Equal Time Rule*, 41–42. In the early 1960s, WLBT allowed a black minister to conduct a program at 6:45 A.M. on Sundays (Friendly, *The Good Guys, the Bad Guys and the First Amendment*, 91). In addition to WLBT (NBC), Jackson had a CBS affiliate, WJTV, which was also negative and unfair to black viewers. It generally came in second to WLBT in the ratings war for total number of viewers in the market (ibid.). In 1966 Anselm Finch, black principal at Wilkinson County Training School in southwest Mississippi, developed a television program shown on WJTV called "The Mississippi Negro." The program also appeared in Louisiana. See *Clarion-Ledger*, August 6, 1966.

56. Friendly, *Good Guys*, 92, 101; Ford, *Broadcast Fairness*, 57. To win FCC approval previously, Lamar Life's WLBT management added several black-interest programs after 1964, including "a Negro student apprentice program," the appearance of black ministers during midday devotional services (rotating with white religious representatives). WLBT's management claimed to support integrated local and network programs on the station. Friendly, *The Good Guys, the Bad Guys and the First Amendment*, 99. On the WLBT case, see also Willard D. Rowland, Jr., *The Illusion of Fulfillment: The Broadcast Reform Movement* (Columbia, S.C.: Journalism Monographs, Association for Education in Journalism and Mass Communication, Number 79, December 1982), 12–14.

57. Washington, "Speech at the Atlanta Exposition," 675.

58. *Close-Up Magazine* (First Quarter 1967): 24. For this period see also Yates, *Mississippi Mind*, 68–78.

Chapter 5

1. Loewen and Sallis, *Mississippi*, 330; Arnold H. Taylor, *Travail and Triumph: Black Life and Culture in the South since the Civil War*, 258; *Clarion-Ledger*,

June 16, 1977; *Times Picayune*, July 4, 1977. See also Lawson, *Black Ballots*, 331. Even with the vote, many black Mississippians did not believe that real changes would occur through voting. Leslie W. Dunbar notes in *The South of the Near Future* (Atlanta: Clark College, Southern Center for Studies in Public Policy, 1980), 283, that during the 1970s black voter participation decreased in the South. See also Edwin Dorn, *Rules and Racial Equality* (New Haven: Yale University Press, 1979), 78.

2. *Time*, September 27, 1976, 40. See also Mack H. Jones, "Black Politics: From Civil Rights to Benign Neglect," in *In Negotiating the Mainstream*, ed. Harry A. Johnson (Chicago: American Library Association, 1978), 180–81.

3. *U. S. News and World Report*, May 14, 1979, 53; Daniel C. Thompson, *Sociology and the Black Experience* (Westport, Conn.: Greenwood Press, 1974), 177, 204–13; Taylor, *Travail and Triumph*, 253–55; Loewen and Sallis, *Mississippi*, 323–28. See also Roger Johnson, "Coping with Semiliteracy in Mississippi Education," in *Mississippi 1990*, ed. Walter M. Mathews, 80–91. The Mississippi Sovereignty Commission existed until 1973, when Governor Bill Waller refused to approve a funding bill for the agency. The state legislature abolished the commission in 1977 and sealed its records for fifty years. The American Civil Liberties Union filed suit in 1977 to force the State of Mississippi to open the commission's files. The case did not come to trial during the 1970s. (See chapter 6.) *Clarion-Ledger/Jackson Daily News*, February 21, 1982. See also *Jackson Daily News*, March 7, 1977; Dunbar, *The South of the Near Future*, 21; Daniel M. Johnson and Rex Campbell, *Black Migration in America: A Social Demographic History*, 170; John N. Burrus, "Urbanization in Mississippi," in McLemore, *A History of Mississippi*, 2:366–74; *Jackson Daily News*, February 15, 1971, July 27, 1977; *Clarion-Ledger/Jackson Daily News*, July 30, 1978; L. Alex Swan, *Survival and Progress: The Afro-American Experience* (Westport, Conn.: Greenwood Press, 1981), 104; *New York Times*, July 25, 1971.

4. *Social and Economic Profile of Black Mississippians* (Jackson: Mississippi Research and Development Center, 1977), 9.

5. On the general history of this period, see Woodward, *The Strange Career of Jim Crow*, 210–20; H. V. Savitch, "The Politics of Deprivation," in *Racism and Inequality: The Policy Alternatives*, ed. Harrell R. Rodgers, Jr., 5–35; Frances Fox Piven and Richard A. Cloward, *Poor People's Movements: Why They Succeed, How They Fail* (New York: Vintage Books, 1979).

6. *Ayer's Directory*, 1970, 1143; 1971, 1430; 1972, 987; 1973, 5; 1974, 1043; 1976, 1204; 1978, 494; *The Black Press Periodical Directory, 1975*, 11–12; Mitchell Memorial Library, *Mississippiana: Union List of Newspapers*, 31; interview with Henry Kirksey.

7. See *Social and Economic Profile of Black Mississippians*, 5–6, 9, 41.

8. The black educational press remained active in the 1970s at the historically black colleges and universities. For this period, see Thompson, *The History of the Mississippi Teachers Association*, 164–65.

9. On the issues, events, movements, and problems of the 1970s, see "Special Issue on the Bakke Case," *Freedomways* 18 (1st quarter 1978); Sloan, *The Blacks in America*, 62–80; "The Ebony Years," 112; "Mississippi Professor

Sues Alex Haley," *Chronicle of Higher Education*, May 2, 1977, 2; "Fannie
Lou Hamer Remembered," *Delta Democrat-Times*, March 16, 1977; Chokwe
Lumumba, "Short History of the U.S. War on the R.N.A."; Harry A. Ploski
and James Williams, eds., *The Negro Almanac*, 59; Tim Spofford, *Lynch
Street: The May 1970 Slayings at Jackson State College* (Kent, Ohio: Kent
State University Press, 1988).

10. On the national black press during the 1970s see Wolseley, *The Black Press,
U.S.A.*, 181–211, 321–32; Taylor, *Travail and Triumph*, 241–52; Suggs, *The
Black Press in the South*; Charlotte G. O'Kelly, "The Black Press: Conserva-
tive or Radical, Reformist or Revolutionary?," *Journalism History*; L.F.
Palmer, Jr., "The Black Press in Transition," 31–36; Ernest C. Hynds,
American Newspapers in the 1970s, 104–8.

11. *Mississippi Manufacturing Atlas* (Jackson, Mississippi Research and Development Center, 1975), 33; *Mississippi Statistical Abstract, 1977* (December
1977), 308–11; *Jackson Daily News*, August 5, 1977. A 1970 study found that
the *Clarion-Ledger* remained extremely weak in its treatment of black Mississippians. See Edwin N. Williams, "Dimout in Jackson," in *Our Troubled
Press, Ten Years of the Columbia Journalism Review*, ed. Alfred Balk and
James Boylan, 81–86. In addition, beginning in 1971, Mississippi's Choctaw
Indians published the *Choctaw Community News*, a twelve-page tabloid
based in Philadelphia, Mississippi. See James E. Murphy and Sharon M.
Murphy, *Let My People Know: American Indian Journalism, 1828–1978*, 96.
On the Choctaw Indians, see Catherine W. Cole, *Minority Organizations: A
National Directory* (Garrett Park, Md.: Garrett Park Press, 1978); John H.
Peterson, Jr., *Socio-Economic Characteristics of Mississippi Choctaw Indians*
(Starkville: Mississippi State University, 1970). On the white press's negative
treatment of Afro-Americans during the 1970s, see Vincent Harding, *The
Other American Revolution*, 204.

12. Wilson, "Voices from Mississippi," 62–71; *Commercial Appeal*, October 1,
1972, August 18, 1978; *Jackson Daily News*, April 5, 1972; *Clarion-Ledger/
Jackson Daily News*, May 2, 1982; Spahn, Spahn, and Miller, *From Radical
Left to Extreme Right*, 1:102; *Kudzu*, May 1970; *Reporter*, July 22, 1976; Jo-
seph P. Kahn, "Once a Week, but Never Weakly," 9–10; Silver, *Running
Scared*, 129–34; Charles Evers, *Evers*, 23–24, 172; Chet Fuller, *I Hear Them
Calling My Name: A Journey through the New South*, 210–15.

13. Spahn, Spahn, and Miller, *From Radical Left to Extreme Right*, 1:282, 2:820.
Elements of the extreme right displayed violent tendencies even toward the
moderate white press in Mississippi. On a cross burning at the *Capital
Reporter*, see "Editor Sees Klan, Vandalism Link," *Clarion-Ledger*, January
9, 1978.

14. Williams, "Dimout in Jackson," 86; Ray Jenkins, "Mass Media Changes in the
South since the World War," in *The Rising South*, ed. Robert H. McKenzie,
2:1290.

15. *Jackson Advocate*, January 3, 1970, October 23, 1976.

16. Ibid.; LaBrie, *The Black Newspaper in America*, 47. I recall discovering copies of the paper at the front door while in Jackson in 1974.

17. Greene hired Charles Tisdale during this period to serve as a roaming adver-

tising salesman for the *Advocate*, but this relationship did not always remain happy. Greene fired Tisdale in 1973 but later rehired him (*Jackson Advocate*, July 14, 1973).

18. Ibid., February 6, 1971. See also April 17, July 10, 1971. On Charles Evers, the first elected black mayor in a biracial town in the South since Reconstruction, see Jason Berry, *Amazing Grace: With Charles Evers in Mississippi.*

19. *Jackson Advocate*, January 3, 1970. Greene still criticized communism on the international scene during the 1970s. See ibid., March 27, 1976.

20. Ibid., April 4, 1970, August 30, 1975.

21. Ibid., April 7, 1976. Greene similarly viewed the NAACP during this period as the most significant organization working for black progress in the United States (ibid., May 10, 1976).

22. Ibid., January 19, 1977. At this time, the paper sold for twenty-five cents a copy and eight dollars for a one-year subscription, with an average issue ranging from eight to sixteen pages. On the end of the Sovereignty Commission and Greene's relationship to it, see Johnston, *Mississippi's Defiant Years*, 231–32, 375–83.

23. *Jackson Advocate*, January 3, 1970. In total, fifty-one advertisements appeared in this issue. The September 5, 1970, issue contained twenty-four advertisements. Whites purchased all of the ads in these two issues, demonstrating the continuation of the black boycott of the 1960s. Few black advertisements appeared in the paper during the early 1970s; of the nineteen advertisements in the January 6, 1973, issue, white advertisers paid for all but three—Denton Funeral Home, *Soul Silhouette* (a Compton, California, black publication), and a local house sale.

24. *Atlanta Daily World*, April 19, 1977; *Clarion-Ledger*, April 19, 1977.

25. *Atlanta Daily World*, April 22, 1984.

26. The central problem lay in the huge amount of reprint material that appeared during this period and in the underdevelopment of the editorial page and of special sections of the paper, such as the sports pages, women's pages, and book reviews.

27. *Jackson Advocate*, May 6, 1978. The *Advocate* was especially concerned about the plight of black businesses and the black press (ibid., April 29, May 20, 1978).

28. Ibid., January 10, 1978.

29. Ibid., June 17, 24, 1978. The *Advocate* also disliked bigotry expressed by any racial group (ibid., May 13, 1978).

30. Ibid., July 8, 1978. The change of the *Advocate*'s motto as early as April 1978 reflects Tisdale's influence at the paper (ibid., April 1, 1978).

31. Ibid., July 8, 29, October 5, 1978. These developments also included a growth in the number of advertisements in the paper. In comparison to eighteen advertisements per week in 1977, the July 22, 1978, issue contained forty-four (ibid., July 23, 1977, July 22, 1978).

32. Ibid., September 21, 1978.

33. For the period of LaFayette's first editorship at the *Advocate*, July–October, 1978, see the following issues on its positions on politics: "Charles Evers, What Chance Does He Have?," August 5, 1978; "Women Change to Chal-

lenge," August 31, 1978; "Killers of the Dream," August 31, 1978; on press freedom, September 7, 1978; on black leadership, September 14, 1978; on peace issues, September 21, 1978; on voting and the black community, September 29, 1978; on economic matters, October 5, 1978; on social concerns, "Minorities . . . Who Are They?," August 17, 1978, and "Education—A Deeper Meaning," September 7, 1978; on race relations, September 14, 1978; on black entertainment, July 22, August 24, 1978.

34. Ibid., July 8, 1978.
35. Interview with Colia L. LaFayette, Jackson, May 10, 1980.
36. *Jackson Advocate*, January 4, 1979.
37. Ibid., February 8, 1979. See also January 30, 1979.
38. On the *Advocate*'s major political, economic, and social positions during this period, see "What the Black Community Wants," January 11, 1979; on the Wilmington Ten Case, March 1, 1979; on voting, March 22, 1979; on black Republicans, May 31, 1979; on black leadership, May 17, 1979; on black landholdings, March 8, 15, 1979; on health care for minorities, January 29, February 1, March 29, 1979; on black spending habits, March 22, 1979; on housing in Mississippi, March 31, 1979; on education, May 10, 1979; on crime, February 15, 1979; on black prisoners and the death penalty, February 22, 1979; on race relations, April 12, 1979.
39. Ibid., July 12, August 2, 9, December 6, 1979.
40. On the array of positions taken during this period by the *Jackson Advocate* see the following issues: on politics, August 2, 12, 23, September 27, October 25, November 1, 29, December 6, 1979; on economic matters, August 9, September 27, 1979; on social issues, June 7, August 30, September 13, 20, 27, October 11, December 6, 1979; on the fate of black colleges, December 6, 1979. The *Advocate* continued its policy of opposition to homosexuality, especially with reference to black men (October 11, 1979).
41. The predominantly black National Newspaper Publishers Association (NNPA) twice awarded the *Jackson Advocate* national recognition in 1979 (for the best business section and the best Women's Page in the black press), reflecting the admiration that LaFayette's work had generated. The *Advocate* became "the first newspaper in the NNPA history to win two first place awards after less than a year of publication." See *Jackson Advocate*, June 20, 1979; interview with Colia L. LaFayette.
42. Interview with Robert E. Williams, February 16, 1980, Meridian; Robert E. Williams, questionnaire, March 18, 1980. Percy Greene, editor of the *Jackson Advocate*, gave suggestions to Robert Williams on how to run a newspaper during the early years of the *Memo Digest*. In the opinion of some individuals at the NNPA, Williams incorporated some of these ideas into the paper because Greene had such a good reputation for keeping the *Advocate* alive (interview with Robert E. Williams).
43. Interview with Robert E. Williams; LaBrie, *The Black Newspaper in America*, 48; *The Black Press Periodical Directory, 1975*, 11; *Memo Digest*, January 14, November 18, 1970, January 6, 1971, January 5, 1972, December 26, 1973, December 24, 1975, January 21, 1976, January 5, 1977, January 4, 1978, October 3, 1979. Between 1970 and 1978, an average issue of the *Digest* con-

tained between twelve and sixteen pages; in 1979, this number rose to twenty.

44. *Memo Digest*, October 3, 1979. Advertising (local open rate) cost $2.25 per column inch in the *Digest* in 1978. The paper belonged to the NNPA throughout the decade. *Memo Digest* advertising card, 1978.

45. *Memo Digest*, October 17, 1979. On January 14, 1970, four advertisements appeared in the *Digest*. (The paper had just resumed publication.) By November 10, 1971, this figure had increased to twenty-one, then to thirty-two on March 19, 1975; but by October 19, 1977, it had declined to twenty. The *Digest* could be purchased at newstands and at twenty-four businesses throughout Meridian. *Memo Digest*, October 19, 1977, October 3, 1979.

46. *Standard Map and Guide of Mississippi*, 14. Lauderdale County had a population of 65,451 in 1970. In 1980, blacks represented 32.2 percent of the county's population. *Ayer's Directory*, 1978, 490; *Clarion-Ledger*, August 20, 1970; *Jackson Advocate*, January 13, 1983.

47. Interview with Robert E. Williams.

48. *Memo Digest*, January 28, 1970, January 13, 1971. See also January 5, 15, 1972, December 25, 1974, January 4, 1978.

49. Ibid., January 14, 1970. In general, the paper followed a moderate course that included support for Democratic party candidates for public office. It supported the 1976 presidential campaign of Jimmy Carter. Interview with Robert E. Williams.

50. *Memo Digest*, January 13, 20, 27, 1971. As an expression of its economic concerns, the *Digest* joined the Meridian Chamber of Commerce in 1970 (January 21, 1970).

51. Ibid., October 3, 17, November 14, December 19, 1979.

52. *Natchez News Leader*, September 19, 1971, December 9, 1973; *Bluff City Post*, November 9, 23, 1979; *Mississippi News*, March 13, 1976; *Brotherhood*, August 20, 1976; *Pas-Point Journal*, August 30, September 30, November 1977, January, March, April 1978; *Metropolitan Observer*, June 10, July 1, 22, August 25, 1976. In 1977, black-owned business firms in Mississippi numbered 4,872, employed 2,767 individuals, and had yearly gross receipts of $164,848,000. See Barbara Taylor, Cliff Kuhn, and Marc Miller, "Research Report after Twenty-Five Years," 122.

53. *Ayer's Directory*, 1970, 1443; 1971, 1430; 1972, 987; 1979, 487; *Pascagoula–Moss Point 50/50*, July 26, 1979; *Tutwiler Whirlwind*, nos. 27 and 32 (no date [1979?]); letter from Jene David Rayford, Jr., to the author, February 7, 1980; LaBrie, *The Black Newspaper in America*, 47; *Mississippi Enterprise*, December 24, 1979; *Weekly Communicator*, June 6, July 18, October 16, November 7, December 12, 1976, January 2, August 12, September 23, October 7, 1977; *Highlighter*, October 24, 1975, February 20, April 5, 1976, May 1976; Subscriber letter from Gene L. Mosley to the author, February 8, 1974.

54. Mound Bayou *Voice*, June 17, May 27, July 12, 1970, January 17, February 11, May 27, July 1971; *The Drummer*, June 15, October 30, 1971; *Mississippi Mirror*, October, December 1978; interview with Henry Kirksey. In the words of its motto, the *Voice* was "Dedicated to the Total Freedom and Independence of the African American People in this country" (July 12, 1970).

55. *Close-Up Magazine*, April 1971; *Outlook*, February 1976; *Reaction Magazine*, 1976; *Street Talk*, May 1979; *Sunbelt*, December 1979.
56. *Outlook*, March, November 1976, June, December 1978; *Street Talk*, February, December 1979. The personal statements in *Outlook* included a monthly reprint of sections of James Meredith's book, *Three Years in Mississippi* (Bloomington: Indiana University Press, 1965).
57. *Reaction Magazine*, 1976. The magazine attempted to reach black college students in particular by devoting a large section of each issue to them.
58. *Sunbelt*, October, November 1979; Lynette J. Shelton, questionnaire, spring 1980. *Sunbelt's* excellent advertisement base included First National Bank, Gavin-Robinson Travel Agency, Tramot Computer Service, Village Book Store, Clinton Motion Machines, Golden Deeds Realty, Jackson State University, Century Funeral Home, and First Mississippi National Bank (October, November 1979).
59. *Sunbelt*, November 1979, 2.
60. On black magazines of this period in general, see also "Black Magazines' Popularity Up," *Commercial Appeal*, January 12, 1975; Eugene Redmond, "Stridency and the Sword: Literary and Cultural Emphasis on Afro-American Magazines," in *The Little Magazine on America: A Modern Documentary History*, ed. Elliott Anderson and Mary Kinzie (Yonkers, N.Y.: Pushcart Press, 1978), 538–73.
61. See *Black List*, 1:363; Mary Lee Bundy and Irvin Gilchrist, *The National Civil Rights Directory*, 104.
62. The RNA aimed to acquire five southern states (Alabama, Georgia, Louisiana, Mississippi, and South Carolina) for a new black nation in the Western Hemisphere. On its history see Imari Abubakari Obadele I, *Foundations of the Black Nation: A Textbook of Ideas behind the New Black Nationalism and the Struggle for Land in America*.
63. *New African*, June 29, 1971, June 26, 1976. The organ also took special interest in the general issue of oppression in the United States (e.g., Native Americans and the historical burden of black oppression) and in the black freedom struggle worldwide. In 1976, Sister Chinyere Abubakari edited the *New African* at Detroit; however, the journal still listed Jackson as the RNA's principal office (June 26, 1976).
64. *New African*, June 26, 1976.
65. *Clarion-Ledger*, May 12, 1980.
66. Lumumba, "Short History of the U.S. War on the R.N.A.," 75. An RNA Legal Defense Fund and Newsletter were created in the early 1970s to aid the defense of the RNA Eleven. See Mary Lee Bundy, ed., *The National Prison Directory* 72. See also *The New African P.O.W. Committee Newsletter* and the *R.N.A. Newsletter*, created in 1974 (*R.N.A. Newsletter*, March 1975).
67. *40 Acres and a Mule*, June 1978; editorial statement from Jessie Morris and Regina Banks to the author, January 1980.
68. *40 Acres and a Mule*, September 1978, December 1979.
69. Ibid., September 1978. Largely subsidized by the Emergency Land Fund, *40 Acres and a Mule* faced economic difficulties during its first two years of ex-

istence. Because of its focus on low-income farmers and landowners, advertisers hesitated to advertise in the journal. This problem continued after 1979. See also *Clarion-Ledger*, July 4, 1979; Earl Caldwell, "Gaining Ground on Black Property," 23.

70. Subscriber letter from *40 Acres and a Mule*, January 1980. On the Emergency Land Fund, see also Bundy and Irvin, *The National Civil Rights Directory*, 104.

71. Mississippi Industrial College also existed during the 1970s, but its viability came into question during this period because it had a weak economic base and few students. See George A. Sewell, "A Hundred Years of History: Alcorn A&M College Observes Centennial (1871–1971)," *Negro History Bulletin* 34 (1971): 78–80; Orde Coombs, "Jackson State College," *Change* 5 (October 1973): 34–39; Sammy Tinsley, "A History of Mississippi Valley State College" (Ed.D. diss., University of Mississippi, 1972).

72. In 1973, the *Herald*, a monthly, had an average press run of 4,100 copies. John I. Hendericks served for many years as its faculty adviser. See *Directory of the College Student Press in America, 1973* (New York: Oxbridge Communications, Inc., 1973), 192; *Alcorn Herald*, May 8, 1976, February 3, 1977; interview with John I. Hendericks, Lorman, Miss., March 24, 1977.

73. Sharon D. Luvene, director of public information, Rust College, letter to the author, March 24, 1981; *Directory of the College Student Press in America, 1973*, 194–95. At Rust, Brankley Spight served as the faculty editorial adviser to the *Rustorian*, the *Rust College Sentinel*, and the *Bearcat*. The *Rustorian* had a press run of 900 in 1973. *Directory of the College Student Press of America, 1973*, 194–95.

74. *Directory, 1973*, 193; *Blue and White Flash*, December 18, 1975, February 12, 1976, September 12, 1977, October 26, 1978, October 4, December 6, 1979. An additional thirty-plus publications produced at Jackson State University in the 1970s included *New Visions: A Journal of Contemporary Literature*; *Social Science Speaks*; the *Jackson Rodet*; *JSU Now*; *Faculty Resource Center Newsletter*; *The Gospel Truth*; *JSU Focus*; the *Campus Communicator*; and the *JSU Faculty News*. See also Rhodes, *Jackson State University*, 137, 203.

75. *Directory, 1973*, 194. See also *What's Happening: Faculty/Staff Newsletter*, active at Mississippi Valley State University since 1970 (July 7, 1981), 1; *Clarion-Ledger*, March 30, 1975.

76. *Directory of the College Student Press of America, 1980*, 127; *The Harambee*, November–December 1977, January–February 1978, November 13, 1979; *Tougaloo News*, October 1977. See also the press materials of the United Black Students of Mississippi, organized at Tougaloo College on December 3–4, 1971, dedicated to finding solutions to the problems of black Americans. See *The Drummer*, February 23, 1972. Tougaloo College also constituted a significant center for black Mississippi press activity because it served as the base for a key civil rights movement organ, *The Mississippi Newsletter*, issued by the Freedom Information Center, located at the institution. See James P. Danky, *Undergrounds: A Union List of Alternative Periodicals in Libraries of the United States and Canada*, 175.

77. *Directory of the College Student Press in America, 1973*, 192–95; Alferdteen Harrison, letter to the author, February 26, 1981; *Pine Torch*, October 1972, 1; *Prentissite*, January–March, 1978, *Black List*, 1:296–97; *Maroon and Gold Flash*, September 1979. See also Walter Washington, "Utica (Mississippi) Junior College, 1903–1947: A Half Century of Education for Negroes" (Ed.D. diss., University of Southern Mississippi, 1970).

78. *Directory of the College Student Press in America, 1973*, 192–95.

79. *Afro-Times Newsletter*, 1971, 1; Wilhoit, *The Politics of Massive Resistance*, 305.

80. See *Clarion-Ledger*, March 15, 1970. As a part of its work, the Mississippi Teachers Association also published the biweekly newsletter *Mississippi Teachers Association—NOW* at Jackson in the early 1970s and *Insight*, a legislative bulletin that aimed to keep black teachers informed about educational matters pending before the state legislature.

81. *Clarion-Ledger*, July 5, 1980; *Clarion-Ledger/Jackson Daily News*, February 19, 1983; *The Black Press Periodical Directory, 1975*, 24.

82. W. Augustus Low and Virgil A. Clift, eds., *Encyclopedia of Black America*, 725; *Minority Group Media Guide U.S.A., 1976–77: Ethnic and Minority Media and Markets in the United States*, 115–17; *Black List*, 1:169–70, 875–87; *National Black Business Directory, 1971*, 52. The thirteen black-oriented stations existed in the following cities: Bay Springs (WHII), Belzoni (WFLZ), Clarksdale (WROX), Cleveland (WCLD), Hattiesburg/Laurel (WNSL), Jackson (WJMI, WKXI, WOKJ), Greenville (WESY), Meridian (WQIC), Natchez (WNAT), West Point (WROB), and Yazoo City (WYAX) (*National Black Business Directory, 1971*, 52). In 1976, Mississippi's radio industry employed 520 people, 19 percent of them black. See Quida C. Drinkwater, "Discrimination against Women in Mississippi Newsrooms: An Exploratory Study," 52.

83. On black Mississippi personalities of this period, such as Beverly Johnson, Herb Anderson, J.D. Black, and Vernon Floyd, see *Jackson Advocate*, January 21, February 18, November 30, 1978; *Mississippi Enterprise*, August 23, 1975. On other personalities, see *Jackson Advocate*, March 5, 1981. A 1971 advertisement for Jackson's WKXI noted that the station brought black listeners "Music with the Soul professionals, Soul Generation news, Jackson State Football and basketball, Community service features, Fun contests daily" (*The Drummer*, December 15, 1971).

84. WJSU was established in 1976 as a student-operated and training station under the direction of the faculty of the Department of Mass Communications. It began as a 10-watt station in 1975 but increased in 1977 to 100 watts. Besides standard music, the station emphasized American jazz (the only station in the Jackson metropolitan area to do so) and development of new educational programs, such as a black history documentary series called "Family Tree." In 1979 the station won the Mississippi Broadcasters Association's Public Service Award for the series. See *Jackson Advocate*, July 1, 1980, April 8, 1982; *Catalogue of Jackson State University, 1979–1981* (Jackson, 1979), 27; interview with Bruce Payne.

85. The National Black Network (with seventy-three affiliates in 1974) included

programs such as "The Ossie Davis and Ruby Dee Story Hour," "Black Issues and the Black Press," and "One Black Man's Opinion." Another black-oriented news agency of this period was the Mutual Black Network, part of the Mutual Broadcasting System, with ninety-eight affiliates in 1974. See *Black List*, 1:157; Hal Bennet and Lew Roberts, "National Black Network: Black Radio's Big Brother," 141–47; Jackie Jones, "Spotlight On: Mutual Black Network," 31, 79.

86. Drinkwater, "Discrimination against Women in Mississippi Newsrooms," 52. In 1971 blacks represented 36.8 percent of Mississippi's popuation.

87. *Television and Radio Directory: The 1979 Media Encyclopedia Working Press of the Nation*, vol. 3 (Burlington, Iowa: National Research Bureau, 1979), part 1, 26, part 2, 26–27; *Black List*, 1:85–86. The eleven commercial television stations in Mississippi during the 1970s operated in Greenwood (WABG-TV), Hattiesburg/Laurel (WDAM-TV), Jackson (WAPT-TV, WJTV-TV, WLBT-TV), Biloxi (WLOX-TV), Meridian (WHTV-TV, WTOK-TV), Tupelo (WIWV-TV, WHTV), and Columbus (WCBI-TV). The state's eight educational stations were located at Jackson (WMAA-TV), Biloxi (WMAH-TV), Booneville (WMAE-TV), Bude (WMAU-TV), Greenwood (WMAO-TV), Meridian (WMAW-TV, Starkville (WMAB-TV), and Oxford (WMAV-TV) (*Television and Radio Directory*, part 1, 26, part 2, 26–27).

88. On blacks and the television industry in the 1970s see Denise Nicholas, "Blacks in Television: A Personal View from Inside Outside," *Black World* 25 (April 1976): 36-42; Lerone Bennett, "The Crisis of the Black Spirit," 141–44.

89. Vaughncille Molden, *Telecommunications and Black Americans: A Survey of Ownership, Participation and Control*, 137, 141; Lloyd Gite, "Broadcast News," *Black Enterprise* 20 (December 1989): 106.

90. Molden, *Telecommunications*, 141. See also "Reverse Migration," *Time*, September 27, 1976, 50.

91. On Dilday's role at the station, including his contract difficulties during the late 1970s with the station's owners, see "Dilday Case Still Unresolved," Jackson *Reporter*, June 16, 1977; "Black Leaders Contend 'Racism' in WLBT Board", ibid., July 28, 1977; "Dilday, WLBT Settle Controversy," ibid., August 18, 1977; "Dilday Contracts to Resume Duties," *Clarion-Ledger*, August 17, 1977; *Jackson Daily News*, August 17, 1977. On other areas of black interest in Mississippi television, see *Jackson Daily News*, May 21, 1973; *Clarion-Ledger*, August 14, October 8, 1975, September 2, 1977; *Jackson Advocate*, November 9, 1978, January 11, 1979.

92. The new owners of the station, TV-3 Inc., consisted of four of the original petitioning groups. See Molden, *Telecommunications*, 141–43; *Clarion-Ledger*, November 30, 1978.

93. 1977 study on employment trends among white Mississippi media companies found that of the respondents' 242 journalistic positions, blacks held 17 percent. See Gale S. Denley and Allyn C. Boone, "Mississippi Study Finds Media Hiring More Blacks," 375–79.

94. On this period, see also Francis Ward, "The American Press: Money, Power, Control," *Black Books Bulletin* 7 (Summer 1977): 16–19.

95. See "Little Changes for Blacks in an Unpredictable Economy," *American Libraries* 7 (December 1976): 680.

96. See Dennis Moore, "Mississippi Featured in CBS Examination of Blacks, Integration," *Clarion-Ledger*, July 22, 1979.

97. On the national crisis facing the black press in the late 1970s, see James D. Williams, "How Power Can Slip Away," *Black Enterprise* 8 (June 1977): 149–57. For excellent summaries of this period, see Vincent Harding, "So Much History, So Much Future: Martin Luther King, Jr., and the Second Coming of America," and Lerone Bennett, Jr., "Have We Overcome?," in *Have We Overcome? Race Relations since Brown*, ed. Michael V. Namorato, 31–78, 189–200; Anne Janowitz and Nancy J. Peters, eds., *The Campaign against the Underground Press* (San Francisco: City Lights Books, 1981).

Chapter 6

1. *Clarion-Ledger/Jackson Daily News*, February 22, March 8, May 3, June 28, 1981; February 7, April 25, May 9, 1982; March 6, May 14, August 7, 1983; November 4, 18, 1984; January 15, December 8, 1985; *Wall Street Journal*, June 16, 1981. Although Mississippi continued to possess the largest black population in the United States in 1980, 887,000, the percentage of blacks declined from 36.8 percent of the total population in 1970 to 35.2 percent in 1980 (*Jackson Daily News*, May 2, 1983).

2. *Jackson Daily News*, January 3, 1980, December 5, 1981, January 13, December 10, 1983, January 1, March 11, 1984; *Jackson Advocate*, January 13, 1983; *New York Times*, September 7, 1981, December 12, 1985. Intimidation of some black voters continued in Mississippi in the eighties; see J.H. O'Dell, "The South since Memphis," 76–77.

3. *New York Times*, August 18, 31, 1983; *Wall Street Journal*, November 17, 1980, June 16, 1981; *Jackson Daily News*, February 29, 1980; *Clarion-Ledger/Jackson Daily News*, June 11, 1981, May 2, 1982, January 1, December 10, 1983, June 24, 1984.

4. *The Standard Periodical Directory, 1981–1982* (New York: Oxbridge Communications, Inc., 1980), 1076; Carol Todd Robinson and Inez Wells, eds., *The 1984 Annual Minority Business Directory*, 55–56; McGhee, "Mississippi Black Newspapers," 66–67.

5. *Keynotes* 1 (February 1982): 1; *Jackson Advocate*, May 21, 1981; *Natchez Democrat*, January 3, 1980; *Southern Black Cultural Alliance Newsletter* 1 (November 1980): 1; interview with Robert Walker, Jackson, July 9, 1982. Also note the Afro-American Culture Organization, Columbus, Miss.; Opera/South, Jackson; Mahogany Performing Arts, Meridian American Muslim Mission Center, Hattiesburg; *The Douglass Report*, Jackson. See *Mississippi Muslim Journal* (May 20, 1983): 4; *The Douglass Report* 1 (February 1983): 1; Deborah LeSure, letter to the author, December 19, 1983; *Monitor* 2 (August 1984): 2. Although blacks in Mississippi prisons did not produce a publication during the early 1980s, they did contribute letters and commentaries to black newspapers such as the *Jackson Advocate*. For an

institutional publication of the Mississippi Department of Corrections, see *Inside World*, established at Parchman Prison in 1980 (*Inside World*, 1 [February 1, 1981]: 24; L. C. Dorsey, letter to the author, March 20, 1981).

6. On the economic conditions of black publishing and related concerns in the 1980s, see Jill Nelson, "NY Paper in Trouble," *Black Enterprise* 13 (May 1983): 20; *New York Times*, May 13, July 26, November 30, 1981, October 16, 1984; Sheila Tefft, "Threat to Minority Business Cited," *Clarion-Ledger/Jackson Daily News*, April 3, 1982; *Wall Street Journal*, June 14, 1981; Richard F. America, "How Minority Business Can Build on Its Strength," *Harvard Business Review* 58 (May–June 1980): 116–21; *Washington Post*, August 27, 1981; *Miami Herald*, November 1, 1981; Audreen Ballard, "Looking at Ourselves: What Do Blacks Think of Black Business?," *Black Enterprise* 10 (June 1980): 85–90.

7. *Ayer's Directory*, 1981, 512; 1984, 541.

8. *Clarion-Ledger/Jackson Daily News*, December 26, 1982, January 2, March 4, 1983. On student publications at historically white Mississippi colleges and universities see ibid., March 14, 1980, December 12, 1982, March 4, 1983.

9. *The Reporter* closed because of economic difficulties. See *Clarion-Ledger*, September 10, 11, 1981; *Ayer's Directory*, 1978, 494. On three other white Mississippi papers, the *Tishomingo County News*, the *Greenwood Commonwealth*, and the *Biloxi Herald*, see *Clarion-Ledger*, May 6, June 3, 17, 1984. In 1982, the printing and publishing industry in Mississippi employed 6,060 individuals in 275 establishments and had an annual payroll of $86,032,000. Most establishments had between one and four employees. See U.S. Bureau of the Census, *County Business Patterns, 1980: Mississippi*, 5.

10. *Delta Democrat-Times*, January 30, 1980; *Commercial Appeal*, January 31, 1980; *New York Times*, July 25, 1983; *Clarion-Ledger*, January 31, 1980.

11. *Clarion-Ledger/Jackson Daily News*, April 4, 1982.

12. *New York Times*, April 2, 1982.

13. The daily circulation of the *Clarion-Ledger* (a morning paper) stood at 71,624 in 1983, while that of the *Jackson Daily News* (an afternoon paper) reached more than 40,000. The Sunday edition, jointly published by the two papers, had a circulation of 123,000 in 1980. *Clarion-Ledger/Jackson Daily News*, April 3, November 13, 1983; Richard Weiner, *News Bureaus in the United States*. On the positive response to the new management at the *Clarion-Ledger/Jackson Daily News*, see *New York Times*, April 2, 1982; *Clarion-Ledger/Jackson Daily News*, April 18, August 15, November 7, 1982, March 13, 20, 1983 (on a Pulitzer Prize for distinguished public service for the *Clarion-Ledger*), April 24, June 12, 18, July 31, November 6, 1983, June 16, December 1, 1984. On the negative response to the new management of the paper, see *Clarion-Ledger*, November 16, December 26, 1982.

14. Gerald R. Gill, *Meanness Mania: The Changed Mood*, 33. On the appointment of a black, Bennie L. Ivory, as managing editor of the *Jackson Daily News*, see *Clarion-Ledger/Jackson Daily News*, March 3, 1985.

15. For the 1980s see especially *Jackson Advocate*, 1980–85, *Mississippi Enterprise*, *Memo Digest*, and the *Bluff City Post*.

16. Several editors worked at the *Jackson Advocate* in the 1980s, including Deborah LeSure, Colia LaFayette, Raymond E. Yancey, and Alice Thomas, all with college degrees. Charles Tisdale, publisher of the *Advocate*, holds a master's degree in the social sciences from the University of Chicago. The *Bluff City Post* had two editors, W.H. Terrell and T.C. Johnson. Johnson had completed one year of college study. The other papers each had one primary editor during this period; these editors held degrees from such schools as the University of Chicago, the University of Southern Mississippi, Tougaloo College, Jackson State University, and LeMoyne-Owen College. See LeSure, letter to the author, March 31, 1981; interview with Colia L. LaFayette; *Jackson Advocate*, April 15, 1982, October 6, 1983; William H. Terrell, questionnaire, March 4, 1981; Theodore C. Johnson, questionnaire, March 4, 1981; *Mississippi Enterprise*, March 21, 1981; Robert Williams, questionnaire, March 18, 1980. On the status of black professionals, see Lois Benjamin, *The Black Elite*.

17. One cannot overestimate the importance of black women at Mississippi newspapers. They often performed essential day-to-day tasks to keep poorly financed operations going.

18. *Mississippi Enterprise*, August 29, 1981; *The 1985 IMS/AYER Directory of Publications* (Fort Washington, Pa.: IMS Press, 1985), 549.

19. *Mississippi Enterprise*, January 17, 1981.

20. Ibid., May 2, 9, 30, 1981, December 18, 1982, February 9, 1985. Published on Fridays in the 1980s, the *Enterprise* continued to espouse Democratic politics during this period. See *Ayer's Directory*, 1984, 541.

21. Meridian *Memo Digest*, January 2, 16, February 6, 27, March 2, 12, 26, April 9, 1980. The *Digest*, published on Wednesdays in the 1980s, remained politically independent during this period. See *Ayer's Directory*, 1984, 542; *The Standard Periodical Directory 1985–1986.*

22. *Bluff City Post*, December 18, 1981, September 24, 1982, February 25, 1983, February 1, 1985.

23. Ibid., February 1, 1985; Theodore C. Johnson and William H. Terrell, questionnaire, March 4, 1980.

24. On August 23, 1984, the *Advocate* claimed that the paper was distributed in 247 cities in 35 states. Of Jackson's total population of 202,895 in 1980, the black population numbered 95,357 (47 percent). See Andrew F. Brimmer, "Black Leadership and the Revolution in Economic Policy," *Black Enterprise* 12 (October 1981): 34; U.S. Bureau of the Census, *1980 Census of Population, General Population Characteristics, Part 26, Mississippi* (Washington: U.S. Government Printing Office, 1982), 6, 8.

25. *Jackson Advocate*, February 23, August 23, 1984. All of the contributing editors held master of arts degrees, and three held Ph.D.'s. Ward held the position of chair of the Department of English at Tougaloo College, Dent worked as a professional writer in New Orleans, Lynch served as a professor of Afro-American Studies at the University of Maryland, and Phillips was a professor and former chair of the Department of Social Science Education and Geography at Jackson State University.

26. Ibid., January 31, 1980, March 5, June 11, 1981, March 18, June 17, 1982,

January 6, 1983, August 2, 1984, November 7, 1985. In general, Tisdale had free rein to operate the *Advocate* under his management style.

27. Letters to the editor occupied a significant amount of space in an average edition of the *Advocate*. For example, the paper published seven letters in October 1982 and three in October 1983. Unlike many newspapers, the *Advocate* generally published the full letters rather than excerpts. *Jackson Advocate*, October 7, 14, 21, 28, 1982, October 6, 13, 20, 27, 1983.

28. The official *Advocate* editorials appeared on January 13 (2), February 2, June 23, August 9, and October 18. For thirty-three weeks during this period, no official editorials appeared. For the period March–April 1980, four unsigned editorials appeared in the *Advocate*; over the same period in 1983, three.

29. "The Need for a Black Newspaper: The Problems of the *Jackson Advocate*," *Open Letter* (1980), Jackson, Mississippi; Deborah LeSure, letter to the author, March 31, 1981. The group's opposition centered on its disgust with the *Advocate* under Tisdale. In 1982 State Senator Henry Kirksey noted that other critics believed that the paper often "tends to deal with only one side of the issue. Traditionally black newspapers, in order to survive, have dealt primarily with the sensational. . . . The *Advocate* has had to do that a great deal" (*Jackson Daily News*, June 1, 1982).

30. *Jackson Daily News*, September 30, 1982; *Clarion-Ledger*, September 9, October 1, 1982. See also Marable, *Race, Reform and Rebellion*, 203.

31. *Jackson Advocate*, July 29, August 26, 1982; see also *Clarion-Ledger/Jackson Daily News*, May 29, 1983; *Clarion-Ledger*, May 4, 5, 1983.

32. *Jackson Advocate*, May 26, 1983. See also *Clarion-Ledger*, January 22, 23, 1982; *Jackson Daily News*, October 1, 1982 (see also August 1, November 7, 1985).

33. On the black agenda see *Jackson Advocate*, January 3, February 7, March 20, May 8, July 3, 1980, December 30, 1981, April 29, 1982, March 10, May 26, 1983, March 17, 1984. On black leadership see April 8, 1981, May 7, September 9, 30, October 21, 1982, February 3, March 10, April 6, 1983, January 19, March 17, July 19, 1984, February 28, March 7, October 19, 1985. An issue of special interest to the *Advocate* during this period was its claim that Eddie Carthan, former mayor of Tchula, suffered political persecution in 1980–81. Carthan's case centered on a number of criminal charges. First, he was convicted of simple assault on a police officer on May 1, 1981, and was sentenced to a three-year prison term. Second, he was convicted on October 7, 1981, on federal charges that he committed fraud in applying for a bank loan for day-care equipment. He received a four-year prison term. Finally, he faced charges that, together with his brother, Joe, he arranged the murder and robbery of a black Tchula alderman, Roosevelt Granderson. Although acquitted on these charges, Carthan remained in Parchman Prison (for the assault conviction) from May 1981 until March 1983, when Governor William Winter suspended his sentence. He immediately began serving the federal sentence but received an early release after serving eight months and twenty-one days at Maxwell Air Force Base in Montgomery, Alabama. The *Advocate* believed that Carthan's problems represented the

degree to which the white Mississippi political system would go to destroy a black leader. See the *Jackson Advocate*, April 30, 1981, May 2, September 9, 30, November 11, 1982, September 8, 1983; Frank Chapman, "The Ordeal of Eddie Carthan and the Fight for Democratic Rights," *Freedomways* 23 (1st quarter 1983): 10–13; *Clarion-Ledger/Jackson Daily News*, May 2, 1981, March 12, October 15, 1983; *Miami Herald*, October 25, 1982. For an assessment of local opinion in Tchula on the Carthan case, see the *Clarion-Ledger/Jackson Daily News*, May 27, 1984, and *Jackson Advocate*, December 12, 1985. On a national level, the *Advocate* criticized Mayor Wilson Goode's actions in Philadelphia during the M.O.V.E. events of 1985 (November 7, 1985).

34. On the *Advocate's* treatment of the Reagan administration, see April 30, December 30, 1981, March 18, June 3, November 25, 1982, November 15, 1984. On the New Right see February 14, 1980, December 9, 1981. On the white American media see May 1, 1980. On white Southern historians see March 18, 1982. The *Advocate* supported the political efforts of white Democratic politicians such as Representative Wayne Dowdy of Mississippi's Fourth Congressional District and Walter Mondale, 1984 Democratic presidential candidate (November 1, 1984).

35. Ibid., May 29, 1980. See also July 8, 1982, November 1, 1984.

36. See, on the Ku Klux Klan, ibid., February 7, July 10, 1980, March 19, 1981. On redistricting in Mississippi, June 17, July 1, 1982, June 16, 1983. On the political condition of blacks in Jackson, February 21, 1980, April 8, August 13, 1981, January 6, February 3, 1983. After a long campaign led by State Senator Henry Kirksey, the composition of Jackson's city council was changed from two at-large members to seven members, each representing a ward. In June 1985, the first elections held under the new system resulted in the election of three blacks—Louis Armstrong, Doris Smith, and E.C. Foster, to represent wards two, three, and five, respectively. See *Clarion-Ledger/Jackson Daily News*, June 2, 1985; *Jackson Advocate*, May 23, June 6, 1985.

37. *Jackson Advocate*, September 5, 1985. See, on Africa, August 27, 1981, July 14, October 21, 1982, September 20, 27, November 22, 1984, August 1, 15, November 7, 21, 1985; on the Third World, April 24, 1980, September 30, December 9, 1982, January 13, 1983, May 24, November 8, 1984, January 17, 24, February 28, April 4, 18, 1985. The *Advocate* viewed the plight of the American Indians with great distress (July 11, 1985).

38. See, on the need for black unity for economic progress, ibid., February 7, April 17, 24, June 19, July 17, 1980, June 3, July 29, August 5, 1982, June 30, 1983, September 6, 1984, February 21, March 14, 1985. For the *Advocate's* support for affirmative action, see February 14, 21, March 6, 1980, March 22, 1984. On the issue of high utility bills for Mississippians, July 31, 1980, January 27, 1983. The *Advocate* applauded the U.S. Supreme Court's ruling allowing a series of boycotts of white merchants in Port Gibson, Mississippi, during the 1960s (July 29, August 5, 1982). For the *Advocate's* attitudes toward the Carter administration, see April 24, 1980.

39. Ibid., March 5, August 6, December 17, 1981, April 1, June 24, July 29, 1982,

February 24, March 17, September 23, December 1, 1983, May 17, 1984, January 17, March 21, October 17, 1985. Outside of Mississippi, the *Advocate* was especially concerned about the financial difficulties of Fisk University, in Nashville (see November 24, 1983, January 26, February 2, 1984).

40. Ibid., February 7, 14, 1980, June 24, 1982, February 24, May 12, 19, December 1, 1983, August 9, September 6, 1984, July 18, 25, September 12, 1985. The *Advocate* criticized the Mississippi State College Board, the official body that regulated the public institutions of higher education (February 24, 1983, March 21, May 17, 1985). The paper also remained unconvinced about the extent of black progress at the University of Mississippi (April 28, May 5, 1983). On problems at Jackson State University during this period, especially the destruction of parts of the Department of Foreign Language, see November 26, 1981, September 22, 1983.

41. Ibid., January 17, February 21, March 6, 13, April 24, June 12, 1980, August 6, 1981, June 24, July 29, 1982, October 20, December 8, 1983, January 3, 10, February 21, March 7, 1985. As noted previously, the case of Robert Earl "Bubba" May, a fourteen-year-old boy who received a forty-eight-year prison term for armed robbery, drew the special attention of the *Advocate* (February 21, 1980).

42. See, especially, ibid., April 16, 1981, May 12, 1983; Jerry W. Ward, questionnaire, August 23, 1982. The paper expressed outrage about the multiple murders of black children in Atlanta (March 19, 1981). See also Toni Cade Bambara, "What's Happening in Atlanta?," *Race and Class* 24 (1982): 111–24.

43. *Jackson Advocate*, February 23, 1984; see also February 21, 1980, February 24, 1983, January 3, 1984, February 21, 28, 1985.

44. The *Advocate* supported national efforts to establish a holiday in honor of Martin Luther King, Jr.; see February 6, 1980, May 6, November 6, 1982, September 22, October 13, 1983, January 10, 1985. On Marcus Garvey, see August 12, 1982. On Malcolm X, see May 17, 20, 1982, February 28, 1985. On black women, see especially September 22, 1983, March 22, 1984; see also August 13, 1981. On the *Advocate*'s use of the work of a prominent black historian, Vincent Harding, see "God Is for White Folks," January 6, 13, 1983.

45. On the theme of Afro-American studies in the *Advocate*, see March 6, June 19, 1980. On American popular culture, see March 20, April 24, May 15, 1980, March 26, 1981, January 20, 1983. The *Advocate* praised the career and life of pianist Arthur Rubinstein on his death in early 1983. The paper believed that "in fighting for freedom for Poland, he inspired many to fight for Black freedom in America and the world" (January 20, 1983).

46. For 1981, see ibid. for works by poets Winston (March 12), Randall (April 16), Dorsey (August 27), and Thompson (December 17). For 1982, see Baraka (April 1), Dorsey (June 24), P. Mack (July 1), and Dorothy Whitley (September 23). For 1983, see Virgia Brocks-Shedd (February 24), Watkins (June 2), Braxton (November 10), and Chiplin (December 22). For 1984, see Herbert Harris, Jr. (January 12), Wesley (February 23), Brocks-Shedd

(March 22), and Chiplin, April 19, 1984. For 1985, see Ulysses Howard (May 2) and Margaret Walker (July 4).

47. On the black family for this period, ibid., February 17, 1983; on the black church, March 26, 1981, February 24, 1983, October 17, 24, 1985; on the black press, February 21, 1980, April 2, 1981, June 17, 1982. The *Advocate* also concerned itself with the social impact on the black community of prostitution in Jackson (December 17, 1981).

48. On examples of outside support for the *Advocate* from Juanita Jackson Mitchell and John Raye, two Marylanders, see May 5, June 30, 1983. For support from within Mississippi, see March 24, 1983.

49. In October 1984, the *Advocate* informed its readers that the paper's campaign to secure new advertisers had resulted in ads from Gayfers, WJTV-Channel 12, and Ferguson Furniture. Thirty-five other businesses and institutions still refused to advertise with the paper, including J.C. Penney, Deposit Guaranty Bank, Jackson Mall, Westland Plaza, A&P Stores, Winn Dixie, K-Mart, Woolworth's, WAPT-TV, McDonald's, Kentucky Fried Chicken, Dairy Queen, Capital Furniture, Cowboy Maloney, Burger King, the State of Mississippi, Joe's Clothing Store, TG&Y, Super D Drugs, and Eckerd's (October 11, 1984). The economic hardships at the *Advocate* were reflected in the fact that between April 1982 and December 1983, the paper requested bankruptcy proceedings on three different occasions. The paper survived each petition, however, and continued to publish weekly. See *Jackson Daily News*, June 1, 1982, December 16, 1983.

50. The income of blacks nationwide reached $140 billion in the early 1980s. See David Agtor, "Black Spending Power: $140 Billion and Growing," *Marketing Communications* (July 1982): 13–18.

51. Although the *TOF Weekly Magazine* also published, it was more a tabloid than a genuine magazine. Published at Jackson but devoted to Canton, eighteen miles north, it was a division of the Associated Enterprise International. In 1980, Johnnie B. Stevens served as editor, Zettie M. Hamilton as publisher, and Betty D. Smith as editor-at-large. An eight-page organ, priced at thirty-five cents an issue ($13.00 for one year), the *TOF* published black and white celebrity profiles, news briefs, and consumer tips. Advertisements appeared in the paper from Greenwood Food Center, the *Jackson Advocate*, Tate's Department Store in Canton, Anderson's Grocery and Market in Canton, *Sunbelt* magazine, and Robertson's Furniture and Appliance in Canton, among others (March 16, 1980). In 1982, *Chenier's Black Woman Magazine* began to publish at Jackson, edited by its founder, Dorothy Chenier. It put out two forty-page issues per year, each costing $1.50 per copy and containing articles on subjects such as education, religion, sports, fashion, horoscopes, politics, hair styles, and health issues (*Chenier's Magazine* 2 [October 1983]: 2, 9, 41).

52. The following 1982 circulations for black journals provide a good comparison: *The Black Collegian* (monthly), 254,818; *Black Enterprise* (monthly), 230,000; *First World* (quarterly), 20,000; *Freedomways* (quarterly), 10,000; *Sepia* (monthly), 50,000; *Equal Opportunity* (three times a year), 15,000.

Sunbelt, January 1980. See Ploski and Williams, *The Negro Almanac*, 1126–1227; Wolseley, *The Black Press, U.S.A.*, 123.

53. Black advertisements in *Sunbelt* during the first quarter of 1980 included such businesses as Peoples Funeral Home, Concept Ltd., Century Funeral Home, Wright Way Realtor, McLin's Body Shops, Fashion Setters, Sanders Cosmetics, Dillingham Associates, Louis A. Robinson and Associates, the Beauty Hub West, the Black Arts Music Society, Alcorn State University. White advertisements in the magazine included the City of Jackson, Ornamental, Ltd., WOKJ, Mississippi Power and Light Company, Standard Life, WJMI, New York Life, First National Bank, Jackson, First Mississippi Bank, Paul Moak Volvo, Tramot Computer Service, First National Bank of Clarksdale, the U.S. Army, South Central Bell, WJTV, and Jackson Music (*Sunbelt* [January–March 1980]).

54. Ibid.

55. Ibid., June–August, 1980.

56. Barbara Dease, "At What Price Assimilation?" ibid. (July 1980): 46–48.

57. On the historical significance of *Sunbelt*, see *Jackson Advocate*, February 28, 1980, February 23, 1984.

58. *Street Talk*, February, May, December 1980.

59. Ibid., February, March, May, September, December 1980.

60. Ibid., May 1980.

61. Ibid., see also February 1985.

62. *Forty Acres and a Mule*, January 1980, October–November 1980. A one-year subscription to the paper cost four dollars in 1980, and an average issue had between sixteen and twenty-four pages.

63. On the financial difficulties of the Emergency Land Fund and thus of *Forty Acres and a Mule*, see *Clarion-Ledger*, September 13, 1981; *Jackson Daily News*, March 2, 12, 1983. On black landownership see also Joseph Brooks, "The Decline of Black Landownership"; *Wall Street Journal*, October 20, 1982; *Clarion-Ledger*, October 1, 1983; *Clarion-Ledger/Jackson Daily News*, April 14, 1985.

64. *Monitor*, August 1982. *Monitor* should not be confused with *The Monitor*, an eight-page newsletter of the Mississippi Legal Services Coalition, also active during the 1980s at Jackson and edited in 1982 by Louis Armstrong (*The Monitor*, January 1982).

65. *Monitor*, August, September, October, November 1982, February, March, April, June, July, December 1983, January, March, April, July 1984.

66. *Keynotes*, June 1982.

67. Ibid., July–August 1983. The work of the Black Arts Music Society includes "residencies in schools and colleges; lectures/demonstrations/workshops; bookings and receptions for concerts/club dates." See also *Jackson Advocate*, March 24, 1983.

68. *Monitor*, September 1982, May 1983.

69. *Keynotes*, June, July–August 1983. For a complete list of the organizational journals during this period, see Appendix A. On the work of the RNA, see *Clarion-Ledger/Jackson Daily News*, November 8, 15, 1981; *New York Times*, August 9, 1983. *Soul Force!*, a monthly publication of the Oxford

Development Association, represented one significant black social organ during the 1980s (*Soul Force!* [February 1984]: 1, [March 1985]: 1). Local black printers such as the *Advocate* Printing Shop of Greenville and Nu-South Typesetting of Jackson have also aided the organizational publications by offering moderate prices for their services (Nu-South Typesetting flyer, Spring 1983). On other groups such as the Cross Communications Printing, R.E.D. Printing, Shaw Industries, Inc., Graphics and Printing, and Westside Printers, all located in Jackson, see Robinson and Wells, eds., *The 1984 Minority Business Directory*, 54.

70. On the Voice of Calvary Ministries, see John Perkins, *Let Justice Roll Down* (Glendale, Calif.: Regal Books, 1976) and *A Quiet Revolution* (Ventura, Calif.: Regal Books, 1982); *Advocate*, March 8, July 5, 1980; *Clarion-Ledger/Jackson Daily News*, February 20, April 28, 1982, April 30, 1983. In 1985 a new religious organ, *It's the Gospel*, sponsored by the Gospel Group Association, edited by Charles Brinston, appeared in Jackson. The sixteen-page publication appears monthly and is priced at $1.00 for a single issue or $12.70 per year for Mississippi residents and $15.00 outside of the state (*It's the Gospel* 1 [1985]: 1, 8).

71. See also the press work of other black religious groups in Mississippi: the General Missionary Baptist State Convention of Mississippi, the General Missionary and Education Convention, the General Progressive State Baptist Convention of Mississippi, the Progressive Baptist State Convention, and the Northeast Mississippi Baptist State Convention, Upper Mississippi Conference (Methodist). See Jack Winton Gunn, "Religion in the Twentieth Century," in McLemore, *A History of Mississippi*, 2:477–91; *Clarion-Ledger/Jackson Daily News*, February 19, 1983. On fraternal organizations see Harrison, *A History of the Most Worshipful Stringer Grand Lodge*; Alvin J. Schmidt, *Fraternal Organizations*, 100–101, 107–8, 173, 387; Karlton Stuart, *Black History and Achievement in America*, 190–97.

72. The major black educational journals of the 1970s remained active in the 1980s. See the *Blue and White Flash*, Jackson State University; the *Alcorn Herald*, Alcorn State University; *The Harambee*, Tougaloo College; the *Valley Voice*, Mississippi Valley State University; and the *Rustorian*, Rust College. *Directory of the College Student Press in America*, 124–27. For a leading scholarly publication based at a historically black institution in Mississippi, see the *Jackson State University Researcher: A Journal of Interdisciplinary Studies* (formerly, the *Jackson State Review*) 9 (Spring 1981). On the economic difficulties of Mississippi Industrial College at Holly Springs, which failed to produce significant press-related materials in the 1980s, see the *Commercial Appeal*, September 26, 1982. At the University of Mississippi at Oxford, the Afro-American Studies Program has published the *Afro-American Studies Newsletter* (3 [Fall 1984]: 1). See *Oxbridge Directory of Newsletters 1981–1982*, 97, and *New York Times*, November 23, 1985.

73. *Jackson Advocate*, December 10, 1981, March 15, 1984; *Clarion Ledger*, May 21, 1981.

74. Blacks owned 130 radio stations nationwide in 1981, three of them in Missis-

sippi. See Udayan Gupta, "Integrating the Airwaves," 125; *Miami Times,* February 11, 1982; Ploski and Williams, *The Negro Almanac,* 1234. On the importance of radio stations as a source of news, see the *Wall Street Journal,* March 3, 1981; Lynne S. Cross, *See/Hear: An Introduction to Broadcasting* (Dubuque, Iowa: William C. Brown Company, Publishers, 1980), 33–34. On the contribution to black radio of the more than ninety National Black Network stations, see *Wall Street Journal,* March 3, 1981; *Miami Times,* August 27, 1981.

75. *Black Resource Guide,* 39; *Jackson Advocate,* March 5, 1981, July 1, 1982, September 27, November 29, 1984; *Clarion-Ledger,* May 21, 1981; interview with Bruce Payne; *Jackson Advocate,* July 25, 1985. Mississippi had a total of thirteen public radio stations during this period. See *Clarion-Ledger/ Jackson Daily News,* September 16, 1984.

76. *Clarion-Ledger/Jackson Daily News,* May 21, 1981; *Jackson Advocate,* May 7, 1981. It was estimated that black clubs lost 75 percent of their Friday business during this period. For many blacks, WOKJ and WJMI's position reflected the fact that although blacks comprised more than 40 percent of Jackson's population, they did not own a single local radio station in that city.

77. Ibid., November 18, 1982.

78. Ibid., September 1, 8, 1983. The on-the-air staff at WJMI and WOKJ included fifteen blacks and two white sports announcers in 1980. *WOKJ-WJMI Black History Month Announcement* [1980?].

79. *Clarion-Ledger,* May 21, 1981. The paper noted that in 1981, WJMI "was among the highest-rated stations in Jackson with a strong youth audience, which is an important segment for advertisers." Thus, the station focused on music rather than news. In spite of its disagreements with WOKJ-WJMI, on November 8, 1984, the *Advocate* honored Bruce Payne, Jr., public affairs director for the stations, as a black "pioneer broadcaster" in Mississippi. On the role of Project Media—a Hinds County organization of black journalists in sponsoring the affair in honor of Payne, see *Clarion-Ledger/Jackson Daily News,* June 13, 1982.

80. *Jackson Advocate,* September 1, 8, 1983. Many blacks attribute part of WKXI's success to its program director, Tommy Marshall, a white man, and to outstanding on-the-air black performers. On the significance of one such star, Heavy Herb Anderson, who signed a $1 million contract with WKXI on April 18, 1984, see *Jackson Advocate,* April 26, 1984.

81. Ibid., March 15, 1984.

82. Ibid., September 20, 1984. On WOAD's public service efforts in the area of sickle cell anemia, see September 27, 1984. On the growth of the station, see December 6, 1984.

83. *Monitor,* July 1984.

84. *Jackson Advocate,* April 8, June 24, July 1, 1982. On WJSU's success in attracting funding outside of Jackson State University, see December 14, 1981. See also *Clarion-Ledger,* January 30, August 1, 1984; *WJSU Program Guide* (November 1984): 1.

85. *Jackson Advocate*, June 17, 1981, April 8, 1982. On the issue of student protest at the station, see *Clarion-Ledger/Jackson Daily News*, May 16, 1982.

86. *Jackson Advocate*, December 29, 1983, November 29, 1984; Aurelia N. Young, letter to the author, December 15, 1984. A series of problems prevented WMPR from beginning a daily broadcasting schedule before 1984, including funding problems and a flood that damaged the station's office and equipment.

87. *Jackson Advocate*, April 14, 1983. Two grants aided the struggle to create WMPR: $75,000 from the Corporation for Public Broadcasting and $197,000 from the National Telecommunications and Information Administration, both in 1981 (October 14, 1982).

88. Ibid., August 20, December 10, 1981, October 14, 1982. In its struggle with WABG-TV-6, WMPR received aid from the NAACP's board members, who signed a petition in early 1983 in support of the public radio station.

89. Ibid., April 14, 1983.

90. Ibid., November 29, 1984. On WMPR see also January 20, March 17, 1983, August 2, 1984; *Monitor*, December 1982, March 1983, 2; "WMPR-FM 90.1 Maxwell Broadcasting Support Letter," Jackson, 1984; "Sign-On WMPR-FM Fundraising Campaign 1983"; *Clarion-Ledger*, September 8, 1982, October 5, 1983; *Jackson Daily News*, December 28, 1983, June 26, August 22, October 31, 1984.

91. *New York Times*, January 28, 1984. Another study, by the *Television Factbook*, observed that in the United States enough television sets were sold in the early 1980s to distribute two to each family in the country. In 1982, the United States had an estimated 170.8 million sets (*Miami Herald*, September 11, 1982).

92. *San Francisco Examiner and Chronicle*, May 17, 1981; *Miami Herald*, July 31, 1982.

93. *Clarion-Ledger/Jackson Daily News*, June 7, 1981, May 23, 1982, February 27, March 20, 1983, July 14, October 14, 1984, February 3, 1985. WOBN in Bruce holds the distinction of being "the first low-power television station to begin broadcasting in Mississippi, and one of the first built in the nation." On the potential of low-power television, see also *New York Times*, April 11, 1982.

94. Udayan Gupta, "How They Did It: Black Television Station Owners," 106.

95. *Jackson Advocate*, February 19, December 2, 10, 1981, May 3, 1984.

96. For example, blacks in Mississippi and the NAACP alleged that at WAPT-TV in Jackson, "the station's management had discriminated against minorities in its hiring and promotion practices." The station's license was renewed after the FCC did not press the charges, however. See *Clarion-Ledger/Jackson Daily News*, January 16, 1983. A black critic of Mississippi television noted recently that several outstanding black television interview programs in Jackson disappeared from the airwaves in the 1980s. While Ruth Campbell's program, "Faces," still appears on Mississippi PBS, three other programs—"Pumojo," "Ebony Voices" and a program hosted by Phyllis Qualls-Brooks—no longer air. See *Jackson Advocate*, October 25, 1984.

97. *Black Enterprise* 10 (February 1980): 106.

98. *Jackson Advocate,* October 1, 1981, June 2, 1983.

99. Jackson residents E. W. Banks and Dr. Al Britton opposed the station's sale. Civic Communications purchased WLBT for $21 million. See *Clarion-Ledger/Jackson Daily News,* February 1, 1980, June 10, 1983, March 24, April 15, 1984; *Black Enterprise* 10 (February 1980): 106; *Jackson Advocate,* June 26, 1980, September 1, 1983. Also see Jannette L. Dates, "Commercial Television," in *Split Image: African Americans in the Mass Media,* ed. Jannette L. Dates and William Barlow, 253–302.

100. *Jackson Advocate,* February 2, April 12, 1984; *Clarion-Ledger/Jackson Daily News,* August 18, 1984. Walsh had resigned his position while Dilday was still in office—two days before Melton fired him.

101. The coalition was established in 1964 to deal with the Lamar Insurance Company, the original owners of WLBT. The boycott leaders included such black leaders as Bennie Thompson, a Hinds County supervisor, and Dr. James Anderson and whites such as Ken Lawrence, a local activist and an original coalition member and state AFL-CIO president Claude Ramsay. *Clarion-Ledger,* March 26, 1984.

102. Ibid. WLBT was cited in April 1984 "for several unfair labor practices" growing out of the station's handling of an effort on the part of some staff members "who petitioned to decertify a union at the station" (*New York Times,* May 29, 1984).

103. Melton reported in April 1984 that he received a television call from Dilday that "he took to be a threat on his life." Nothing developed from this allegation, however (*Jackson Advocate,* April 22, 1984).

104. *New York Times,* May 29, 1984. On Thompson, see also *Clarion-Ledger/Jackson Daily News,* May 27, 1984; Joe Klein, "The Emancipation of Bolton, Mississippi," *Esquire,* December 1985, 258–62.

105. *New York Times,* May 29, 1984, "Who Controls WLBT?," 48.

106. *Clarion-Ledger/Jackson Daily News,* July 14, 1984.

107. Ibid., August 18, 1984. See also July 13, 17, September 6, 1984. In late 1985, Buford Television Corporation, which owned 26 percent of WLBT, sold its shares to the other owner of Civic Communications. By 1985 Dilday had joined Sadler at WJTV, a CBS affiliate (*Clarion-Ledger/Jackson Daily News,* September 28, 1985).

108. On cable television and blacks, see Jeff Greenfield, "Hidden Treasures on Cable TV," *Saturday Review,* July 1980, 22–24. See also *Clarion-Ledger/Jackson Daily News,* June 4, 1980; *Los Angeles Times,* May 17, 1981; *New York Times,* June 25, 1981, January 24, 1985; Ploski and Williamson, *The Negro Almanac,* 1233–34.

109. Some experts believe that a low-power station can be created for a minimum investment of $20,000, a very low figure. WOBN's equipment alone cost $52,000. Low-power television signals generally reach a radius of ten to twenty miles. *Clarion-Ledger/Jackson Daily News,* February 27, 1983; *New York Times,* March 7, April 11, 1982. On the FCC and minority-controlled television stations, see Lloyd Gite, "Blacks at a Standstill in Tele-

vision." Gupta, "How They Did It"7; *New York Times*, May 27, July 27, August 10, 1984.

110. This information comes from data received by the author from journalists, editors, and publishers, including Tom Dent, Dilla E. Irwin, Theodore Johnson, Henry Kirksey, Colia L. LaFayette, Deborah LeSure, Bruce Payne, Ivory Phillips, William H. Terrell, Jerry W. Ward, Jr., and Robert E. Williams.

111. Jerry W. Ward, questionnaire, August 23, 1982; Ivory Phillips, questionnaire, August 23, 1982.

112. Tom Dent, questionnaire, August 23, 1982.

113. Deborah LeSure, questionnaire, March 31, 1981; Interview with Henry Kirksey; Theodore C. Johnson, questionnaire, March 4, 1980.

114. Robert E. Williams, questionnaire, March 18, 1980.

115. Ivory Phillips, questionnaire, August 23, 1982.

116. Mari Evans, *I Am a Black Woman* (New York: William Morrow and Company, 1970), 91.

Conclusion

1. Sheila Hobson-Smith, "The New World Information Order," *Freedomways* 21 (2d quarter 1981): 109.

Selected Bibliography

Manuscripts and Newspapers

The collections of vertical file material at a number of libraries in Mississippi and elsewhere in the South constitute the major manuscript sources available for study on the black press in the state. In Mississippi, the collections held by the public libraries of Natchez, Jackson, Meridian, Cleveland, Greenville, and Vicksburg proved especially helpful for this work, as did the collections at Tougaloo College, Jackson State University, Utica Junior College, Prentiss Institute, Alcorn State University, Rust College, Mississippi Valley State University, Mississippi State University, the University of Southern Mississippi, the University of Mississippi, Millsaps College, and the Department of Archives and History, Jackson. Important holdings outside of Mississippi included those at Atlanta University, Howard University, Amistad Research Center in New Orleans, the Library of Congress, and the Schomburg Collection for Research in Black Culture of the New York Public Library. This study also profited from work in the special collections on Afro-Americans at the Detroit Public Library, Princeton University Library, Indiana University Library, Butler University Library, Columbia University Library, Fisk University Library, the University of Pennsylvania Library, the University of Miami Library, Florida Memorial College Library, and the State University of New York at Albany Library.

The Department of Archives and History, Jackson, represents the major repository for the black press in Mississippi. They possess either the originals of the following journals or microfilm of them: *Jackson Advocate*, 1940–85; *Mississippi Enterprise*, 1939–85; *Highlighter*, 1976; *Taborian Star*, 1941–45; *Natchez News Leader*, 1971–74; *Mississippi Newsletter*, 1966–68; *Tougaloo News*, 1930–35, 1939–41; *The Harambee*, 1976–85; *Sentinel* (Mound Bayou), 1952–54; *Southern Advocate*, 1938–41; *Mississippi Educational Journal*, 1934–35, 1937–41; *Delta Leader*, late 1930s–early 1940s.

Interviews

Hendericks, John I. Interview with author, Lorman, Mississippi, March 24, 1977.
Irwin, Dilla E. Interview with author, Vicksburg, Mississippi, April 16, 1981.
Kirksey, Henry. Interview with author, Jackson, Mississippi, March 15, 1981.
LaFayette, Colia L. Interview with author, Jackson, Mississippi, May 10, 1980.
Payne, Bruce. Interview with author, Jackson, Mississippi, March 20, 1981.
Walker, Robert. Interview with author, Jackson, Mississippi, July 9, 1982.
Williams, Robert E. Interview with author, Meridian, Mississippi, February 16, 1980.

Secondary Sources

Alston, Roland. "Black-Owned Radio: Taking to the Airwaves in a Hurry." *Black Enterprise* 8 (July 1978): 20–26.

American Newspaper Catalogue. Cincinnati: Edwin Alden Brothers, 1882.

American Newspaper Directory. New York: George P. Rowell and Co., 1870.

Anthearn, Robert G. *In Search of Canaan: Black Migration to Kansas, 1879–1880.* Lawrence: Regents Press of Kansas, 1978.

Ayer, N.W., and Sons. *American Newspaper Annual.* Philadelphia: N.W. Ayer, and Sons, 1880–1985.

Barbeau, Arthur E., and Florette Henri. *The Unknown Soldiers: Black American Troops in World War I.* Philadelphia: Temple University Press, 1974.

Bardolph, Richard. *The Negro Vanguard.* New York: Vintage Books, 1959.

Bastron, Ellen Kay. "Black Oriented Radio: Analysis of Broadcast Content and Policies: A Case Study." Master's thesis, University of Illinois, 1975.

Baymor, Karl Michael. "An Analysis of Newspaper Uses and Gratifications by Blacks and Whites in Greenwood, Mississippi." Master's thesis, University of Mississippi, 1981.

Benjamin, Lois. *The Black Elite.* Chicago: Nelson-Hall, 1991.

Bennet, Hal, and Lew Roberts. "National Black Network: Black Radio's Big Brother." *Black Enterprise* 7 (June 1977): 141–47.

Bennett, Lerone. "The Crisis of the Black Spirit." *Ebony Magazine* 32 (October 1977): 140–44.

Benn's Guide to Newspapers and Periodicals of the World: Newspaper Press Directory, 1966. London: Benn Brothers, 1965.

Bergman, Peter M., and Mort N. Bergman. *The Chronological History of the Negro in America.* New York: New American Library, 1969.

Berry, Jason. *Amazing Grace: With Charles Evers in Mississippi.* New York: Saturday Review Press, 1973.

Berry, Mary Frances, and John W. Blassingame. *Long Memory: The Black Experience in America.* New York: Oxford University Press, 1982.

Black, Earl. *Southern Governors and Civil Rights: Racial Segregation as a Campaign Issue in the Second Reconstruction.* Cambridge: Harvard University Press, 1976.

Black List: The Concise Reference Guide to Publications and Broadcasting Media of Black America, Africa and the Caribbean. 2 vols. New York: Panther House, 1975.

The Black Press Periodical Directory, 1975. New York: Amalgamated Publishers, 1975.

Black Resource Guide. Washington, D.C.: Black Resource Guide, 1982.

Brisbane, Robert H. *Black Activism.* Valley Forge, Pa.: Judson Press, 1974.

———. *The Black Vanguard: Origins of the Negro Social Revolution, 1900–1960.* Valley Forge, Pa.: Judson Press, 1970.

Brooks, Joseph. "The Decline of Black Landownership." *Freedomways* 24 (3d quarter 1984): 191–94.

Brown, Geneva, Blalock White, and Eva Hunter Bishop, eds. *Mississippi's Black*

Women: A Pictorial Story of Their Contributions to the State and Nation. Jackson: Mississippi State Federation of Colored Women's Clubs, 1976.

Brown, Sterling A., Arthur P. Davis, and Ulysses Lee, eds. *The Negro Caravan.* New York: Arno Press, 1969.

Brown, Warren, comp. *Check List of Negro Newspapers in the United States, 1827–1946.* Jefferson City, Mo.: Lincoln University, School of Journalism, 1946.

Bundy, Mary Lee, ed. *The National Prison Directory.* College Park, Md.: Urban Information Interpreters, 1975.

Bundy, Mary Lee, and Irvin Gilchrist. *The National Civil Rights Directory.* College Park, Md.: Urban Information Interpreters, 1979.

Buni, Andrew. *Robert L. Vann of the Pittsburgh Courier: Politics and Black Journalism.* Pittsburgh: University of Pittsburgh Press, 1974.

Butt, Charles L. "Mississippi: The Vacuum and the System." In *Black, White, and Gray: Twenty-one Points of View on the Race Question,* edited by Bradford Daniel, 103–14. New York: Sheed and Ward, 1964.

———. *Mississippi Free Press.* Jackson: Hico Publishing n.d.

———. *Philosophy of the Mississippi Free Press.* Jackson: Hico, 1963.

Caldwell, Earl. "Gaining Ground on Black Property." *Black Enterprise* 8 (May 1978): 20–24, 48.

Campbell, Clarice T., and Oscar Allan Rogers, Jr. *Mississippi: The View from Tougaloo.* Jackson: University Press of Mississippi, 1979.

Campbell, Georgetta Merritt. "Extant Collections of Black Newspapers, 1880–1915 in the Libraries of the United States: The Need for a Scholarly Index." Ed.D. diss., Fairleigh Dickinson University, 1977.

Carson, Clayborne. *In Struggle: SNCC and the Black Awakening of the 1960s.* Cambridge: Harvard University Press, 1981.

Carter, Dan T. *Scottsboro: A Tragedy of the American South.* New York: Oxford University Press, 1969.

Carter, Hodding. *Their Words Were Bullets: The Southern Press in War, Reconstruction, and Peace.* Athens: University of Georgia Press, 1969.

Chambliss, Rollin. "What Negro Newspapers of Georgia Say about Some Social Problems." Master's thesis, University of Georgia, 1934.

Chapple, Levye, Jr. *History of Blacks in Greenville, Mississippi, 1868–1975.* Greenville: Greenville Travel Club, 1971.

Clark, Benjamin F. "The Editorial Reaction of Selected Southern Black Newspapers to the Civil Rights Movement, 1954–1968." Ph.D. diss., Howard University, 1989.

Cohn, David L. *Where I Was Born and Raised.* Boston: Houghton Mifflin, 1948. Reprint, Notre Dame, Ind.: University of Notre Dame Press, 1967.

Cortner, Richard C. *A "Scottsboro" Case in Mississippi: The Supreme Court and Brown v. Mississippi.* Jackson: University Press of Mississippi, 1986.

Crawford, I.W., P.H. Thompson, and J.H. Ballou, eds. *Multum in Parvo.* Jackson: privately printed, 1912.

Daniel, Pete. *The Shadow of Slavery: Peonage in the South, 1901–1969.* New York: Oxford University Press, 1972.

Danky, James P. *Undergrounds: A Union List of Alternative Periodicals in Li-*

braries of the United States and Canada. Madison: State Historical Society of Wisconsin, 1974.

Dates, Jannette, and William Barlow, eds. *Split Image: African Americans in the Mass Media*. Washington, D.C.: Howard University Press, 1990.

DeMond, Albert L. *Certain Aspects of the Economic Development of the American Negro, 1865–1900*. Washington, D.C.: Murray and Heister Publishers, 1946.

Denley, Gale S., and Allyn C. Boone. "Mississippi Study Finds Media Hiring More Blacks." *Journalism Quarterly* 54 (Summer 1977): 375–79.

Detweiler, Frederick G. *The Negro Press in the United States*. Chicago: University of Chicago Press, 1922.

Directory of the College Student Press in America, 1973. New York: Oxbridge Communications, 1973.

Drinkwater, Quida C. "Discrimination against Women in Mississippi Newsrooms: An Exploratory Study." Master's thesis, University of Mississippi, 1978.

DuBois, W.E.B. *Black Reconstruction in America*. New York: Russell and Russell Co., 1935.

———. *The Souls of Black Folk*. Chicago: McClurg, 1903. Reprint, Greenwich, Conn.: Fawcett Publications, 1968.

East, P.D. *The Magnolia Jungle: The Life, Times and Education of a Southern Editor*. New York: Simon and Schuster, 1960.

The Ebony Handbook, 1966. Chicago: Johnson Publishing Co., 1966.

"The Ebony Years: Significant Dates." *Ebony* 35 (November 1980): 110–12.

Emmerich, J. Oliver. *Two Faces of Janus: The Saga of Deep South Change*. Jackson: University and College Press of Mississippi, 1973.

Evers, Charles, *Evers*. Edited by Grace Halsell. New York: World Publishing Co., 1971.

Evers, Myrlie. *For Us the Living*. Garden City, N.Y.: Doubleday, 1967.

Fleener, Nickieann. "'Breaking Down Buyer Resistance': Marketing the 1935 Pittsburgh *Courier* to Mississippi Blacks." *Journalism History* 13, nos. 3–4 (Autumn–Winter 1986): 78–85.

Foner, Eric, ed. *A Reader in Afro-American History*. New York: Harper and Row, 1970.

Foster, E.C. "A Reflection on Afro-Mississippi Political Reconstruction from a 1980 Perspective: A Tribute to Mississippi Black Legislators." *Jackson State University Researcher* 7 (Summer 1980): 50–55.

Franklin, John Hope. *From Slavery to Freedom: A History of Negro Americans*. New York: Alfred A. Knopf, 1980.

Franklin, John Hope, and August Meier, eds. *Black Leaders of the Twentieth Century*. Urbana: University of Illinois Press, 1982.

Fraser, Walter J., Jr., and Winfred B. Moore, Jr. *The Southern Enigma: Essays on Race, Class, and Folk Culture*. Greenwich, Conn.: Greenwood Press, 1983.

Friendly, Fred W. *The Good Guys, the Bad Guys and the First Amendment: Free Speech vs. Fairness in Broadcasting*. New York: Random House, 1976.

Fuller, Chet. *I Hear Them Calling My Name: A Journey through the New South*. Boston: Houghton Mifflin Co., 1981.

Garland, Phyl. "The Black Press: Down but Not Out." *Columbia Journalism Review* 21 (September–October 1982): 43–50.

Garner, James W. *Reconstruction in Mississippi*. New York: Macmillan, 1901. Reprint, Gloucester, Mass.: Peter Smith, 1964.

Giddings, Paula. *When and Where I Enter: The Impact of Black Women on Race and Sex in America*. New York: William Morrow and Co., 1984.

Gill, Gerald R. *Meanness Mania: The Changed Mood*. Washington, D.C.: Howard University Press, 1980.

Gite, Lloyd. "Blacks at a Standstill in Television." *Black Collegian* 11 (November 1980): 84, 86, 186, 188–89.

Goldman, Eric F. *The Crucial Decade and After: America, 1945–1960*. New York: Vintage Books, 1960.

Gravely, William. *Gilbert Haven, Methodist Abolitionist: A Study in Race, Religion and Reform, 1850–1880*. Nashville: Abingdon Press, 1973.

Gross, Lynne S. *See/Hear: An Introduction to Broadcasting*. Dubuque, Iowa: William C. Brown, 1980.

Guerin, Daniel. *Negroes on the March: A Frenchman's Report on the American Negro's Struggle*. New York: George L. Weissman, 1956.

Gupta, Udayan. "How They Did It: Black Television Station Owners." *Black Enterprise* 10 (February 1980): 106–11.

———. "Integrating the Airwaves." *Black Enterprise* 12 (June 1982): 125–27.

Guyot, Lawrence, and Mike Thelwell. "The Politics of Necessity and Survival in Mississippi." *Freedomways* 6 (Spring 1966): 120–32.

Guzman, Jessie Parkhurst, ed. *The Negro Year Book, 1941–1946*. Tuskegee, Ala.: Tuskegee Institute, 1947.

Hall, Raymond L. *Black Separatism in the United States*. Hanover, N.H.: University Press of New England, 1978.

Harding, Vincent. *The Other American Revolution*. Los Angeles: Afro-American Culture Society, 1980.

———. *There Is a River: The Black Struggle for Freedom in America*. New York: Vintage Books, 1983.

Harkey, Ira B. *The Smell of Burning Crosses: An Autobiography of a Mississippi Newspaperman*. Jackson, Ill.: Harris-Wolfe and Co., 1967.

Harlan, Louis R. *Booker T. Washington: The Wizard of Tuskegee, 1901–1915*. New York: Oxford University Press, 1983.

Harris, William C. *The Day of the Carpetbagger: Republican Reconstruction in Mississippi*. Baton Rouge: Louisiana State University Press, 1979.

Harrison, Alferdteen. *A History of the Most Worshipful Stringer Grand Lodge: Our Heritage Is Our Challenge*. Jackson: Most Worshipful Stringer Grand Lodge of Mississippi, 1977.

———. *Piney Woods School: An Oral History*. Jackson: University Press of Mississippi, 1982.

———, ed. *Black Exodus: The Great Migration from the American South*. Jackson: University Press of Mississippi, 1992.

Hemmingway, Theodore. "Booker T. Washington in Mississippi: October, 1908." *Journal of Mississippi History* (February 1984): 29–42.

Henderson, Lloyd T. "Black Land Ownership in the South: Some Ways to Alter its Decline." *Sunbelt* 1 (December 1979): 26, 46.

Hendricks, Ruby N. *Profile of Mississippians by Race.* Jackson: Mississippi Research and Development Center, 1984.

Henri, Florette. *Black Migration: Movement North, 1900–1920.* Garden City, N.Y.: Anchor Press/Doubleday, 1975.

Herman, Janet Sharp. *Black Utopias: The Pursuit of a Dream.* New York: Oxford University Press, 1981.

Hogan, Lawrence D. *A Black National News Service: The Associated Negro Press and Claude Barnett, 1919–1945.* Rutherford, N.J.: Fairleigh Dickinson University Press, 1984.

Holtzclaw, Robert Fulton. *Black Magnolias: A Brief History of the Afro-Mississippian, 1865–1980.* Shaker Heights, Ohio: Keeble Press, 1984.

Hooker, Robert. "Race and the Mississippi Press." *New South* (Winter 1971): 55–62.

Huey, Gary. *Rebel with a Cause: P.D. East, Southern Liberalism, and the Civil Rights Movement, 1953–1971.* Wilmington, Del.: Scholarly Resources, 1985.

Hynds, Ernest C. *American Newspapers in the 1970s.* New York: Hasting House, 1975.

Jackson, Kenneth T. *The Ku Klux Klan in the City, 1915–1930.* New York: Oxford University Press, 1967.

Jackson, Luther P. "Race and Suffrage in the South since 1940." *New South* 3 (June–July 1948): 3–4.

Jacoway, Elizabeth, and David R. Colburn, eds. *Southern Businessmen and Desegregation.* Baton Rouge: Louisiana State University Press, 1982.

James, Arthur. "A Historical Look at Black Business in Mississippi." *Sunbelt* 1 (April 1980): 13, 35.

Johnson, Anthony W., ed. *Black Families and the Medium of Television.* Ann Arbor: Bush Program in Child Development, University of Michigan, 1982.

Johnson, Daniel M., and Rex Campbell. *Black Migration in America: A Social Demographic History.* Durham, N.C.: Duke University Press, 1981.

Johnson, Harry A., ed. *In Negotiating the Mainstream.* Chicago: American Library Association, 1978.

Johnson, Haynes. *Dusk at the Mountain: The Negro, the Nation, and the Capital—A Report on Problems and Progress.* Garden City, N.Y.: Doubleday, 1963.

Johnston, Erle. *Mississippi's Defiant Years, 1953–1973: An Interpretive Documentary with Personal Experiences.* Forest, Miss.: Lake Harbor Publishers, 1990.

Jones, Jackie. "Spotlight On: Mutual Black Network." *Black Books Bulletin* 5 (Summer 1977): 31, 79.

Jones, Laurence C. *The Bottom Rail: Addresses and Papers on the Negro in the Low Lands in Mississippi and on Inter-Racial Relations in the South during Twenty-Five Years.* London: Fleming H. Revell, 1935.

Kahn, Joseph P. "Once a Week but Never Weakly." *Quest* 44 (July–August 1979): 9–10.

Kerlin, R.T. *The Voice of the Negro.* New York: E.P. Dutton and Co., 1920. Reprint, New York: Arno Press and the *New York Times*, 1968.

King, Martin Luther, Jr. *Stride toward Freedom: The Montgomery Story.* New York: Harper and Row, 1958.

Kinzer, Robert H., and Edward Sagarin. *The Negro in American Business.* New York: Greenberg, 1950.

Kirwan, Albert D. *Revolt of the Rednecks: Mississippi Politics, 1876–1925.* Lexington: University of Kentucky Press, 1951. Reprint, Gloucester, Mass.: Peter Smith, 1964.

LaBrie, Henry. *The Black Newspaper in America: A Guide.* Iowa City: University of Iowa, Institute for Communication Studies, 1970.

_____. *A Survey of Black Newspapers in America.* Kennebunkport, Maine: Mercer House Press, 1979.

_____, ed. *Perspectives of the Black Press: 1974.* Kennebunkport, Maine: Mercer House Press, 1974.

Lawson, Steven F. *Black Ballots: Voting Rights in the South, 1944–1969.* New York: Columbia University Press, 1976.

The Leading Afro-Americans of Vicksburg, Mississippi: Their Enterprises, Churches, Schools, Lodges and Societies. Vicksburg: Biographical Publishing Co., 1908.

"Leads 400,000 Baptists." *US Magazine* (February 1954): 24–26.

Litwack, Leon. *Been in the Storm So Long: The Aftermath of Slavery.* New York: Vintage Books, 1978.

Litwack, Leon, and August Meier, eds. *Black Leaders of the Nineteenth Century.* Urbana: University of Illinois Press, 1988.

Loewen, James W. *The Mississippi Chinese: Between Blacks and Whites.* Cambridge: Harvard University Press, 1971.

Loewen, James W., and Charles Sallis, eds. *Mississippi: Conflict and Change.* New York: Pantheon Books, 1974.

Loewenberg, Bert James, and Ruth Bogin, eds. *Black Women in Nineteenth-Century American Life: Their Words, Their Thoughts, Their Feelings.* University Park: Pennsylvania State University Press, 1976.

Logan, Rayford W., ed. *The Attitude of the Southern White Press toward Negro Suffrage.* Washington, D.C.: Foundation Publishers, 1940.

Logan, Rayford W., and Michael R. Winston, eds. *Dictionary of American Negro Biography.* New York: W.W. Norton and Co., 1982.

Logue, Calvin M., and Howard Dorgan, eds. *The Oratory of Southern Demagogues.* Baton Rouge: Louisiana State University Press, 1981.

Long, Howard Rusk, ed. *Main Street Militants: An Anthology from Grassroots Editors.* Carbondale: Southern Illinois University Press, 1977.

Low, W. Augustus, and Virgil A. Clift, eds. *Encyclopedia of Black America.* New York: McGraw-Hill Book Co., 1981.

Lumumba, Chokwe. "Short History of the U.S. War on the R.N.A." *Black Scholar* 12 (January–February 1981): 72–81.

Lyle, Jack, ed. *The Black American and the Press.* Los Angeles: Ward Ritchie Press, 1968.

Lynch, John Roy. *Reminiscences of an Active Life: The Autobiography of John Roy Lynch.* Edited by John Hope Franklin. Chicago: University of Chicago Press, 1970.

MacDonald, J. Fred. *Blacks and White T.V.: Afro-Americans in Television since 1948.* Chicago: Nelson-Hall, 1983.

McFadden, Roland. "A Study of the *Jackson Advocate* Newspaper Reports of Specific Change in Mississippi from 1954–1974." Master's thesis, Jackson State University, 1981.

McGhee, Flora Ann Caldwell. "Mississippi Black Newspapers: Their History, Content, and Future." Ph.D. diss., University of Southern Mississippi, 1985.

McKenzie, Robert H., ed. *The Rising South.* 2 vols. Tuscaloosa: University of Alabama Press, 1976.

McLemore, Richard Aubrey, ed. *A History of Mississippi.* 2 vols. Hattiesburg: University and College Press of Mississippi, 1973.

McMillen, Neil R. "Black Enfranchisement in Mississippi: Federal Enforcement and Black Protest in the 1960s." *Journal of Southern History* 43 (August 1977): 351–72.

———. *Dark Journey: Black Mississippians in the Age of Jim Crow.* Urbana: University of Illinois Press, 1989.

McPherson, James M. *The Negro's Civil War.* New York: Vintage Books, 1965.

McRaney, Bob, Sr. *The History of Radio in Mississippi.* West Point, Miss.: History of Radio in Mississippi Fund, 1979.

Marable, Manning. *Race, Reform and Rebellion: The Second Reconstruction in Black America, 1945–1982.* Jackson: University Press of Mississippi, 1984.

Mars, Florence. *Witness in Philadelphia.* Baton Rouge: Louisiana State University Press, 1977.

Martin, Tony. *Race First: The Ideological and Organizational Struggles of Marcus Garvey and the Universal Negro Improvement Association.* Westport, Conn.: Greenwood Press, 1976.

Mathews, Walter M., ed. *Mississippi 1990.* Jackson: University Press of Mississippi, 1981.

Meier, August. *Negro Thought in America, 1880–1915: Racial Ideologies in the Age of Booker T. Washington.* Ann Arbor: University of Michigan Press, 1963.

Meier, August, and Elliott Rudwick. *From Plantation to Ghetto.* New York: Hill and Wang, 1970.

———. *Along the Color Line: Explorations in the Black Experience.* Urbana: University of Illinois Press, 1976.

Minority Group Media Guide U.S.A., 1976–1977: Ethnic and Minority Markets in the United States. Los Angeles: Chester L. Washington, 1977.

Mitchell Memorial Library. *Mississippiana: Union List of Newspapers.* Starkville: Mississippi State University, 1971.

Molden, Vaughncille. *Telecommunications and Black Americans: A Survey of Ownership, Participation and Control.* St. Louis: Washington University, Center for Development Technology and Program in Technology and Human Affairs, 1975.

Moody, Ann. *Coming of Age in Mississippi.* New York: Dell Publishers, 1970.

Murphy, James E., and Sharon M. Murphy. *Let My People Know: American Indian Journalism, 1828–1978.* Norman: University of Oklahoma Press, 1981.

Murray, Florence, ed. *The Negro Handbook.* New York: W. Malliet, 1944.

Myrdal, Gunnar. *An American Dilemma*. New York: Harper and Row, 1944.

Namorato, Michael V., ed. *Have We Overcome? Race Relations since Brown*. Jackson: University Press of Mississippi, 1975.

National Black Business Directory, 1971. Minneapolis: National Buy-Black Campaign, National Minority Business Directories, 1970.

Negro Newspapers on Microfilm: A Selected List. Washington, D.C.: Library of Congress, 1953.

Newby, I. A. *Jim Crow's Defense: Anti-Negro Thought in America, 1900–1930*. Baton Rouge: Louisiana State University Press, 1965.

Nielson, David Gordon. *Black Ethos: Northern Urban Negro Life and Thought, 1890–1930*. Westport, Conn.: Greenwood Press, 1977.

Oak, Vishnu V. *The Negro Newspaper*. Westport, Conn.: Negro Universities Press, 1948.

Obadele, Imari Abubakari, I. *Foundations of the Black Nation: A Textbook of Ideas behind the New Black Nationalism and the Struggle for Land in America*. Detroit and San Francisco: House of Songhay and Julian Richardson Associates, 1975.

O'Dell, J. H. "Climbin' Jacob's Ladder: The Life and Times of the Freedom Movement." *Freedomways* 9 (Winter 1969): 7–23.

———. "The South since Memphis." *Freedomways* 22 (2d quarter 1982): 68–80.

O'Kelly, Charlotte G. "The Black Press: Conservative or Radical, Reformist or Revolutionary?" *Journalism History* 4 (Winter 1977–78): 114–16.

Ottley, Roi. *"New World a-Coming": Inside Black America*. Boston: Houghton Mifflin Co., 1943.

Oxbridge Directory of Newsletters, 1981–1982. New York: Oxbridge Communications, 1981.

Painter, Nell Irvin. *Exodusters: Black Migration to Kansas after Reconstruction*. New York: Alfred A. Knopf, 1977.

Palmer, L. F., Jr. "The Black Press in Transition." *Columbia Journalism Review* 9 (Spring 1970): 31–36.

Patterson, James T. *America's Struggle against Poverty, 1900–1980*. Cambridge: Harvard University Press, 1981.

Payne, Cleveland. *Laurel: A History of the Black Community, 1882–1962*. Laurel, Miss.: privately printed, 1990.

Payne, Les. "Black Reporters, White Press and the Jackson Campaign." *Columbia Journalism Review* 28 (July–August 1984): 32–37.

Penn, I. Garland. *The Afro-American Press and Its Editors*. Springfield, Mass.: Willey, 1891. Reprint, New York: Arno Press and the *New York Times*, 1969.

Peters, William. *The Southern Temper*. Garden City, N.Y.: Doubleday, 1959.

Pickney, Alphonso. *The Myth of Black Progress*. Cambridge and New York: Cambridge University Press, 1984.

Ploski, Harry A., and James Williams, eds. *The Negro Almanac: A Reference Work on the Afro American*. New York: John Wiley and Sons, 1983.

Ploski, Harry A., Otto J. Lindenmeyer, and Henry Kaiser, eds. *Reference Library of Black America*. New York: Bellwether, 1971.

Prenshaw, Peggy W., and Jesse O. McKee, eds. *Sense of Place: Mississippi*. Jackson: University Press of Mississippi, 1979.

Pride, Armistead Scott. "Negro Newspapers: Yesterday, Today and Tomorrow." *Journalism Quarterly* 28 (Spring 1951): 179–88.

———. "A Register and History of Negro Newspapers in the United States: 1827–1950." Ph.D. diss., Northwestern University, 1950.

Rabinowitz, Howard N. *Race Relations in the Urban South, 1865–1890.* New York: Oxford University Press, 1978.

Randel, William Peirce. *The Ku Klux Klan: A Century of Infamy.* Radnor, Pa.: Clifton Book Co., 1965.

Range, Leslie G., ed. *Selected Proceedings of the Symposium on the State of the Black Economy in Mississippi.* Jackson: Office for Black Economic Development, Mississippi Research and Development Center, 1978.

Record, Wilson. *The Negro and the Communist Party.* Chapel Hill: University of North Carolina Press, 1951.

Report of the National Advisory Commission on Civil Disorders. Presidential Report. Washington, D.C.: Government Printing Office, 1968.

Rhodes, Lelia G. *Jackson State University: The First Hundred Years, 1877–1977.* Jackson: University Press of Mississippi, 1979.

Richards, Dona. "With Our Minds Set on Freedom." *Freedomways* 5 (Spring 1965): 324–42.

Robinson, Carol Todd, and Inez Wells, eds. *The 1984 Annual Minority Business Directory.* Clinton, Miss.: Robinson-Wells and Co., 1984.

Rodgers, Harrell R., Jr., ed. *Racism and Inequality: The Policy Alternatives.* San Francisco: W.H. Freeman and Co., 1975.

Roebuck, Julian B. *Lotus among the Magnolias: The Mississippi Chinese.* Jackson: University Press of Mississippi, 1982.

Rowan, Ford. *Broadcast Fairness Doctrine, Practice, Prospects: A Reappraisal of the Fairness Doctrine and Equal Time Rule.* New York: Longman, 1984.

Salter, John R., Jr. *Jackson, Mississippi: An American Chronicle of Struggle and Schism.* Hicksville, N.Y.: Exposition Press, 1979.

Sangins, David, ed. *What Was Freedom's Price?* Jackson: University Press of Mississippi, 1978.

Sawyer, Frank B., and Ruth Castor, eds. *U.S. Negro World, 1966: Directory of U.S. Negro Newspapers, Magazines and Periodicals.* Ann Arbor: University Microfilms, 1970.

Schmidt, Alvin J. *Fraternal Organizations.* Westport, Conn.: Greenwood Press, 1980.

Schuyler, George S. "Freedom of the Press in Mississippi." *Crisis* 43 (October 1936): 302–4.

Seligmann, Herbert J. *The Negro Faces America.* New York: Press of Clarence S. Nathan, 1920.

Sewell, George Alexander, and Margaret L. Dwight. *Mississippi Black History Makers.* Jackson: University Press of Mississippi, 1984.

Sherrill, Robert. *Gothic Politics in the Deep South: Stars of the New Confederacy.* New York: Ballantine Books, 1968.

Silver, James. *Mississippi: The Closed Society.* New York: Harcourt, Brace and World, 1964.

_____. *Running Scared: Silver in Mississippi.* Jackson: University Press of Mississippi, 1984.

Simmons, William J. *Men of Mark.* Chicago: George M. Rewell and Co., 1887. Reprint, New York: Arno Press and the *New York Times,* 1968.

Sitkoff, Harvard. *A New Deal for Blacks: The Emergence of Civil Rights as a National Issue.* Vol. 1: *The Depression Decade.* New York: Oxford University Press, 1978.

Skates, John R. "Mississippi." In *The Encyclopedia of Southern History,* edited by David C. Roller and Robert W. Twyman, 282–36. Baton Rouge: Louisiana State University Press, 1976.

Sloan, Irving J., ed. *The Blacks in America, 1492–1977: A Chronology and Fact Book.* Dobbs Ferry, N.Y.: Oceana Publications, 1977.

Smead, Howard. *Blood Justice: The Lynching of Mack Charles Parker.* New York: Oxford University Press, 1986.

Smith, Frank E. *Congressman from Mississippi.* New York: Pantheon Books, 1964.

Smith-Hobson, Sheila. "The New World Information Order." *Freedomways* 21 (2d quarter 1981): 106–14.

Social and Economic Profile of Black Mississippians. Jackson: Mississippi Research and Development Center, 1977.

Spahn, Theodore J., Janet M. Spahn, and Robert H. Miller. *From Radical Left to Extreme Right.* 2 vols. Metuchen, N.J.: Scarecrow Press, 1970.

Spofford, Tim. *Lynch Street: The May 1970 Slayings at Jackson State College.* Kent, Ohio: Kent State University Press, 1988.

The Standard Periodical Directory, 1985–1986. New York: Oxbridge Communications, 1985.

Stead, Alma Henley. "The Media as Viewed by Fifteen Black Journalists in Mississippi." Master's thesis, University of Mississippi, 1979.

Stuart, Karlton. *Black History and Achievement in America.* Phoenix, Ariz.: Phoenix Books, 1982.

Suggs, Henry Lewis, ed. *The Black Press in the South, 1865–1979.* Westport, Conn.: Greenwood Press, 1983.

_____. *P.B. Young, Newspaperman: Race, Politics, and Journalism in the New South, 1910–1962.* Charlottesville: University Press of Virginia, 1988.

Taylor, Arnold H. *Travail and Triumph: Black Life and Culture in the South since the Civil War.* Westport, Conn.: Greenwood Press, 1976.

Taylor, Barbara, Cliff Kuhn, and Marc Miller. "Research Report after Twenty-Five Years." *Southern Exposure* 9 (Spring 1981): 120–24.

Thompson, Cleopatra. *The History of the Mississippi Teachers Association.* Washington, D.C.: NEA Teacher Rights and Mississippi Teachers Association, 1973.

Thompson, Julius E. *The Black Press in Mississippi, 1865–1985: A Directory.* West Cornwall, Conn.: Locust Hill Press, 1988.

_____. *Hiram R. Revels, 1827–1901: A Biography.* New York: Arno Press and the *New York Times,* 1982.

Thompson, Patrick H. *The History of Negro Baptists in Mississippi.* Jackson: R.W. Bailey Printing Co., 1898.

Thornbrough, Emma Lou. "American Negro Newspapers, 1880–1914." *Business History Review* 41 (1st quarter 1966): 467–90.

———, ed. *Black Reconstructionists.* Englewood Cliffs, N.J.: Prentice-Hall, 1972.

Tinney, James S., and Justine J. Rector, eds. *Issues and Trends in Afro-American Journalism.* Washington, D.C.: University Press of America, 1980.

U.S. Bureau of the Census. *Census of Population.* Washington, D.C.: Government Printing Office, 1860, 1950, 1980.

———. *County Business Patterns, 1980: Mississippi.* Washington, D.C.: Government Printing Office, 1982.

U.S. Department of Justice. *Directory of Organizations Serving Minority Communications.* Washington, D.C.: Government Printing Office, 1971.

Vorspan, Albert. "The Iconoclast of Petal, Mississippi." *The Reporter* 16 (March 21, 1957): 33–35.

Wade, F. John. "The Development of Mississippi's Economy since 1950." In *Sense of Place: Mississippi,* edited by Peggy W. Prenshaw and Jesse O. McKee. Jackson: University Press of Mississippi, 1979.

Wallace, Jesse Thomas. *A History of the Negroes of Mississippi from 1865 to 1890.* Jackson: published by the author, 1927. Reprint, Chicago: Johnson Reprint, 1970.

Washburn, Patrick S. *A Question of Sedition: The Federal Government's Investigation of the Black Press during World War II.* New York: Oxford University Press, 1986.

Washington, Booker T. "Progress of the Negro Race in Mississippi." *World's Work* 13 (March 1909): 409–13.

Weiner, Richard. *News Bureaus in the United States.* New York: Public Relations Publishing Co., 1981.

Wells, Ida B. *Crusade For Justice.* Edited by Alfreda M. Duster. Chicago: University of Chicago Press, 1970.

Wharton, Vernon Lane. *The Negro in Mississippi, 1865–1890.* Chapel Hill: University of North Carolina Press, 1947. Reprint, New York: Harper and Row, 1965.

White, John, "Veiled Testimony: Negro Spirituals and the Slave Experience." *Journal of American Studies* 17 (August 1983): 251–63.

Whittemore, L.H. *Together: A Reporter's Journey into the New Black Politics.* New York: William Morrow and Co., 1971.

Who's Who among Black Americans, 1977–1978. 2 vols. Northbrook, Ill.: Who's Who Among Black Americans, 1977.

Who's Who of the Colored Race. Chicago: Half-Century Anniversary of Negro Freedom in United States, 1915. Reprint, Detroit: Gale Research Co., 1976.

Wilhoit, Francis M. *The Politics of Massive Resistance.* New York: George Braziler, 1973.

Wilkerson, Doxey A. "The Negro Press." *Journal of Negro Education* 16 (Fall 1947): 511–21.

Williamson, Joel. *The Crucible of Race: Black-White Relations in the American South since Emancipation.* New York: Oxford University Press, 1984.

Wilson, C.J. "Voices from Mississippi." *New South* 28 (Spring 1973): 62–71.

Witherspoon, St. Cloud. "Who Controls WLBT?" *Black Enterprise* 15 (September 1984): 45–48.

Wolseley, Roland E. *The Black Press, U.S.A.* Ames: Iowa State University Press, 1971.

Woodson, Carter G. *A Century of Negro Migration.* Washington, D.C.: Associated Publishers, 1919.

Woodward, C. Vann. *The Strange Career of Jim Crow.* New York: Oxford University Press, 1974.

Woodward, D.W. *Negro Progress in a Mississippi Town: Being a Study of Conditions in Jackson, Mississippi.* Cheyney, Pa.: Biddle Press, 1908.

Work, Monroe. *Negro Year Book.* Tuskegee, Ala.: Negro Year Book Publishing Co., 1912, 1918–19, 1922, 1947.

Wynar, Lubomyr R. *Encyclopedic Directory of Ethnic Organizations in the United States.* Littleton, Colo.: Libraries Unlimited, 1975.

Wynn, Neil. *The Afro-American and the Second World War.* New York: Holmes and Meier, 1976.

Yates, Gayle Graham. *Mississippi Mind: A Personal Cultural History of an American State.* Knoxville: University of Tennessee Press, 1990.

Yette, Samuel F. *The Choice: The Issue of Black Survival in America.* New York: G.P. Putnam and Sons, 1971.

INDEX

Advance Dispatch (Mound Bayou), 9, 15, 24
Advertising. *See* Black press, commercial
Advocate. See Jackson Advocate
Afro-American (Baltimore), 56
Afro-Times Newsletter (Miss. State University), 107
Akuchu, Gemuh, 91, 92
Alcorn A & M College (later Alcorn State University), 5, 6, 24
Alcorn Herald, 42, 104, 105
Alcornite, 42, 105
Allen's News Agency, 13
American Baptist Home Mission Society, 5
American Missionary Association, 3
Armstrong, Louis, 83, 94
Associated Negro Press (ANP), 13, 19
Atlanta Exposition Address of 1895, 30

Bakara, Imamu Amiri, 128
Banks, Regina, 103, 135. *See also* Black women editors; Devoual, Regina
Bannerman, Charles, 125
Baptist Echo (Mound Bayou), 9
Baptist Signal, 4, 10–11
Barnes, Jai, 83, 99
Barnes, Bernard, 83
Barnett, Ross, 41, 69
Barron, Zee Anderson, 108
Batesville Panolian, 66
Bearcat (Rust College), 42, 105
Black Arts Music Society, 135
Black Baptist Convention, 3–4
Black editors and publishers: background of, 5–6, 12, 14, 29, 118, 195nn.16, 25; conservative views of, 10, 31; hardships of, 13–14; as leaders and publishers, 5–6, 28; as ministers, 18; as part-time journalists, 25; as "peace keepers," 20, 22; resilience

of, 55; responsibility of, 38; during World War II, 30. *See also* Black press
Black elected officials, 113–15
Black History Month, 127
Black life: effects of school desegregation on, 42; in 1950s, 40–41; in 1960s, 59–60; in 1970s, 82, 85, 111, 112; in 1980s, 113, 115
Black Man (Vicksburg), 24
Black media, 149–50
Black organizations, news publishing of, in 1950s, 42
Black press: advertising support of, 76, 77; beginning of communication during slavery, 1–2; black business, support by, 51; commercial, in 1970s, 83, 96–97; commercial, in 1980s, 128–29; commercial growth of, 24; community-oriented papers, 97, 121–22; concerns of, in the 1960s, 61; decline of, 7, 15–16, 22, 42, 56–57, 115; early problems of, 5; economic problems of, 10–12, 15, 24, 83, 85, 116; educational institutions active in, 24; effect of national issues on, 42–43; emergence of, 2, 3; future role of, 146–47; growth of noncommercial, 7, 8, 11–12; historical view of, 148–50; impact of white terrorism on, 41; male control and dominance of, 25, 119; national support of state's black media, 86–87; new publications of, in 1970s, 85; organizational activity of, in 1980s, 134–35; organizational increase of, 116; religious, fraternal, social, 2, 4, 7, 8, 11–13, 24, 60, 61, 63, 108, 116; renewed interest in, in 1970s and 1980s, 82–83, 116, 136, 201nn.70, 71; significance of, 83, 110, 145–46; social conditions and decline of,

221